Beyond Disney

THE *unofficial* **GUIDE**®

TO Universal®, SeaWorld®, and the Best of Central Florida

4TH EDITION

D0112273

Beyond Disney

THE *unofficial* **GUIDE**®

TO Universal®, SeaWorld®, and the Best of Central Florida

4TH EDITION

BOB SEHLINGER *and*
KATIE BRANDON

WILEY

Please note that prices fluctuate in the course of time, and travel information changes under the impact of many factors that influence the travel industry. We therefore suggest that you write or call ahead for confirmation when making your travel plans. Every effort has been made to ensure the accuracy of information throughout this book, and the contents of this publication are believed correct at the time of printing. Nevertheless, the publishers cannot accept responsibility for errors or omissions or for changes in details given in this guide or for the consequences of any reliance on the information provided by the same. Assessments of attractions and so forth are based upon the author's own experience, and therefore, descriptions given in this guide necessarily contain an element of subjective opinion, which may not reflect the publisher's opinion or dictate a reader's own experience on another occasion. Readers are invited to write the publisher with ideas, comments, and suggestions for future editions.

Published by:
John Wiley & Sons, Inc.
111 River Street
Hoboken, NJ 07030

Produced by Menasha Ridge Press

Cover design by Michael J. Freeland

Interior design by Michele Laseau

For information on our other products and services or to obtain technical support please contact our Customer Care Department within the U.S. at (800) 762-2974, outside the U.S. at (317) 572-3993 or fax (317) 572-4002.

John Wiley & Sons, Inc. also publishes its books in a variety of electronic formats. Some content that appears in print may not be available in electronic formats.

ISBN 0-7645-8339-5

Manufactured in the United States of America

5 4 3 2 1

CONTENTS

ABOUT *the* AUTHORS

BOB SEHLINGER is the author of *The Unofficial Guide to Walt Disney World* and the executive publisher of the *Unofficial Guide* series.

KATIE BRANDON is a 2004 graduate of the University of Florida college of Journalism. This is her first book.

Beyond Disney

THE
unofficial **GUIDE**®

TO Universal®, SeaWorld®, and the Best of Central Florida

4TH EDITION

INTRODUCTION

WHY "UNOFFICIAL"?

THE AUTHORS AND RESEARCHERS of this guide specifically and categorically declare that they are and always have
been totally independent. The material in this guide origi-
nated with the authors and has not been reviewed, edited,
or in any way approved by the companies whose travel
products are discussed. The purpose of this guide is to provide you with the information necessary to tour central
Florida with the greatest efficiency and economy and with
the least hassle and stress. In this guide we represent and
serve you, the consumer. If a restaurant serves bad food, or
a gift item is overpriced, or a certain ride isn't worth the
wait, we can say so, and in the process we hope to make
your visit more fun, efficient, and economical.

THERE'S *another* WORLD
out THERE

IF YOU THINK THAT CENTRAL FLORIDA consists only of
Walt Disney World, you're wrong. What's more, you're passing up some great fun and amazing sights. Admittedly, it's
taken a while, but Walt Disney World now has plenty of competition that measures up toe-to-toe. And though it may
sound blasphemous to suggest a whole vacation in central
Florida without setting foot on Disney property, it's not only
possible but also in many ways a fresh and appealing idea.

The big four non-Disney theme parks are Universal Studios
Florida, Universal Islands of Adventure, SeaWorld, and Busch

Gardens. Each is unique. Universal Studios Florida, a long-time rival of the Disney-MGM Studios, draws its inspiration from movies and television and is every bit the equal of the Disney movie-themed park. Universal Islands of Adventure is arguably the most modern, high-tech theme park in the United States, featuring an all-star lineup of thrill rides that make it the best park in Florida for older kids and young-at-heart adults. SeaWorld provides an incomparable glimpse into the world of marine mammals and fish, served up in a way that (for the most part) eliminates those never-ending lines. Finally, Busch Gardens, with its shows, zoological exhibits, and knockout coasters, offers the most eclectic entertainment mix of any theme park we know. All four parks approximate, equal, or exceed the Disney standard without imitating Disney, successfully blending distinctive presentations and personalities into every attraction.

In addition to the big four, there are several specialty parks that are also worthy of your attention. The Kennedy Space Center Visitor Complex at Cape Canaveral provides an inside look at the past, present, and future of America's space program, and Gatorland showcases the alligator, one of the most ancient creatures on Earth. Splendid China features dozens of meticulously created miniature dioramas and buildings, some with thousands of individually sculpted human figures. SeaWorld's Discovery Cove offers central Florida's first-ever dolphin swim, and the Holy Land Experience is the first Christian theme park in the state and quite likely the most elaborate one in the world. All of these places offer an experience that is different from a day at one of the big theme parks, including a respite from standing in line, all of the walking, and the frenetic pace.

But these are just for starters. In central Florida, you'll also find a vibrant dinner-theater scene, two excellent non-Disney water parks, nightlife, and great shopping, all surrounded by some of the best hiking, biking, fishing, and canoeing available anywhere.

THE ATTRACTION *that* ATE FLORIDA

BEFORE WALT DISNEY WORLD, FLORIDA was a happy peninsula of many more or less equal tourist attractions. Distributed around the state in great profusion, these attractions constituted the nation's most perennially appealing vacation opportunity. There were the Monkey Jungle, the Orchid Jungle, venerable Marineland, the St. Augustine Alligator Farm, Silver Springs, the Miami Wax Museum, the Sunken Gardens, the Coral Castle, and the Conch Train Tour. These, along with Cypress Gardens, Busch Gardens, and others, were the attractions that ruled Florida. Now, like so many dinosaurs, those remaining survive precariously on the leavings of the greatest beast of them all, Walt Disney World. Old standbys continue to welcome tourists, but when was the last time you planned your vacation around a visit to Jungle Larry's Safari Park?

When Walt Disney World arrived on the scene, Florida tourism changed forever. Before Disney (BD), southern Florida was the state's and the nation's foremost tourist destination. Throngs sunned on the beaches of Miami, Hollywood, and Fort Lauderdale and patronized such nearby attractions as the Miami Serpentarium and the Parrot Jungle. Attractions in the Ocala and St. Augustine areas upstate hosted road travelers in great waves as they journeyed to and from southern Florida. At the time, Orlando was a sleepy central Florida town an hour's drive from Cypress Gardens, with practically no tourist appeal whatsoever.

Then came Disney, snapping up acres of farm- and swampland before anyone even knew who the purchaser was. Bargaining hard, Walt demanded improved highways, tax concessions, bargain financing, and community support. So successful had been his California Disneyland that whatever he requested, he received.

Generally approving, and hoping for a larger aggregate market, the existing Florida attractions failed to discern the cloud on the horizon. Walt had tipped his hand early, however, and all the cards were on the table. When Disney bought 27,500 central Florida acres, it was evident he didn't intend to raise cattle.

The Magic Kingdom opened on October 1, 1971, and was immediately successful. Hotel construction boomed in Orlando, Kissimmee, and around Walt Disney World. Major new attractions popped up along recently completed Interstate 4 to cash in on the tide of tourists arriving at Disney's latest wonder. Walt Disney World became a destination, and suddenly nobody cared as much about going to the beach. The Magic Kingdom was good for two days, and then you could enjoy the rest of the week at SeaWorld, Cypress Gardens, Circus World, Gatorland, Busch Gardens, the Stars Hall of Fame Wax Museum, and the Kennedy Space Center.

These attractions, all practically new and stretching from Florida's east to west coasts, formed what would come to be called the Orlando Wall. Tourists no longer poured into Miami and Fort Lauderdale. Instead they stopped at the Orlando Wall and exhausted themselves and their dollars in the shiny attractions arrayed between Cape Canaveral and Tampa. In southern Florida, venerable attractions held on by a parrot feather, and more than a few closed their doors. Flagship hotels on the fabled Gold Coast went bust or were converted into condominiums.

When Walt Disney World opened, the very definition of a tourist attraction changed. Setting new standards for cleanliness, size, scope, grandeur, variety, and attention to detail, Walt Disney World relegated the majority of Florida's headliner attractions to comparative insignificance almost overnight. Newer attractions such as SeaWorld and the vastly enlarged Busch Gardens successfully matched the standard Disney set. Cypress Gardens, Weeki Wachi, and Silver Springs expanded and modernized. Most other attractions, however, slipped into a limbo of diminished status. Far from being headliners or tourist destinations, they plugged along as local diversions, pulling in the curious, the bored, and the sunburned for mere two-hour excursions.

Many of the affected attractions were and are wonderful places to spend a day, but even collectively they don't command sufficient appeal to lure many tourists beyond the Orlando Wall. We recommend them, however, not only for a variety of high-quality offerings but also as a glimpse of Florida's golden age, a time of less sophisticated, less plastic pleasures before the Mouse. Take a day or two and drive three-and-a-half hours south of Orlando. Visit the Miami Seaquarium, Vizcaya Museum and Gardens, Fairchild Tropical Garden, and Lion Country Safari. Drive Collins Avenue along the Gold Coast. You'll be glad you did.

When Epcot opened in Walt Disney World on October 1, 1982, another seismic shock reverberated throughout the Florida attractions industry. This time it wasn't only the smaller and more vulnerable attractions that were affected but the newer large-scale attractions along the Orlando Wall. Suddenly, Disney World swallowed up another one or two days of each tourist's vacation week. When the Magic Kingdom stood alone, most visitors had three or four days remaining to sample other attractions. With the addition of Epcot, that time was cut to one or two days.

Disney ensured its market share by creating multiday admission passes, which allowed unlimited access to both the Magic Kingdom and Epcot. More cost-efficient than a one-day pass to a single park, these passes kept the guest on Disney turf for three to five days.

Kennedy Space Center and SeaWorld, by virtue of their very specialized products, continued to prosper after Epcot opened. Most other attractions were forced to focus on local markets. Some, like Busch Gardens, did very well, with increased local support replacing the decreased numbers of Walt Disney World tourists coming over for the day. Others, like Cypress Gardens, suffered badly but worked diligently to improve their product. Some, like Circus World and the Hall of Fame Wax Museum, passed into history.

Though long an innovator, Disney turned in the mid-1980s to copying existing successful competitors. Except *copying* is not exactly the right word. What Disney did was to take a competitor's concept, improve it, and reproduce it in Disney style and on a grand scale.

The first competitor to feel the heat was SeaWorld, when Disney added the Living Seas pavilion to the Future World section of Epcot. SeaWorld, however, had killer whales, the Shark Encounter, and sufficient corporate resources to remain preeminent among marine exhibits. Still, many Disney patrons willingly substituted a visit to the Living Seas for a visit to SeaWorld.

One of Disney's own products was threatened when the Wet 'n' Wild water park took aim at the older and smaller but more aesthetically pleasing River Country. Never one to take a challenge sitting down, Disney responded in 1989 with the opening of Typhoon Lagoon, then the world's largest swimming theme park.

Also in 1989, Disney opened Pleasure Island, a single-cover multi-nightclub entertainment complex patterned on Orlando's successful Church Street Station. Tourist traffic around the theme parks starting gravitating to Pleasure Island for nightlife rather than traveling to Church Street.

The third big Disney opening of 1989 was Disney-MGM Studios, a combination working motion picture and television production complex and theme park. Copying the long-lauded Universal Studios tour in southern California, Disney-MGM Studios was speeded into operation after Universal announced its plans for a central Florida park.

Disney-MGM Studios, however, affected much more than Universal's plans. With the opening of Disney-MGM, the Three-Day World Passport was discontinued. Instead, Disney patrons were offered a single-day pass or the more economical multiday passports, good for either four or five days. With three theme parks on a multiday pass, plus two swimming parks, several golf courses, various lakes, and a nighttime entertainment complex, Disney effectively swallowed up the average family's entire vacation. Break away to SeaWorld or the Kennedy Space Center for the day? How about a day at the ocean (remember the ocean)? Fat chance.

In 1995, Disney opened Blizzard Beach, a third swimming theme park, and began plans for a fourth major theme park, the Animal Kingdom, designed to compete directly with Busch Gardens. During the same year, the first phase of Disney's All-Star resorts came online, featuring (by Disney standards) budget accommodations. The location and rates of the All-Star resorts were intended to capture the market of the smaller independent and chain hotels along US 192. Disney even discussed constructing a monorail to the airport so that visitors wouldn't have to set foot in Orlando.

As time passed, Disney continued to consolidate its hold. With the openings in 1996 of Disney's BoardWalk, Fantasia Gardens miniature golf, and the Walt Disney World Speedway; in 1997 of Disney's Wide World of Sports, Disney's West Side shopping and entertainment district, and a new convention center; and in 1998 of the Animal Kingdom, Disney attracted armies of central Floridians to compensate for decreased tourist traffic during off-season. For people who can never get enough, there is the town of Celebration, a Disney residential land-development project where home buyers can live in Disney-designed houses in Disney-designed neighborhoods, protected by Disney-designed security.

In 1999, however, for the first time in many years, the initiative passed to Disney's competitors. Universal Studios Florida became a bona fide destination with the opening of its second major theme park (Islands of Adventure), on-property hotels, and the CityWalk dining and entertainment complex that directly competed with Pleasure Island (and Church Street Station, which was promptly forced out of business). SeaWorld announced the 2000 debut of its Discovery Cove park, and Busch Gardens turned up the heat with the addition of new roller coasters. The latest additions bring Busch Gardens' total to six coasters, making them the roller-coaster capital of Florida. Cypress Gardens briefly closed, then had a face-lift and reopened will all-new rides and attractions. Giving Disney some of its own medicine, Busch Gardens, SeaWorld, and Universal combined with Wet 'n' Wild to offer multiday passes good at any of the parks. Although it may be too early to say that Disney's hegemony is at an end, one thing's for sure: Disney's not the only 800-pound gorilla on the block anymore.

The tourism slump that began during the collapse of the Internet bubble economy peaked during post-9/11 paranoia, affected the big players in central Florida, but has gotten incrementally better as of this writing. While the big boys tightened their belts and cut corners where they could, some had to call it quits. The classic Ocean World in Fort Lauderdale was shut down for good shortly after the turn of the millennium. Splendid China, a vast landscaped garden filled with miniature recreations of Chinese buildings, monuments, palaces, cities, temples, and landmarks, closed its doors in 2003.

Even with these recent bad patches, most attractions and theme parks in central Florida are just learning how to become more adaptive and creative. Those that survive will be leaner, cleaner, and even more competitive than ever before. All this competition, of course, is good for central Florida, and it's good for you. The time, money, and energy invested in developing ever-better parks and attractions boggle the mind. Nobody, including Disney, can rest on their laurels in this market. And as for you, you're certain to find something new and amazing on every visit.

TRYING TO REASON WITH THE TOURIST SEASON

CENTRAL FLORIDA THEME PARKS and attractions are busiest Christmas Day through New Year's Day. Thanksgiving weekend, the week of Washington's birthday, Martin Luther King Jr. holiday weekend, and spring break for colleges, plus the two weeks around Easter are also extremely busy. What does "busy" mean? More than 90,000 people can tour one of the larger theme parks on a single day during these peak times! Although this level of attendance isn't typical, it is possible, and only the ignorant or foolish challenge the major Florida theme parks at their peak periods.

The least busy time extends from after the Thanksgiving weekend until the week before Christmas. The next slowest times are November up to the weekend preceding Thanksgiving, January 4 through the first week of February, and the week after Easter through early June. Late February, March, and early April are dicey. Crowds ebb and flow according to spring break schedules and the timing of Presidents' Day weekend. Though crowds have grown markedly in September and October as a result of special promotions aimed at

locals and the international market, these months continue
to be good for weekday touring.

IT TAKES *more than* ONE BOOK *to* DO *the* JOB RIGHT

WE'VE BEEN COVERING CENTRAL FLORIDA TOURISM for
over 20 years. We began by lumping everything into one
guidebook, but that was when the Magic Kingdom was the
only theme park at Walt Disney World, at the very beginning
of the boom that has made central Florida the most visited
tourist destination on Earth. As central Florida grew, so did
our guide, until eventually we needed to split the tome into
smaller, more in-depth (and more portable) volumes. The
result is a small library of six titles, designed to work both
individually and together. All six provide specialized information tailored to very specific central Florida and Walt
Disney World visitors. Although some tips (like arriving at
the theme parks early) are echoed or elaborated in the all the
guides, most of the information in each book is unique.

The Unofficial Guide to Walt Disney World is the centerpiece of our central Florida coverage because, well, Walt
Disney World is the centerpiece of most central Florida
vacations. *The Unofficial Guide to Walt Disney World* is
evaluative, comprehensive, and instructive—the ultimate
planning tool for a successful Walt Disney World vacation.
The Unofficial Guide to Walt Disney World is supplemented
and augmented by five additional titles, including this guide:

*Mini-Mickey: The Pocket-Sized Unofficial Guide to Walt
Disney World,* by Bob Sehlinger

*Inside Disney: The Incredible Story of Walt Disney World
and the Man behind the Mouse,* by Eve Zibart

The Unofficial Guide to Walt Disney World with Kids, by
Bob Sehlinger

*The Unofficial Guide to Walt Disney World for Grown-
Ups,* by Eve Zibart

Mini-Mickey is a nifty, portable, *Cliffs Notes* version of
The Unofficial Guide to Walt Disney World. Updated semi-
annually, it distills information from this comprehensive
guide to help short-stay or last-minute visitors decide
quickly how to plan their limited hours at Disney World.
Inside Disney is a behind-the-scenes, unauthorized history

of Walt Disney World, and it is loaded with all the amazing facts and great stories that we can't squeeze into *The Unofficial Guide to Walt Disney World*. *The Unofficial Guide to Walt Disney World for Grown-Ups* helps adults traveling without children make the most of their Disney vacation, and *The Unofficial Guide to Walt Disney World with Kids* presents a wealth of planning and touring tips for a successful Disney family vacation. Finally, this guide, B*eyond Disney,* is a complete consumer guide to the non-Disney attractions, hotels, restaurants, and nightlife in Orlando and central Florida. All of the guides are available from Wiley Publishing and at most bookstores.

LETTERS AND COMMENTS FROM READERS

MANY OF THOSE WHO USE *The Unofficial Guides* write us to make comments or share their own strategies for visiting central Florida. We appreciate all such input, both positive and critical, and encourage our readers to continue writing. Readers' comments and observations are frequently incorporated into revised editions of *The Unofficial Guides* and have contributed immeasurably to their improvement. If you write us, you can rest assured that we won't release your name and address to any mailing lists, direct-mail advertisers, or other third party.

How to Write the Authors

Bob Sehlinger and Katie Brandon
The Unofficial Guides
P.O. Box 43673
Birmingham, AL 35243
UnofficialGuides@menasharidge.com

When you write by mail, put your address on both your letter and envelope, as sometimes the two get separated. It is also a good idea to include your phone number. And remember, as travel writers, we're often out of the office for long periods of time, so forgive us if our response is slow.

PART ONE

ACCOMMODATIONS

ORLANDO LODGING OPTIONS

SELECTING AND BOOKING A HOTEL

LODGING COSTS IN ORLANDO vary incredibly. If you shop around, you can find a clean motel with a pool for as low as $35 a night. You also can find luxurious, expensive hotels with all the extras. Because of hot competition, discounts abound, particularly for AAA and AARP members.

There are three primary areas to consider:

I. INTERNATIONAL DRIVE AREA This area, about 15 to 20 minutes east of Walt Disney World, parallels Interstate-4 on its southern side and offers a wide selection of both hotels and restaurants. Accommodations range from $40 to $320 per night. The chief drawbacks of the International Drive area are its terribly congested roads, countless traffic signals, and inadequate access to westbound I-4. Though the biggest bottleneck is the intersection with Sand Lake Road, the mile of International Drive between Kirkman Road and Sand Lake Road stays in nearly continuous gridlock. It's common to lose 25–35 minutes trying to navigate this stretch.

Regarding International Drive (known locally as I-Drive) traffic, the following comments are representative.

From a Seattle mom:

> After spending half our trip sitting in traffic on International Drive, those Disney hotels didn't sound so expensive after all.

Hotel Concentrations around Walt Disney World

A convention-goer from Islip, New York, weighed in:

We wasted huge chunks of time in traffic on International Drive. Our hotel was in the section between the big McDonald's [at Sand Lake Drive] and Wet 'n' Wild [at Universal Boulevard]. There are practically no left turn lanes in this section, so anyone turning left can hold up traffic for a long time. Recently, I returned to Orlando for a trade show and stayed at a hotel on International Drive near the convention center. This section was much saner and far less congested.

If you stay on I-Drive, you can avoid the worst traffic as well as the infamous Sand Lake Road intersection by using Universal Boulevard. Universal Boulevard originates north of I-4, crosses the interstate, and then intersects International Drive. It continues south, crossing Sand Lake Road, and eventually reconnects with I-Drive south of the Orange County Convention Center. Turning left onto I-Drive, it's a short hop (about one-third mile) to the I-Drive/Beeline Expressway interchange. Get on the Beeline Expressway heading west (no toll), and it will drop you right onto I-4. Proceed west on I-4 to the exits for Walt Disney World.

Hotels in the International Drive area are listed in an Orlando vacation planning kit published by the Orlando/ Orange County Convention and Visitors Bureau. For a copy, call ☎ 800-255-5786 or 407-363-5872.

2. LAKE BUENA VISTA AND THE I-4 CORRIDOR A number of hotels are situated along FL 535 and north of I-4 between Walt Disney World and I-4's intersection with the Florida Turnpike. These properties are easily reached from the interstate and are near a large number of restaurants, including those on International Drive. Most hotels in this area are listed in the Orlando vacation planning kit.

3. US 192 This is the highway to Kissimmee, southeast of Walt Disney World. In addition to a number of large, full-service hotels, there are many small, privately owned motels that are often a good value. The number and variety of restaurants on US 192 has increased markedly in the past several years, easing the area's primary shortcoming.

We're happy to report that the construction project on US 192 was completed: widened and landscaped medians and shoulders, lined with stately palms, were added. The flow of traffic has improved considerably, and the improved appearance of the highway is remarkable. What once looked like an endless strip mall has now assumed the lush appearance of a resort area.

unofficial **TIP**
If your hotel on US 192 is east of the Walt Disney World entrance, you can bypass the lights by using the Osceola Parkway toll road that parallels US 192 to the north.

Although traffic now moves fluidly along US 192, there remain a number of traffic signals. From US 192 take FL 535 or Poinciana Boulevard north to access the parkway.

A senior citizen from Brookfield, Connecticut, was surprised and pleased with lodging in the US 192/Kissimmee area:

> *We were amazed to find that from our cheaper and supe-*
> *rior accommodations in Kissimmee it took only five*
> *minutes longer to reach the park turnstiles. . . . Kissimmee*
> *is the way to go, in our opinion.*

Hotels on US 192 and in Kissimmee are listed in the *Offi-cial Kissimmee Vacation Planner,* available at ☎ 800-327-9159 or **www.floridakiss.com.**

GETTING A GOOD DEAL ON A ROOM IN ORLANDO

HOTEL DEVELOPMENT IN ORLANDO has sharpened the competition among lodgings throughout the area. Hotels out-side Disney World, in particular, struggle to fill their guest rooms. Unable to compete with Disney resorts for convenience or perks, off-World hotels lure patrons with bargain rates. The extent of the bargain depends on the season, day of the week, and area events. In high season, during holiday periods, and during large conventions at the Orange County Convention Center, even the most modest lodging properties are sold out. Here are tips and strategies for getting a good deal on a room.

The following list may seem intimidating and may refer to travel-market players unfamiliar to you, but many tips we provide for getting a good deal work equally well almost any place you need a hotel. Once you understand these strate-gies, you'll routinely be able to obtain rooms at the best hotels for the lowest possible rates.

1. ORLANDO MAGICARD Orlando Magicard is a discount program sponsored by the Orlando/Orange County Con-vention and Visitors Bureau. Cardholders are eligible for discounts of 20–50 percent at about 50 participating hotels. The Magicard is also good for discounts at area attractions, including SeaWorld, the Universal parks, several dinner the-aters, and Disney's Pleasure Island. Valid for up to six persons, the card isn't available for groups or conventions.

To obtain an Orlando Magicard and a list of participating hotels and attractions, call ☎ 800-255-5786 or 407-363-5874, or find a printable version online at **www.orlandoinfo.com/magicard.** Anyone older than 18 years is eligible, and the card is free. If you miss getting a card before you leave home, you can get one at the Conven-tion and Visitors Bureau at 8723 Interna-tional Drive in Orlando.

unofficial **TIP**
When you call for a vacation planning kit, you'll receive a Magicard.

2. TRAVELER DISCOUNT GUIDE Traveler Discount Guide is a book of discount coupons for bargain rates at hotels statewide. The book is free in many restaurants and motels on main highways leading to Florida. Because most travelers make reservations before leaving home, picking up the coupon book en route doesn't help much. If you call and use a credit card, TDG will send the guide first class for $3 ($5 U.S. for Canadian delivery). The guide is available at ☎ 352-371-3948 or **www.travelerguide.com.**

3. HOTEL SHOPPING ON THE INTERNET To read the popular press, you'd think hotels were giving away rooms on the Internet. While they're not, of course, it is true that hotels are increasingly using the Internet to fill rooms during slow periods and advertise time-limited specials. The Internet is one of many communications tools in the hotel's toolbox, and hotels use it along with more traditional practices, such as promoting specials through travel agents. If you enjoy cyber shopping, by all means have at it, but hotel shopping on the Internet is not nearly as quick or convenient as handing the task to your travel agent. You'll be hard-pressed to find a deal that is not also available through your agent. When we bump into a great deal on the Web, we call our travel agent. Often our agent can beat the deal or improve on it (as in the case of an upgrade). Although a good travel agent working alone can achieve great things, the same agent working with a savvy, helpful client can work wonders.

Web sites we've found most dependable for Orlando hotel discounts are:

Expedia.com	An Internet travel superstore
FloridaKiss.com	Operated by Kissimmee–St. Cloud Visitors Bureau
HotelKingdom.com	Will beat the prices you find elsewhere
RoomSaver.com	Specializes in budget accommodations
Travelocity.com	An Internet travel superstore
2000orlando-florida.com	A wholesale company runs the site and uses its bulk-buying power to negotiate discounted rates with local hotels
ValueTrips.com	Specializes in budget accommodations

4. HALF-PRICE PROGRAMS Larger discounts on rooms (35–60 percent), in the Orlando area or anywhere else, are available through half-price hotel programs, often called travel clubs. Program operators contract with hotels to provide rooms at a deep discount, usually 50 percent off the rack rate, on a space-available basis. Generally, space available means you can reserve a room at the discount whenever the hotel expects occupancy will be less than 80 percent. To increase your chances for the discount, check the calendar to avoid high season, big conventions, holidays, and special events.

Most half-price programs charge an annual membership or directory subscription fee of $25 to $125. Once enrolled, you're mailed a membership card and a directory listing participating hotels. There are lots of restrictions and exceptions. Some hotels, for instance, "black out" (exclude) certain times. Others may offer the discount only on certain days of the week or may require you to stay a certain number of nights. Still others may offer a discount much smaller than 50 percent.

More established programs offer members up to 4,000 hotels in the United States. All of the programs have a heavy concentration of hotels in California and Florida. Offerings elsewhere in the United States vary considerably. The programs with the largest selection of hotels in the Orlando area are Encore, at ☎ 800-638-0930, and Entertainment Publications, at ☎ 800-285-5525.

One problem with half-price programs is that not all hotels offer a full 50-percent discount. Another is the base rate against which the discount is applied. Some hotels figure the discount on an exaggerated rack rate that virtually no one pays. A few participating hotels may deduct the discount from the rate for a "superior" or "upgraded" room, though the room assigned is the hotel's standard accommodation. The majority of participants base discounts on rates published in the *Hotel & Travel Index* (a quarterly reference journal used by travel agents) and work within the spirit of their agreement with the program operator.

unofficial **TIP**
As a rule, if you travel several times a year, your savings will more than pay for your program membership.

A footnote to this information is that rooms through half-price programs aren't commissionable to travel agents. This means you usually must make your own inquiries and reservations. If you work frequently with your agent, however, he or she will probably do your legwork, lack of commission notwithstanding.

5. WHOLESALERS, CONSOLIDATORS, AND RESERVATION SERVICES Wholesalers and consolidators buy rooms, or options on rooms (room blocks), from hotels at a low, negotiated rate. They then resell the rooms at a profit through travel agents and tour packagers, or directly to the public. Most wholesalers and consolidators make provisions for returning unsold rooms to participating hotels but are disinclined to do so. The wholesaler's or consolidator's relationship with any hotel is tied to volume. If unsold rooms are returned, the hotel might not make as many rooms available the next time. So wholesalers and consolidators often offer rooms at rates from 15 to 50 percent off rack rate, occasionally sacrificing profit to avoid returning the rooms unsold.

When wholesalers and consolidators deal directly with the public, they frequently represent themselves as "reservation services." When you call, ask for a rate for your chosen hotel or for the best deal in the area where you'd like to stay. Say if there's a maximum amount you're willing to pay. The service likely will find something for you, even if it has to shave off a dollar or two of profit. You may have to pay by credit card when you reserve a room. Other times, you pay when you check out. Here are three services that frequently offer substantial discounts:

Accommodations Express ☎ 800-444-7666 or www.accommodationsexpress.com

Hotel Reservations Network/ ☎ 800-715-7666 or
Hotel Discounts www.hoteldiscounts.com

6. IF YOU MAKE YOUR OWN RESERVATION Always call the hotel in question, not the hotel chain's national toll-free number. Often, reservationists at the toll-free number are unaware of local specials. Always ask about specials before you inquire about corporate rates. Don't hesitate to bargain, but do it before you check in. If you're buying a hotel's weekend package, for example, and want to extend your stay, you can often obtain at least the corporate rate for the extra days.

7. CONDOMINIUM DEALS A large number of condo resorts, time-shares, and all-suite properties in the Kissimmee/Orlando area rent to vacationers for a week or less. Look for bargains, especially during off-peak periods. Reservations and information can be obtained from:

Condolink ☎ 800-733-4445

Holiday Villas ☎ 800-344-3959

Kissimmee–St. Cloud	
Reservations	☎ 800-333-5477
Vistana Resort	☎ 800-877-8787
Ramada Suites by SeaWorld	☎ 407-239-0707
Holiday Inn Family Suites	☎ 877-387-KIDS

We frequently receive letters from readers extolling the virtues of renting a condo or vacation home. This endorsement by a family from Ellington, Connecticut, is typical:

> *We found over the last couple of years that our children can't share the same bed. We have also gotten tired of having to turn off the lights at 8 p.m. and lie quietly in the dark waiting for our children to fall asleep. With this in mind, we needed a kind of condo/suite layout. . . . We decided on the Sheraton Vistana Resort. We had a two-bedroom villa with full kitchen, living room, three TVs, and washer/dryer. I packed for half the trip and did laundry almost every night. The facilities offered a daily children's program and several pools, kiddy pools, and "playscapes." Located on FL 535, we had a 5–10-minute drive to most attractions, including SeaWorld, Disney, and Universal.*

A majority of rental condos are listed with travel agents. Condo owners often pay an enhanced commission to agents who rent the units for reduced consumer rates.

ORLANDO'S BEST HOTELS *for* FAMILIES

International Drive Area

Doubletree Castle Hotel
8629 International Drive, Orlando; ☎ **407-345-1511 or 800-952-2785; www.doubletreecastle.com**

Rate per night $150. **Pool** ★★★. **Fridge in room** Yes. **Shuttle to parks** Yes (Disney, Universal, and SeaWorld). **Maximum persons per room** 4. **Special comments** Add $20 to room rate and up to four people receive a full, cooked-to-order breakfast; two chocolate-chip cookies come with every room. You can purchase park tickets through the hotel when you reserve your room online.

DESCRIPTION AND COMMENTS You can't miss this one—it's the only castle on I-Drive. Inside you'll find royal colors (purple dominates), opulent fixtures, European art, Renaissance music, and, of course, a mystical Castle Creature at the door. The 216 guest rooms also receive the royal treatment when it comes to decor, and some may find them on the gaudy side; however, they are fairly large and well equipped with TV and Sony PlayStation, fridge, three phones, coffee maker, iron and board, hair dryer, and safe. Guests can enjoy full or continental breakfast in the Castle Cafe located off the lobby. A court jester appears at breakfast four days a week to entertain with juggling and balloon sculptures. For lunch or dinner, you might walk next door to either Vito's Chop House or Café Tu Tu Tango (an *Unofficial* favorite). The heated circular pool is five feet deep and features a fountain in the center, a poolside bar, and a whirlpool. *Note:* there is no separate kiddie pool. Other on-site amenities include a fitness center, arcade, gift shop, lounge, valet laundry service and facilities, and guest services desk with park passes for sale and baby-sitting recommendations. All elevators require an electronic guest card key, a nice security feature.

Hard Rock Hotel

kids
5800 Universal Boulevard, Orlando
☎ **407-503-ROCK; www.loewshotels.com**

Rate per night $260. **Pool** ★★★★. **Fridge in room** No, but available for $10 per day. **Shuttle to parks** Yes (Universal, SeaWorld, and Wet 'n' Wild). **Maximum persons per room** 5. **Special comments** Microwaves available for $15 per day.

DESCRIPTION AND COMMENTS Located on the Universal property, the 650-room Hard Rock Hotel is nirvana for any kid over age eight, especially those interested in music. The hotel's architecture is California mission style, and rock memorabilia is displayed throughout. If you're planning to spend at least a few days at the Universal parks, this is an excellent upscale option. Hotel guests receive special theme-park privileges, such as early admission on select days and all-day access to the Universal Express line-breaking program, plus delivery of packages to their hotel room and priority seating at select Universal restaurants. The music-filled pool area is a big draw, with a white-sand beach, water slide, underwater audio system, and ultra-hip pool bar. You'll also find two restaurants, including the world-renowned Palm Restaurant, a chic lounge, a fitness center, and a Hard Rock merchandise store (watch your teens closely here). Guest rooms are ultra-hip, too, of course, with cutting-edge contemporary decor, a CD sound system, TV with pay-per-view movies and video games, coffee maker, iron and board, robes, hair dryer, and two phones. There's also a supervised children's activity center for kids ages 4–14.

Nickelodeon Family Suites by Holiday Inn

kids 14500 Continental Gateway, Orlando
☎ 866-GO-2-NICK; www.nickhotel.com

Rate per night $137–$535. **Pools** ★★★★★. **Fridge in room** Yes.
Shuttle to parks Yes (Disney, Universal, SeaWorld, Wet 'n' Wild).
Maximum persons per room Varies. **Special comments** The kids may
never want to leave.

DESCRIPTION AND COMMENTS   In late 2004, the Holiday Inn Family
Suites underwent a major renovation that transformed it into
a Nickelodeon-themed all-suite kid-friendly resort. The all-
new resort reopened in spring 2005. The place is dedicated to
all things Nick and includes two- and three-bedroom suites
themed after SpongeBob SquarePants, Jimmy Neutron,
Rugrats, the Fairly Oddparents, and Danny Phantom. For
grownups, there are one-bedroom Nick-at-Nite suites with
heart-shaped whirlpool tubs. The two-bedroom suites include
semi-private kids rooms with bunk or twin beds, TV, video
game system, CD/cassette player, and activity table with
chairs. The family room has a microwave, fridge, coffee maker,
pull-out sofa, high-speed Internet access, and a TV with video
game player. Though the rooms are fun, there are myriad
activities on the premises to keep kids entertained, like a
3,000-square-foot game room, nightly entertainment in the
Nick Studio (from live performers to interactive games), and
Sparkle Kids Spa, with treatments just for children. But the
very best amenity this hotel offers might be the huge pool
areas. The Lagoon area includes a free-form pool at the base
of a four-story interactive water tower with a 400-gallon
dump tank. Seven waterslides swoop through the tower, and
several times a day, a recreation staff member leads games
and activities poolside. There's also a restaurant with burgers,
hot dogs, sandwiches, and salads. The Oasis area has an
Olympic-sized pool, more waterslides, a shaded kids area
designed specifically for preschoolers, a sandy play area, and
two giant whirlpool tubs. The Oasis snack bar serves prepack-
aged sandwiches, drinks, and ice cream. With five restaurants
to choose from, most families will find something that suits
them, including a food court with a Pizza Hut and A&W Hot-
dog stand. A character buffet-style breakfast is served daily
from 7 to 11 a.m. and is $16 for adults, $8 for kids age 12 and
under. Kids eat free with a paying adult at every restaurant,
except the character breakfast and food court. This resort is a
great choice if you don't mind the cartoon-saturated decor—
kids will be so consumed with the activities, you may be able
to forgo the theme parks a day or two.

Ritz Carlton Orlando
4012 Central Florida Parkway, Orlando
☎ **407-206-2400; www.ritzcarlton.com**

Rate per night $279–$509. **Pools** ★★★½. **Fridge in room** No. **Shuttle to parks** No. **Maximum persons per room** 6.

DESCRIPTION AND COMMENTS   A bit of a departure from the resorts that pack the I-4 corridor and Lake Buena Vista, this is the perfect place to stay if you are the type who needs a respite from the hectic theme parks. The kids club here has enough to keep little ones busy for the day while parents partake in the lavish spa services or 18-hole golf course—a great break from a day at the parks. The Ritz Kids program offers supervised activities for kids 5–12, including crafts and dive-in movie pool parties. The Ritz Teen Spa Adventures offer spa services catered to young clients through age 18. Kids Nite Out has supervised adventures like treasure hunts and a Mexican fiesta and are available every night for $10 per hour per child. Other on-site amenities include horse-drawn carriage rides, tennis courts, fitness room, and three kid-friendly dining options. For casual dining there's a poolside cafe; for something a little fancier, there are two very nice choices: Norman's, a AAA four-star restaurant, and a casually elegant steakhouse. If you have the bank account to pay for it and you want to spend a day (or two) away from the parks, you can't go wrong here.

Renaissance Orlando Resort
6677 Sea Harbor Drive, Orlando; ☎ **407-351-5555 or 800-327-6677; www.renaissancehotels.com**

Rate per night $189. **Pool** ★★★½. **Fridge in room** Yes. **Shuttle to parks** Yes (Disney, Universal, SeaWorld). **Maximum persons per room** 4. **Special comments** Baby-sitting and child care services available, and pets are permitted.

DESCRIPTION AND COMMENTS   The Renaissance Orlando Resort does a lot of convention business. However, its large size and convenience to SeaWorld and Universal make it an acceptable alternative if the more family-friendly options are sold out or not to your liking. Rooms are decorated in light and bright colors, albeit in a largely ho-hum style. In-room amenities for families are limited; although the staff will help by arranging child care or bringing up cribs, you'll have to largely make do with repurposed business amenities (i.e., cramming your own perishables in the minibar). Dining options range from casual sandwiches at the poolside bar and grill to a continental restaurant serving dinner only. The sizable pool is the main draw for kids, because it has enough square footage to exhaust even the most determined small fry. The large central atrium of the hotel also has a small tropical bird aviary; local songbirds, perhaps drawn by their imprisoned kin, are often seen flitting about the wide central space and stealing potato chips from abandoned lunches.

Sheraton Studio City
5905 International Drive, Orlando; ☎ **407-351-2100 or 800-327-1366; www.sheratonstudiocity.com**

Rate per night $129. **Pool** ★★½. **Fridge in room** No. **Shuttle to parks** Yes (Universal, SeaWorld, and Wet 'n' Wild). **Maximum persons per room** 4. **Special comments** Across the street from Wet 'n' Wild.

DESCRIPTION AND COMMENTS It's not for little ones, but preteens and teens will love the hip atmosphere at Sheraton Studio City. Movie buffs will appreciate the theme—a tribute to feature films of the 1940s and 1950s. The lobby is reminiscent of a 1950s movie-house lobby, with a slick black-and-white color scheme, cool Art Deco furnishings, and photos of classic movie stars. The Art Deco theme continues in the 302 guest rooms, which also offer subdued teal and silver hues, elegant marble baths, TV with Sony PlayStation, two phones, iron and board, coffee maker, hair dryer, and safe. The 21-story hotel is round, which makes guest rooms somewhat pie-shaped but still spacious enough. Request a room on one of the upper floors for an outstanding view. The heated pool is on the smallish side but has a jumping fountain over it, a kiddie pool, and a très cool poolside bar with more movie motif. The Starlight Room serves breakfast, lunch, and dinner, while Oscar's Lounge features a nightly champagne celebration for adults. Other major on-site amenities and services include fitness center, arcade, gift shop, hair salon, car rental, one-hour photo service, and Universal park passes for sale in the lobby.

Sheraton World Resort

10100 International Drive, Orlando; ☎ **407-352-1100 or 800-327-0363; www.sheratonworld.com**

Rate per night $159. **Pools** ★★★½. **Fridge in room** Yes. **Shuttle to parks** Yes (Disney only). **Maximum persons per room** 4. **Special comments** A good option if you're visiting SeaWorld.

DESCRIPTION AND COMMENTS Set on 28 acres, the Sheraton World Resort offers plenty of room for kids to roam. With three heated pools, two kiddie pools, a small playground, an arcade, and a complimentary mini-golf course (very mini, indeed), this resort offers more than enough kid-friendly diversions. The main pool is especially pleasant, with fountains, lush landscaping, and a poolside bar. Other on-site amenities and services include fitness center, massage therapy, gift shop, guest services desk, and lounge. A golf club is located one mile away. We recommend booking a room in the new tower if possible, even though it's set away from the kiddie pools and playground. The tower rooms are a bit larger and more upscale than the low-rise rooms, some of which could use a renovation. All 1,102 guest rooms include fridge, coffee maker, TV with Nintendo, iron and board, hair dryer, and safe. The Sheraton has one restaurant and a deli with a Pizza Hut. If your family loves SeaWorld, you're in luck here—Shamu and friends are within walking distance.

Lake Buena Vista and I-4 Corridor

Hilton Disney Village

1751 Hotel Plaza Boulevard, Lake Buena Vista; ☎ 407-827-4000 or 800-782-4414; www.hilton-wdwv.com

Rate per night $150. **Pools** ★★★½. **Fridge in room** Minibar. **Shuttle to parks** Yes (Disney theme and water parks only). **Maximum persons per room** 4. **Special comments** Sunday character breakfast and Surprise Mornings program available.

DESCRIPTION AND COMMENTS Located in the Disney Village, the Hilton offers 814 guest rooms and suites set on 23 landscaped acres. As an official Walt Disney World hotel, guests can take advantage of the Surprise Mornings program, which allows hotel guests to enter a selected Disney park one hour before official opening time. Hilton guest rooms are spacious, luxurious, and tasteful. Decorated in earth tones and complete with marble baths, all standard rooms are equipped with iron and board, hair dryer, two phones, desk, minibar, coffee maker, and cable TV with pay-per-view movies and video games. One big family amenity offered by the Hilton is its character breakfast. Offered on Sunday only from 8:30 to 11 a.m., the food is served buffet style, and four characters attend, but only two are present at a time. When we visited the characters were Minnie Mouse, Brer Bear, Donald Duck, and Pluto. Reservations are not accepted. Other important family amenities include the Hilton Vacation Station, where kids ages 4–12 can take part in supervised activities; baby-sitting services; an arcade and pool table; and two beautifully landscaped heated swimming pools, as well as a kiddie pool. Adults and older children can blow off steam after a long day at the parks in the fitness center. Nine on-site restaurants, including Benihana, add to the hotel's convenience.

Holiday Inn SunSpree Resort

kids

13351 FL 535, Lake Buena Vista; ☎ 407-239-4500 or
800-366-6299; www.kidsuites.com

Rate per night $109. **Pool** ★★★. **Fridge in room** Yes. **Shuttle to parks** Yes (Disney only). **Maximum persons per room** 4–6. **Special comments** The first hotel in the world to offer Kidsuites.

DESCRIPTION AND COMMENTS Put on your sunglasses—you'll know you're there when the hot pink, bright blue, green, and yellow exterior comes into view. Once inside, kids get into the action from the very beginning at their own check-in counter, where they'll receive a free goody bag. Max, Maxine, and the Kidsuite Gang, the character mascots here, come out to play with the kids at scheduled times during the day. But the big lure is the Kidsuites, which are 405-square-foot rooms with a separate area for kids. Themes include a tree house, circus tent, jail, space capsule, igloo, fort, and many more. The kids' area has either two sets of bunk beds or one bunk bed and a twin, plus a cable TV and VCR, Nintendo, radio/cassette or CD player, fun phone, and game table and chairs. The separate adult area has its own TV and VCR, safe, hair dryer, and a mini kitchen with fridge, microwave, sink, and coffee maker. Standard guest rooms are also available and offer the same amenities found in the adult areas of the Kidsuites. Other kid-friendly amenities include free bedtime tuck-in service by a member of the Kidsuite Gang (reservations required); the tiny Castle Movie Theater, which shows continuous movies daily and clown and magic shows nightly; a playground; a state-of-the-art arcade; a basketball court; and Camp Holiday, a free supervised-activities program for kids ages 3–12. There are also a large, attractive, free-form pool, complete with kiddie pool and two whirlpools, and a fitness center. You won't go hungry with Maxine's Food Emporium on site. Open 7 a.m.–10 p.m., it includes Little Caesars, A&W Restaurant, Otis Spunkmeyer Cookies and Muffins, TCBY, and more. There's also a mini mart. Kids age 12 and under eat free from a special menu when dining with one paying adult; there's a maximum of four kids per paying adult.

Hyatt Regency Grand Cypress

One Grand Cypress Boulevard, Lake Buena Vista;
☎ 407-239-1234; www.hyattgrandcypress.com

Rate per night $209. **Pool** ★★★★★. **Fridge in room** Minibar; fridge available on request. **Shuttle to parks** Yes (Disney only). **Maximum persons per room** 4. **Special comments** Wow, what a pool!

DESCRIPTION AND COMMENTS There are myriad reasons to stay at this 1,500-acre resort, but in our book, the pool ranks as number one. It's a sprawling, 800,000-gallon tropical paradise with a 125-foot waterslide, ubiquitous waterfalls, caves and grottos, and a suspension bridge. The only problem is your kids may never want to leave the pool to visit the theme parks. The Hyatt is also a golfer's paradise. With a 45-hole championship Jack Nicklaus–designed course, an 18-hole course, a 9-hole pitch-and-putt course, and a golf academy, there's something for golfers of all abilities. Other recreational perks include a racquet facility with hard and clay courts, a private lake complete with beach, a fitness center, and miles of nature trails for biking, walking or jogging, and horseback riding. The 750 standard guest rooms are 360 square feet and provide a casual but luxurious Florida ambience, with green and reddish hues, touches of rattan, and private balconies. In-room amenities include minibar, iron and board, safe, hair dryer, ceiling fan, and cable TV with pay-per-view movies and video games. Suite and villa accommodations offer even more amenities. Camp Hyatt provides supervised programs for kids, and in-room baby-sitting is also available. Five restaurants provide plenty of dining options, and four lounges offer nighttime entertainment. If outdoor recreation is high on your family's list, the Hyatt is an excellent high-end choice.

Marriott Village at Little Lake Bryan

kids

8623 Vineland Avenue, Lake Buena Vista
☎ **407-938-9001 or 877-682-8552**
www.marriott-village.com

Rate per night $79–$159. **Pools** ★★★. **Fridge in room** Yes. **Shuttle to parks** Yes (Disney, Universal, SeaWorld, and Wet 'n' Wild). **Maximum persons per room** 4. **Special comments** Complimentary continental breakfast at Fairfield Inn and Spring Hill Suites.

DESCRIPTION AND COMMENTS This brand-new, fully gated community includes a 388-room Fairfield Inn, a 400-suite Spring Hill Suites, and a 312-room Courtyard. Whatever your travel budget, you'll find a room to fit it here. For a bit more space, book the Spring Hill Suites; if you're looking for a good value, try the Fairfield Inn; and if you need limited business amenities, reserve at the Courtyard. In-room amenities at all three properties include fridge, cable TV with Sony PlayStation, iron and board, and hair dryer. Additionally, the Spring Hill Suites have microwaves in all suites, and all Courtyard rooms feature Web TV. Cribs and rollaway beds are available at no extra charge at all locations. Pools at all three hotels are attractive and medium-sized with children's interactive splash zones and whirlpools, and all properties have their own fitness center. A particularly convenient feature here is the Village Marketplace food court, which includes Pizza Hut, TCBY Yogurt, Oscar Mayer Hot Dog Construction Company, Oscar Mayer 1883 Deli, Village Grill, Gourmet Bean Coffee and Pastry Shop, and a 24-hour convenience store. If you're looking for a full-service restaurant experience, Bahama Breeze, Fish Bones, and Golden Corral restaurants are adjacent and within walking distance of the compound. Each hotel also features its own Kids Club. For kids ages 4–8, Kids Clubs have a theme (backyard, tree house, and library) and feature a big-screen TV, computer stations, and three educational centers (math and science, reading, and creative activities). They operate approximately six hours per day at no extra charge. Marriott Village also offers a Kids Night Out program (for ages 4–10), which runs on select nights from 6 to 10 p.m. Cost is $35 per child and includes dinner. And last but not least, shoppers in the family will be pleased to know that Marriott Village is located adjacent to the new Orlando Premium Outlets. You'll get a lot of bang for your buck at Marriott Village.

Sheraton Safari Hotel
12205 Apopka-Vineland Road, Lake Buena Vista;
☎ **407-239-0444 or 800-423-3297; www.sheraton.com**

Rate per night $115. **Pool ★★★**. **Fridge in room** In safari suites only. **Shuttle to parks** Yes (Disney complimentary; other parks for a fee). **Maximum persons per room** 4–6. **Special comments** Cool python waterslide.

DESCRIPTION AND COMMENTS The Sheraton Safari offers a more low-key theme experience. The safari theme is nicely executed throughout the property—from the lobby dotted with African artifacts and native decor to the 79-foot python waterslide dominating the pool. The 393 guest rooms and 90 safari suites also sport the safari theme with tasteful animal print soft goods in brown, beige, and jewel tones and African-inspired art. In-room amenities include cable TV with Sony PlayStation, coffee maker, iron and board, hair dryer, and safe. The safari suites are a good option for families because they provide added space with a separate sitting room and a kitchenette with a fridge, microwave, and sink. The first thing your kids will probably want to do is hit the pool and take a turn on the python waterslide. It's pretty impressive, but as one *Unofficial* researcher pointed out, it's somewhat of a letdown that the python doesn't actually spit you out of its mouth. Instead you're deposited below the snake.

Details, details. Other on-site amenities include a restaurant (children's menu available), deli, lounge, arcade, and fitness center. Should you want to escape for a night of strictly adult fun, baby-sitting services are available.

Sheraton Vistana Resort
8800 Vistana Center Drive, Lake Buena Vista; ☎ 866-208-0003; www.starwoodvo.com

Rate per night $149. **Pools** ★★★½. **Fridge in room** Minibar. **Shuttle to parks** Yes (Disney, Universal, SeaWorld). **Maximum persons per room** 6. **Special comments** Though actually timeshares, the villas are rented nightly as well.

DESCRIPTION AND COMMENTS The Sheraton Vistana is deceptively large, stretching as it does across either side of Vistana Center Drive. Because Sheraton's sales emphasis is on ownership of the timeshares, the rental angle is a small secret in local lodging. But it's worth considering for visiting families, because the Vistana is one of the best properties in Orlando. If you want to have a very serene retreat from your days in the theme parks, this is an excellent home base. You may even have difficulty prying yourself out of here to go to the parks. The spacious "villas" come in one-bedroom, two-bedroom, and two-bedroom-with-lockoff combinations. All are cleanly decorated in simple pastels, but the main emphasis is on the profusion of amenities. Each villa comes with full kitchen (including fridge with freezer, microwave, oven/range, dishwasher, toaster, and coffee maker, with an option to prestock with groceries), clothes washer and dryer, TVs in the living room and each bedroom (one with VCR), stereo with CD player, separate dining area, and private patio or balcony in most. The grounds themselves have resort amenities close at hand, with seven swimming pools (four with poolside bars), four playgrounds, three restaurants, game rooms, fitness centers, a mini-golf course, sport equipment rental (including bikes), and courts for basketball, volleyball, tennis, and shuffleboard. The resort organizes a mind-boggling array of activities for kids (and adults) of all ages, from arts and crafts to a variety of games and sports tournaments. Of special note is the fact that the Vistana is extremely secure, with locked gates bordering all guest areas.

Wyndham Palace
1900 Buena Vista Drive, Lake Buena Vista; ☎ 407-827-2727 or 800-WYNDHAM; www.wyndham.com

Rate per night $129. **Pools** ★★★½. **Fridge in room** Minibar. **Shuttle to parks** Yes (Disney only). **Maximum persons per room** 4. **Special comments** Sunday character breakfast available.

DESCRIPTION AND COMMENTS Located in the Disney Village, the Wyndham Palace is an upscale and convenient if Walt Disney World is on your vacation itinerary. Surrounded by a man-made lake and plenty of palms, the attractive and spacious pool area contains three heated pools, a whirlpool, and a sand volleyball court. Plus, there's even a pool concierge who will fetch your favorite magazine or fruity drink. On Sundays, the Wyndham offers a character breakfast at the Watercress Café. Cost is $19 for adults and $11 for children. Minnie Mouse, Pluto, and Goofy were in attendance when we visited. The 1,014 guest rooms are posh and spacious, and each comes with a desk, coffee maker, hair dryer, cable TV with pay-per-view movies, iron and board, and minibar. There are also 112 suites. Children ages 4–12 can participate in supervised programs through the Wyndy Harbour Kids' Klub, and in-room baby-sitting is available through the All about Kids child-care service. Three lighted tennis courts, a European-style spa offering 60 services, a fitness center, an arcade, a playground, and a beauty salon round out the hotel's amenities. There are also three restaurants and a mini-market on site. And if you're not wiped out after visiting the parks, you might consider the Laughing Kookaburra Good Time Bar for live entertainment and dancing. *Note:* These amenities come at a price—an $8-per-night resort fee is added to your bill.

US 192 Area

Comfort Suites Maingate Resort
7888 West US 192, Kissimmee; ☎ 407-390-9888

Rate per night $89. **Pool ★★★**. **Fridge in room** Yes. **Shuttle to parks** Yes (Disney, Universal, SeaWorld, and Wet 'n' Wild). **Maximum persons per room** 6. **Special comments** Complimentary continental breakfast daily.

DESCRIPTION AND COMMENTS This nice new property has 150 spacious one-room suites with double sofa bed, microwave, fridge, coffee maker, TV, hair dryer, and safe. The suites aren't lavish, but they are clean and contemporary with a muted deep purple and beige color scheme. Extra counter space in the bathroom is especially convenient for larger families. The heated pool is large and amoeba-shaped, with plenty of lounge chairs and moderate landscaping. A kiddie pool, whirlpool, and poolside bar complete the courtyard area. Other on-site amenities include an arcade and gift shop. But the big plus for this place is its location—right next door to a shopping center with just about everything a traveling family could possibly need. Here's what you'll find: seven dining options, including Outback Steakhouse, Dairy Queen, Subway, TGI Friday's, and Chinese, Japanese, and Italian eateries; a Goodings supermarket; one-hour film developing; a hair salon; a bank; a dry cleaner; a tourist information center with park passes for sale; and a Centra Care walk-in clinic, among other services. All this just a short walk from your room.

Gaylord Palms Resort
6000 West Osceola Parkway, Kissimmee; ☎ 407-586-0000; www.gaylordpalms.com

Rate per night $325. **Pool** ★★★★. **Fridge in room** Yes. **Shuttle to parks** Yes (Disney). **Maximum persons per room** 4. **Special comments** Probably the closest thing to Disney-level extravagance off Disney grounds.

DESCRIPTION AND COMMENTS Gaylord Palms is a decidedly upscale resort. Though it has a colossal convention facility and strongly caters to its business clientele, the Gaylord Palms is still a nice (if pricey) family resort. Opened in 2001, the property is also quite new. The hotel wings are defined by the three themed, glass-roofed atriums they overlook. Key West features design reminiscent of island life in the Florida Keys; the Everglades are an overgrown spectacle of shabby swamp chic, complete with piped-in cricket noise and a robotic alligator; and the immense, central St. Augustine hearkens back to old Spanish colonial Florida. Lagoons, streams, and waterfalls cut through and connect all three, and little walkways and bridges abound. The rooms themselves reflect the color schemes of their respective areas, though there's no particular connection in decor (the St. Augustine atrium view rooms are the most opulent, but they're not in any way Spanish). The fourth wing of rooms, the Emerald Tower, overlooks the Emerald Bay shopping and dining area of the St. Augustine atrium; these rooms are the nicest and most expensive, and they're mostly used by convention-goers. Though rooms have fridges, CD stereos, and high-speed Internet access, they really work better as retreats for adults than for kids. However, children will enjoy wandering the themed areas, playing in the family pool (complete with giant water-squirting octopus), or participating in the La Petite Academy Kids Station, which organizes a range of games and activities for wee ones.

Holiday Inn Nikki Bird Resort
kids **7300 West US 192, Kissimmee**
☎ 407-396-7300 or 800-20-OASIS

Rate per night $100. **Pools** ★★★½. **Fridge in room** Yes. **Shuttle to parks** Yes (Disney only). **Maximum persons per room** 5 (2 adults; 3 small children). **Special comments** Kids 12 and under eat free from special menus with a paying adult; room service includes Pizza Hut pizza.

DESCRIPTION AND COMMENTS In the Orlando hotel world, you're nobody unless you have a mascot. Here it's the Nikki Bird and Wacky the Wizard, who stroll the resort, interacting with kids and posing for photos. This Holiday Inn offers standard guest rooms as well as Kidsuites. All rooms feature microwave, fridge, TV with Sony PlayStation, coffee maker, iron and board, hair dryer, and safe. Additionally, Kidsuites offer a themed kids area within the guest room with kid-size bunk beds and twin bed, TV with VCR, Sony PlayStation, and CD stereo. Kidsuites are most suitable for families with children age nine and under, as the kids beds are small. Standard rooms are spacious, but the Kidsuites are a bit cramped. This sprawling resort offers three pools with whirlpools and two kiddie pools with squirt fountains and small playgrounds, so you won't have to walk far to cool off. On-site volleyball and tennis provide more outdoor recreation. Fitness equipment is also available, and a large arcade has air hockey, pool, and Sega games. The resort can arrange a baby-sitter for $10 per hour (four-hour minimum) plus a $10 transportation fee. The full-service Angel's Diner has 1950s-style diner decor and a good buffet with American cuisine and some theme nights. You'll find nightly family entertainment at Nikki's Nest with songs, puppet and magic shows, and games.

Howard Johnson EnchantedLand

kids **4985 West US 192, Kissimmee**
☎ **407-396-4343 or 888-753-4343**

Rate per night $79. **Pool** ★★. **Fridge in room** Yes. **Shuttle to parks** Yes (Disney, Universal, and SeaWorld). **Maximum persons per room** 4. **Special comments** Complimentary ice cream party; free video library.

DESCRIPTION AND COMMENTS Fairies, dragons, and superheroes have invaded the HoJo. If you stay here, be sure you book what they call a Family Value Room. Approximately 300 square feet, these rooms feature a themed kids area (choose from a tree house, fairies, or action heroes) with a twin daybed that converts to two twins or one king, TV and VCR, microwave, fridge, coffee maker, and safe. Note that the kids area is separated from the double bed by a mere half-wall divider, so if you're looking for privacy and space from the kids, this probably isn't the place for you. While you're taking care of the real bill, kids can check in at their own desk in the form of a tree house. For $5 per child, the Adventure Club, based in a small playroom, offers supervised activities, games, and movies on weekend evenings (Thursday–Saturday). There is a small market on site, and breakfast is served every morning from 7 to 11 a.m. (kids age 12 and under eat free with a paying adult). Other on-site amenities include a small arcade and a whirlpool. It may not offer the myriad amenities found in more deluxe properties, but EnchantedLand is a good value for your theme buck.

Radisson Resort Parkway
2900 Parkway Boulevard, Kissimmee; ☎ 407-396-7000 or 800-634-4774

Rate per night $149. **Pool** ★★★★½. **Fridge in room** Minibar. **Shuttle to parks** Yes (Disney, Universal, and SeaWorld). **Maximum persons per room** 4. **Special comments** Kids 10 and under eat free with a paying adult at any hotel restaurant.

DESCRIPTION AND COMMENTS The Radisson Resort gets high marks in all areas, but first the pool. It's a huge, free-form affair with a waterfall and waterslide surrounded by lush palms and flowering plants, plus an additional smaller heated pool, two whirlpools, and a kiddie pool. Other outdoor amenities include two lighted tennis courts, volleyball, a playground, and jogging areas. Kids can also blow off steam at the arcade, while adults might visit the fitness center with a sauna. The recently renovated guest rooms are elegant and feature Italian furnishings with clean lines and marble baths. Rooms are fairly large and include minibar, coffee maker, color TV, iron and board, hair dryer, and safe. Dining options include The Court for breakfast and dinner buffets and a 1950s-style diner serving burgers, sandwiches, shakes, and Pizza Hut pizza, among other fare. A sports lounge with an 11-by-6-foot TV offers nighttime entertainment. Guest services can help with special tours, park passes, car rental, and baby-sitting. The only downside here is the lack of an organized children's program. The good news is parents don't sacrifice their vacation for the kids—all will be equally happy here.

PART TWO

BUSCH GARDENS TAMPA BAY

SPANNING 335 ACRES, BUSCH GARDENS combines elements of a zoo and theme park. The park is divided into eight African-themed regions (as you encounter them moving counterclockwise through the park): Morocco, Crown Colony, Egypt, Nairobi, Timbuktu, Congo, Stanleyville, and Bird Gardens. A haven for thrill-ride fanatics, several of the park's eight roller coasters are consistently rated among the top five in the country. Busch Gardens is more than thrill fare, however, with beautiful landscape, excellent shows, and a really wonderful children's play area.

With the wildlife of Disney's Animal Kingdom and the thrills of Universal Studios Islands of Adventure, some may wonder why leave Orlando for a day at Busch Gardens in Tampa? For those who love roller coasters, Busch Gardens boasts eight, four in the super-coaster category. No other area attraction can top that in terms of thrills. Nor can it be matched in its ability to offer a balanced day of fun for all ages. Those who shy away from roller coasters will find plenty to do at the park, with its abundance of animal exhibits, children's rides, gardens, shows, and shops.

In addition, the drive is easy—about 90 minutes from Orlando. With Florida's fickle weather, it could be raining in Orlando but bright and sunny in Tampa, so it's a good idea to check the weather if you're rained out of O-town. Of course, this holds true in reverse, and, unlike Disney, where most of the rides are indoors, any rain will cause the closing of most of the rides at Busch Gardens.

unofficial **TIP**
Busch Gardens offers proximity to Tampa, including the city's beaches and other attractions.

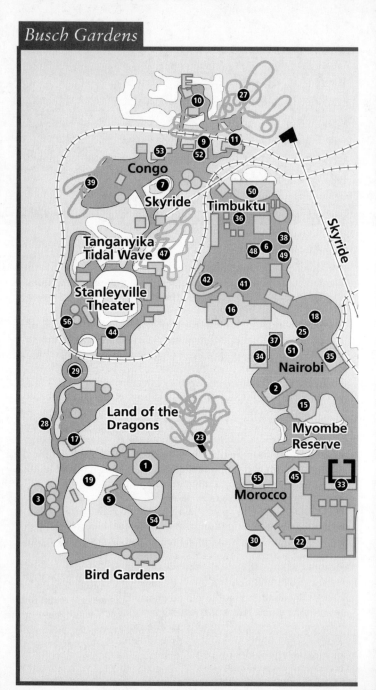

Busch Gardens

Congo

Skyride

Timbuktu

Tanganyika
Tidal Wave

Stanleyville
Theater

Nairobi

Land of the
Dragons

Myombe
Reserve

Morocco

Bird Gardens

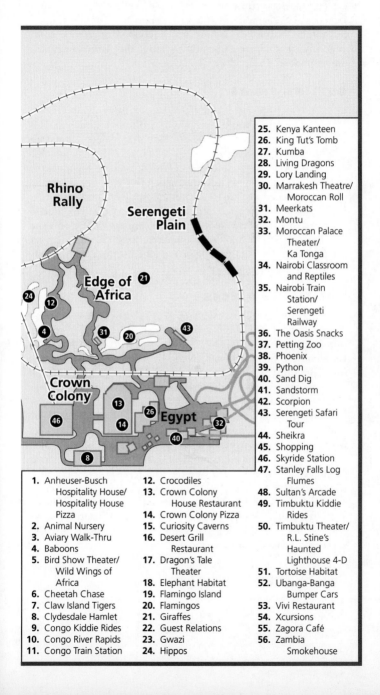

Rhino Rally

Serengeti Plain

Edge of Africa

Crown Colony

Egypt

1. Anheuser-Busch
   Hospitality House/
   Hospitality House
   Pizza
2. Animal Nursery
3. Aviary Walk-Thru
4. Baboons
5. Bird Show Theater/
   Wild Wings of
   Africa
6. Cheetah Chase
7. Claw Island Tigers
8. Clydesdale Hamlet
9. Congo Kiddie Rides
10. Congo River Rapids
11. Congo Train Station
12. Crocodiles
13. Crown Colony
    House Restaurant
14. Crown Colony Pizza
15. Curiosity Caverns
16. Desert Grill
    Restaurant
17. Dragon's Tale
    Theater
18. Elephant Habitat
19. Flamingo Island
20. Flamingos
21. Giraffes
22. Guest Relations
23. Gwazi
24. Hippos

25. Kenya Kanteen
26. King Tut's Tomb
27. Kumba
28. Living Dragons
29. Lory Landing
30. Marrakesh Theatre/
    Moroccan Roll
31. Meerkats
32. Montu
33. Moroccan Palace
    Theater/
    Ka Tonga
34. Nairobi Classroom
    and Reptiles
35. Nairobi Train
    Station/
    Serengeti
    Railway
36. The Oasis Snacks
37. Petting Zoo
38. Phoenix
39. Python
40. Sand Dig
41. Sandstorm
42. Scorpion
43. Serengeti Safari
    Tour
44. Sheikra
45. Shopping
46. Skyride Station
47. Stanley Falls Log
    Flumes
48. Sultan's Arcade
49. Timbuktu Kiddie
    Rides
50. Timbuktu Theater/
    R.L. Stine's
    Haunted
    Lighthouse 4-D
51. Tortoise Habitat
52. Ubanga-Banga
    Bumper Cars
53. Vivi Restaurant
54. Xcursions
55. Zagora Café
56. Zambia
    Smokehouse

The park is only minutes away from the white-sand beaches of St. Petersburg and Tampa Bay, an often-overlooked advantage. A Busch Gardens weekend visit can also be combined with a trip to Adventure Island, the Anheuser-Busch water park in Tampa Bay.

GETTING THERE

BUSCH GARDENS IS ABOUT 70 MILES from Walt Disney World. The trip should take about an hour and a half, depending on traffic and the construction that plagues Interstate 4. The best way to get there is via Interstate 275. Driving west on I-4, there are signs for Busch Gardens, but we recommend ignoring them to avoid a long journey through city streets of Tampa. Proceed instead to the junction of I-275 and go north. Exit at Busch Boulevard (Exit 33), turn right, and drive a little over two miles; the entrance to Busch Gardens will be on your left. Parking is $7 in a lot across the street from the park (trams are provided) and $11 in a preferred lot closer to the main entrance, which fills up quickly.

ADMISSION PRICES

BEFORE PURCHASING TICKETS TO BUSCH GARDENS, consider some of the choices below, which are similar to the options offered by its sister park, SeaWorld (both Busch Gardens and SeaWorld are owned by Anheuser-Busch Brewing Company, which explains why both parks feature beer schools). As with SeaWorld, the best option for most visitors to Busch Gardens is a one-day pass. In fact, Busch Gardens has discontinued most of its multiday tickets in favor of package deals and annual passes. However, Busch Gardens really wants your business, and there are several options that will get you a lot more time in the park for not much more money than the cost of a one-day ticket. If you're planning to spend time at other Orlando theme parks, however, consider the FlexTicket, which includes admission to SeaWorld, Wet 'n' Wild, Universal, and Islands of Adventure. Discounts are available for AAA members, disabled visitors, senior citizens, and military personnel.

One-Day Pass

Adults	$55.95 + tax
Children ages 3–9	$45.95
Children under age 3	Free

Busch Gardens Fun Card

THIS PASS IS BY FAR THE BEST DEAL for admission to Busch Gardens. For $6 more than general admission, you can return to the park an unlimited amount of times for a whole year. Fun Cards aren't valid on Memorial Day weekend or weekends between June 4 and August 7, the park's most popular times of year.

BUSCH GARDENS $61.95

BUSCH GARDENS AND SEAWORLD ORLANDO $99.95

BUSCH GARDENS AND ADVENTURE ISLAND WATER PARK

Adults $99.95
Children ages 3–9 $89.95

BUSCH GARDENS, ADVENTURE ISLAND, AND SEA WORLD

Adults $129.95
Children ages 3–9 $119.95

Busch Gardens/SeaWorld Value Ticket

THIS PASS ALLOWS ONE-DAY ADMISSION to Busch Gardens and one-day admission to SeaWorld.

Adults $94.95 + tax
Children ages 3–9 $84.95

Annual Passports

THESE ALLOW UNLIMITED ADMISSION to either Busch Gardens alone, or Busch Gardens and SeaWorld, or Busch Gardens, Adventure Island, and SeaWorld for one or two years. Unlike the Fun Card, there are no blackout dates.

BUSCH GARDENS SILVER PASSPORT (ONE YEAR)

Adults $94.95
Children ages 3–9 and seniors ages 50+ $84.95

BUSCH GARDENS GOLD PASSPORT (TWO YEARS)

Adults $144.95
Children ages 3–9 and seniors ages 50+ $134.95

BUSCH GARDENS/SEAWORLD SILVER PASSPORT (ONE YEAR)

Adults $144.95;
Children ages 3–9 and seniors ages 50+ $134.95

BUSCH GARDENS/SEAWORLD GOLD PASSPORT (TWO YEARS)

Adults $219.95
Children ages 3–9 and seniors ages 50+ $209.95

BUSCH GARDENS/ADVENTURE ISLAND/SEAWORLD SILVER PASSPORT (ONE YEAR)		
Adults $184.95		
Children ages 3–9 and seniors ages 50+ $174.95		
BUSCH GARDENS/ADVENTURE ISLAND/SEAWORLD GOLD PASSPORT (TWO YEARS)		
Adults $269.95		
Children ages 3–9 and seniors ages 50+ $259.95		

Orlando FlexTicket

THIS PASS IS GOOD FOR UP TO 14 consecutive days at five parks: Busch Gardens, Universal Studios Florida, Universal Islands of Adventure, SeaWorld, and Wet 'n' Wild. There's a version that excludes Busch Gardens, so be sure to get the one you want.

FLEXTICKET
Adults $224.95 + tax
Children ages 3–9 and seniors ages 50+ $189.95
FLEXTICKET WITHOUT BUSCH GARDENS
Adults $184.95 + tax
Children ages 3–9 and seniors ages 50+ $150.95

ARRIVING

NORMAL PARK HOURS VARY month to month and sometimes day to day but are always between 9 a.m. and 8 p.m. The park stays open until 10 p.m. mid-June through the end of July. Unlike other local attractions, Busch Gardens does not allow you through the turnstiles before the scheduled opening time. We recommend checking the Web site (**www.buschgardens.com**) for exact hours of operation, as they change almost daily during certain months. Visiting during peak seasons equals waiting in long lines. Busch Gardens also draws crowds of locals, so avoid visiting on weekends or holidays.

Even when crowds are low, it requires a lot of planning and hustling to see Busch Gardens in one day. In particular, expect to spend a lot of time getting oriented and consulting park maps and signage. With no central hub and few connecting walkways, it's very easy to get lost. Go slow until you have a feel for where you are in the park, or you could spend some frustrating time retracing your steps. Of course, group ages and personal tastes will eliminate some rides and exhibits. Groups without children, for instance, don't need to budget time for kiddie rides. However, even selective touring may not afford enough time to enjoy the park fully. Following are a few tips that may help:

PLAN AHEAD The Busch Gardens map is crammed full of rides and exhibits; the first time many visitors see it, they develop a glazed look in their eyes and begin a crazed tour. Somehow we doubt these folk see even half of what the park offers. Instead, determine in advance what you really want to see. For many groups this involves compromise: parents may not want to spend as much time as children on rides, whereas older kids may want to steer clear of many of the zoological exhibits. If children are old enough, we recommend splitting up after determining a few meeting times and locations for checking in throughout the day. Alternately, parents may want to plan kids rides around the live entertainment schedule, placing children safely in line and then attending a performance of a nearby show while the youngsters wait and ride. Note that bags, cameras, and other belongings are not permitted on most of the thrill rides; for 50 cents, you can temporarily stow such items in lockers near the ride entrances.

> *unofficial* **TIP**
> As with all the theme parks, get to the entrance at or before opening time.

ARRIVE EARLY As with other central Florida attractions, this is the single most effective strategy for efficient touring and avoiding long line waits. Leave Orlando around 7 a.m. to arrive a little before 8:30 a.m. during peak season. Give yourself an extra half hour during other times, when the park doesn't open until 9:30 a.m. Have a quick breakfast before leaving, or eat in the car to save time. Park, purchase tickets (either at windows or through the self-service kiosks), and be at the turnstile ready to roll when the gate opens at either 9 or 9:30 a.m. First thing in the morning, there should be no lines and relatively few people. Rides that require up to an hour (or more) wait later in the day can be experienced in less than 15 minutes first thing in the morning.

There are two ways to hit the three major coasters at prime times for as little waiting as possible:

Route 1: Ride Gwazi (located at the front of the park) first thing, then head to Montu, followed by Kumba, and save SheiKra for mid- to late afternoon.

Route 2: After riding Gwazi first, continue onto Stanleyville to ride SheiKra, followed by Kumba; hit Montu late in the day.

BE READY TO WALK AND WALK AND WALK Busch Gardens is huge and requires lots of walking. Definitely bring strollers for little ones and consider wheelchairs for others who will tire quickly. In addition, have all members in your party grab a park map and show schedule (which, frustratingly, are not combined as at most other attractions). Due to the park's confusing layout, you'll appreciate the navigational help of your entire gang. You might also want to stop for group meals, as eateries are widely spaced and roving snack vendors are sometimes scarce.

AVOID BOTTLENECKS An early arrival will help you avoid the bottlenecks at most of the major attractions. As for smaller rides, if there's a line, don't wait. Go see a show or visit the animal exhibits, which usually have no wait. Then return to the rides later in the day, when lines should subside.

CONTACTING BUSCH GARDENS

FOR MORE INFORMATION, call ☎ 888-800-5447. In addition to park information, the Busch Gardens Web site (**www.buschgardens.com**) also contains an animal information database.

ATTRACTIONS

MOROCCO

Marrakesh Theatre/Moroccan Roll

APPEAL BY AGE	PRESCHOOL ★★½	GRADE SCHOOL ★★	TEENS ★★½
YOUNG ADULTS ★★★		OVER 30 ★★★	SENIORS ★★★½

What it is Song-and-dance show. **Scope and scale** Major attraction. **When to go** Check daily entertainment schedule. **Author's rating** Dorky but amusing; ★★★. **Duration of show** 30 minutes.

DESCRIPTION AND COMMENTS Dancers and singers in vaguely Middle Eastern garb fling themselves around to the beats of contemporary pop and rock songs. The performers don't take themselves or their routines too seriously, and neither does the audience.

TOURING TIPS Rows of wrought-iron patio seats fill this outdoor theater. They are not on an incline, and it is difficult to see the stage from the back. Arrive 10 minutes early to get the best seats near the front of the house. Also, rows to the right or left of the stage don't fill up as quickly and offer great views.

Moroccan Palace Theater/KaTonga

APPEAL BY AGE	PRESCHOOL ★★½	GRADE SCHOOL ★★★½	TEENS ★★★
YOUNG ADULTS ★★★★		OVER 30 ★★★★	SENIORS ★★★★

What it is Musical stage show. **Scope and scale** Headliner. **When to go** Check daily entertainment schedule. **Author's rating** Great music, beautiful puppets, and interesting history ★★★★. **Duration of show** 30 minutes.

DESCRIPTION AND COMMENTS A day in the lives of master African storytellers called Griots, who weave involved and interesting historic tales using music, dance, and impressive, colorful puppets akin to those used in the Broadway version of *The Lion King*. African folklore, traditional music, and dance are all beautiful and well presented.

TOURING TIPS The best time to see this show is either as a first or last stop, depending on the show schedule for the day. Try to sit as close to the stage as possible for the best view.

CROWN COLONY

Skyride

APPEAL BY AGE	PRESCHOOL ★★	GRADE SCHOOL ★★½	TEENS ★★
YOUNG ADULTS ★★		OVER 30 ★★½	SENIORS ★★★

What it is Scenic transportation to Stanleyville. **Scope and scale** Minor attraction. **When to go** In the morning; lines can be long in the afternoon. **Author's rating** Good way to see the Rhino Rally in action; ★★½. **Duration of ride** 4 minutes.

DESCRIPTION AND COMMENTS This aerial tram ride travels to Stanleyville. It goes directly over the Rhino Rally attraction and offers views of the Serengeti Plain as well as the roller coasters. You can board here or in Stanleyville, but you cannot stay on for a round-trip.

TOURING TIPS Unless lines are short, this ride takes longer than walking. It's still faster than the train, though.

kids Rhino Rally

APPEAL BY AGE	PRESCHOOL ★★★½	GRADE SCHOOL ★★★★★
TEENS ★★★★½	YOUNG ADULTS ★★★★½	OVER 30 ★★★★½

What it is Off-road adventure through African-themed terrain. **Scope and scale** Headliner. **When to go** Before 10 a.m. or after 3:30 p.m. **Special comments** Beware if you've got back problems, the ride gets a little bumpy—and wet if you're sitting on the left side of the vehicle. **Author's rating** Great fun, and you see a host of African wildlife; ★★★★½. **Duration of ride** 8–10 minutes.

DESCRIPTION AND COMMENTS Riders board 17-passenger Land Rovers for a safari and wild river adventure across 16 acres, with one "lucky" guest riding shotgun with the wise-cracking driver. The trip—a "competition" for the world's ultimate off-road trophy—gets off to a mild-but-bumpy start, and everyone has a great view of white rhinoceroses, elephants, Cape buffalos, Nile crocodiles, zebras, antelopes, wildebeests, and other species, with running commentary by the driver.

Before too long, of course, the truck comes to a fork in the road, and the driver must make a choice—taking riders on part two of the trip, a surprising journey that involves splashing through riverbeds, a torrential downpour, and raging white waters, with the Land Rover turning into a floating pontoon with an inflatable underside when a flash flood washes out the bridge. Nothing exceptionally thrilling, but everyone is laughing as the SUV-cum-boat delivers everyone back from the rushing waters to dry land.

TOURING TIPS The 8- to 10-minute ride can board about 1,600 guests per hour, but because the attraction is popular, make it one of your early rides (either first thing, or after Gwazi and Montu if you're doing Route #1; second to last if you're doing Route #2). The queue is covered and splits into two lines near the boarding area; pick the shortest line at that point, as the split is only to expedite boarding (there is no difference in the experience).

When you board, request a seat on the right side if you want to stay dry. Youngsters under age 6 may be frightened by some of the heavy water effects.

Edge of Africa

APPEAL BY AGE	PRESCHOOL ★★★½	GRADE SCHOOL ★★★★	TEENS ★★★
YOUNG ADULTS ★★★		OVER 30 ★★★½	SENIORS ★★★½

What it is Walking tour of animal habitats. **Scope and scale** Headliner. **When to go** Crowds are minuscule in the afternoon, and the animals are fairly active. **Author's rating** Good presentation; ★★★½.

DESCRIPTION AND COMMENTS This walking safari features hippopotamuses, giraffes, lions, baboons, meerkats, hyenas, and vultures in naturalistic habitats. The area was designed for up-close viewing, many times with just a pane of glass between you and the animals. Of note are the hippopotamus exhibit and the hyena area. The hippopotamus wade in five-foot-deep water filled with colorful fish, all visible through the glass wall. In the hyena habitat, open safari vehicles are built into the glass, offering a great photo opportunity if you climb in when the animals come near.

TOURING TIPS Animals are most active during feedings, but these are not regularly scheduled, so the animals don't fall into a pattern that would not exist in the wild. Employees are usually willing to tell you feeding times for the day. It might be a hike to return to this area, but seeing the lions chomp into raw meat is definitely worth it.

There is a hidden entrance to this area between Tut's Tomb and the restrooms near Montu. This is useful if you ride the roller coaster before seeing the animals.

Serengeti Safari Tour

APPEAL BY AGE	PRESCHOOL ★★★	GRADE SCHOOL ★★★½	TEENS ★★★
YOUNG ADULTS ★★★★		OVER 30 ★★★½	SENIORS ★★★½

What it is Guided tour. **Scope and scale** Major attraction. **When to go** Call reservation number for a schedule. **Special comments** Costs $30 for everyone age 5 and older. **Author's rating** Worthwhile but might be too expensive for the average visitor; ★★★½. **Duration of tour** 30 minutes.

DESCRIPTION AND COMMENTS If you don't mind spending the extra $30, this guided tour of the Serengeti Plain provides amazing close encounters with the animals. You'll board a flatbed truck and head into an area where no other visitors are allowed. The highlight of the trip is feeding the giraffes. It's amazing to watch their long tongues remove the leaves from a prickly branch while adeptly avoiding thorns. With the construction of the Rhino Rally attraction underneath the Skyride tram, this tour and the train are the only ways to get a good look at the animals on the Serengeti Plain.

TOURING TIPS Only 20 people can fit on the truck, so it's a good idea to make reservations in advance. Call ☎ 813-987-4043 or 813-984-4073 for reservations and more information.

EGYPT

kids Clydesdale Hamlet

APPEAL BY AGE	PRESCHOOL ★★½	GRADE SCHOOL ★★½	TEENS ★½
YOUNG ADULTS ★½		OVER 30 ★★	SENIORS ★★½

What it is Horse stable. **Scope and scale** Diversion. **When to go** Anytime. **Author's rating** Great for kids; ★★.

DESCRIPTION AND COMMENTS This blue-roofed white stable is home to several Clydesdales, huge and beautiful draft horses that are the Anheuser-Busch mascots.

TOURING TIPS These horses are truly amazing to look at, and kids will really enjoy this, but don't waste time here if you're trying to rush through all the coasters and water rides. The horses are sometimes otherwise engaged and the stable may only house one or two horses; sometimes none at all.

King Tut's Tomb

APPEAL BY AGE	PRESCHOOL ★	GRADE SCHOOL ★	TEENS ★½
YOUNG ADULTS ★½		OVER 30 ★★	SENIORS ★★½

What it is Walking tour of a re-created tomb. **Scope and scale** Diversion. **When to go** Anytime; don't wait if there's a line. **Author's rating** Semi-interesting, but often not worth the time; ★. **Duration of tour** 10 minutes.

DESCRIPTION AND COMMENTS The spirit of King Tut leads you on a tour of this re-creation of his tomb. The narration features information about the tomb's artifacts and his life. Objects on display include replicas of Tut's large throne, chariot, and golden sculpted coffin, as well as urns purportedly containing his internal organs.

TOURING TIPS This air-conditioned attraction provides a break from the heat, but it should be skipped if you're in a hurry. Though a bit dull, it does work as a time killer for visitors waiting for the rest of their party to ride Montu.

Montu

APPEAL BY AGE	PRESCHOOL †	GRADE SCHOOL ★★★★	TEENS ★★★★★
YOUNG ADULTS ★★★★½		OVER 30 ★★★½	SENIORS ★★½

† Preschoolers are generally too short to ride.

What it is Inverted, steel super roller coaster. **Scope and scale** Super headliner. **When to go** Before 10 a.m. or after 4 p.m. **Special comments** Riders must be at least 54 inches tall. **Author's rating** Incredible; ★★★★★. **Duration of ride** About 3 minutes. **Loading speed** Quick.

DESCRIPTION AND COMMENTS Seats hang below the track and riders' feet dangle on this intense inverted roller coaster, which is among the top five in the country and among the best we've ever ridden. The fast-paced but extremely smooth ride begins with a 13-story drop. Riders are then hurled through a 104-foot inverted vertical loop. Speeds reach 60 mph as riders are accelerated through more dizzying loops and twists, including an Immelman, an inverse loop named after German World War I fighter pilot Max Immelman.

TOURING TIPS Depending on which route you take, try to ride in the morning or later in the afternoon to avoid waits that can be as long as an hour (or even more). If lines are still long, however, don't be discouraged. As many as 32 riders can pile on to each train, so even the longest line will move quickly and steadily.

If you have time, ride twice, first near the back of the train and then in the front row. In the back, you'll glimpse a sea of dangling feet in front of you and be surprised by each twist and turn because you can't see where the track is headed, just legs swooping through the air. Riding in the front gives you a clear, unobstructed view of everything around you, including the huge trees dozens of feet below you on the first drop. If you have to choose one or the other, we definitely recommend the front row. Look for the special front-seat queue once you enter the load station. The wait for the front is usually an extra 20 minutes, but it's worth it for the thrill.

NAIROBI

Myombe Reserve

APPEAL BY AGE	PRESCHOOL ★★★	GRADE SCHOOL ★★★	TEENS ★★½
YOUNG ADULTS ★★½		OVER 30 ★★★	SENIORS ★★★

What it is Gorilla and ape habitat. **Scope and scale** Major attraction. **When to go** In the morning. **Author's rating** Great theming, informative; ★★★.

DESCRIPTION AND COMMENTS A mist-filled path through lush landscape leads you to this beautiful habitat filled with waterfalls, thick vegetation, and marshlands. The first section is home to several chimpanzees that romp through the trees and greenery. The second area features large gorillas. Only one or two of the animals are regularly visible, but at least one usually can be found napping in front of the glass. Two overhead monitors play a video full of interesting information about each of the animals in the habitat, including how they interact with each other. Chalkboards throughout the exhibit provide facts and figures about the animals.

TOURING TIPS The animals are usually most active before 11 a.m. After riding Montu you can snake through this exhibit, which exits into Nairobi, on your way to Kumba. Bronze sculptures of gorillas and chimpanzees placed throughout the exhibit provide some fun photo opportunities. Climb onto the giant gorilla at the entrance or join the train of chimpanzees combing through each other's hair for a unique snapshot.

Serengeti Railway

APPEAL BY AGE	PRESCHOOL ★★½	GRADE SCHOOL ★★½	TEENS ★★
YOUNG ADULTS ★★		OVER 30 ★★★	SENIORS ★★★½

What it is Train tour through Serengeti Plain and around the park. **Scope and scale** Minor attraction. **When to go** Afternoon. **Author's rating** Relaxing; ★★. **Duration of ride** 12 minutes through animal area exiting at next station; 35 minutes round-trip.

DESCRIPTION AND COMMENTS Riding this train gives your feet a break and provides the best view of the animals along the Serengeti Plain. Because it's quite pokey, we don't recommend it as an alternate means of transportation, but the 12-minute trip from the Nairobi station through the Serengeti Plain to the Congo station is worth the time if you're not racing to ride the coasters. On-board guides provide narration from the front of the train, identifying the animals you see and telling a little about their history and habits.

TOURING TIPS If you board at the Nairobi station, get off at the Congo station for Kumba or the Congo River Rapids; get off at Stanleyville for Tanganyika Tidal Wave or the Land of the Dragons children's area.

Curiosity Caverns

APPEAL BY AGE	PRESCHOOL ★★½	GRADE SCHOOL ★★★½	TEENS ★★½
YOUNG ADULTS ★★★		OVER 30 ★★★	SENIORS ★★½

What it is Walk-through exhibit of "odd" animals. **Scope and scale** Minor attraction. **When to go** Anytime. **Author's rating** A cool break; ★★½.

DESCRIPTION AND COMMENTS This seems to be a catchall for types of animals not exhibited elsewhere in the park. Mostly you'll see snakes and other reptiles behind glass, though there's also a three-toed sloth and a laughing kookaburra bird (the bird did not appear to be in the mood for laughter on our visit).

TOURING TIPS Though the animals are interesting, the best part is how cool and dark the exhibit is. It's a great place to get a break from the heat and brightness outside.

Animal Nursery

APPEAL BY AGE	PRESCHOOL ★★½	GRADE SCHOOL ★★★½	TEENS ★★
YOUNG ADULTS ★★★		OVER 30 ★★½	SENIORS ★★★

What it is Newborns on display. **Scope and scale** Minor attraction. **When to go** Anytime. **Author's rating** Super cute; ★★★½.

DESCRIPTION AND COMMENTS Busch Gardens is home to more than 2,700 animals, many of which often give birth to young. The park also rescues ill or orphaned animal infants, many of which are endangered. Walk by large windows in this animal nursery to glimpse some of these incredibly cute and cuddly babies. The kind of experience depends on which animals have recently been born. During one visit we saw some adorable tiger cubs and scrawny but cute baby birds feeding from an eyedropper.

TOURING TIPS A sign near the entrance usually explains which animals are on display.

Elephant Habitat

APPEAL BY AGE	PRESCHOOL ★★★	GRADE SCHOOL ★★★	TEENS ★★
YOUNG ADULTS ★★		OVER 30 ★★	SENIORS ★★½

What it is Elephant habitat. **Scope and scale** Minor attraction. **When to go** During interaction times. **Author's rating** ★★.

DESCRIPTION AND COMMENTS Endangered Asian elephants roam a dry dirt pen. A large pool is deep enough for these huge animals to submerge themselves and escape the Florida heat. The pen is surprisingly small; it's too bad the elephants can't roam the larger Serengeti Plain.

TOURING TIPS Visit during enrichment times when trainers interact with the animals, sometimes hosing them down. The daily entertainment schedule doesn't list enrichment times for all animals, so you may need to check a detailed sign at the exhibit.

TIMBUKTU

kids Cheetah Chase

APPEAL BY AGE	PRESCHOOL ★★★	GRADE SCHOOL ★★★½	TEENS ★★
YOUNG ADULTS ★★		OVER 30 ★★★	SENIORS ★★

What it is Kiddie coaster. **Scope and scale** Minor attraction. **When to go** Line is usually relatively short compared to the big coasters, but an early stop would be wise because the line grows as the day goes on. **Special comments** Riders must be at least 6 years old and 46 inches tall. **Author's rating** Fun for the little coaster lovers; ★★★. **Duration of ride** Approximately 3 minutes. **Loading speed** Moderate.

DESCRIPTION AND COMMENTS Hairpin turns and mini drops make this a good choice for thrill seekers who aren't tall enough to take on the big coasters.

TOURING TIPS The line moves quickly here; located near other kiddie rides, this is a good place to wait for the coaster-riders in your party.

Sandstorm

APPEAL BY AGE	PRESCHOOL †	GRADE SCHOOL ★★★	TEENS ★★½
YOUNG ADULTS ★★★		OVER 30 ★★½	SENIORS ★★

† Preschoolers are generally too short to ride.

What it is Carnival ride. **Scope and scale** Minor attraction. **When to go** Anytime. **Special comments** Riders must be at least 48 inches tall. **Author's rating** Amusing, but not worth a long wait; ★★. **Duration of ride** Approximately 3 minutes. **Loading speed** Slow.

DESCRIPTION AND COMMENTS This is Busch Gardens' version of a midway ride commonly known as the Scrambler. Two to three riders sit in an enclosed car. Four of the cars rotate on one of six arms that circle a central pedestal.

TOURING TIPS Though fun, this ride is nothing special. Skip it if lines are long.

Scorpion

APPEAL BY AGE	PRESCHOOL †	GRADE SCHOOL ★★★	TEENS ★★½
YOUNG ADULTS ★★★		OVER 30 ★★★	SENIORS ★★

† Preschoolers are generally too short to ride.

What it is Roller coaster. **Scope and scale** Headliner. **When to go** After 2 p.m. **Special comments** Riders must be at least 42 inches tall. **Author's rating** Quick, but exciting; ★★★. **Duration of ride** 1½ minutes.

DESCRIPTION AND COMMENTS This coaster pales in comparison to big sisters Kumba and Montu. But at speeds of 50 mph with a 360-degree vertical loop and three 360-degree spirals, it's nothing to sneeze at.

TOURING TIPS Lines will be long for this attraction; because it doesn't have the high capacity of Kumba or Montu, they move slowly. Save it for the afternoon, when the wait is almost always shorter.

Kiddie Rides

APPEAL BY AGE	PRESCHOOL ★★★	GRADE SCHOOL †	TEENS †
YOUNG ADULTS †		OVER 30 †	SENIORS †

† Not designed for older kids and adults.

What they are Pint-size carnival rides. **Scope and scale** Minor attraction. **When to go** Anytime. **Author's rating** Good diversion for children; ★★½.

DESCRIPTION AND COMMENTS Nothing fancy, but these attractions help kids that aren't old enough to ride the thrillers feel like they aren't being left out. Another set of kiddie rides can be found in the Congo.

TOURING TIPS These rides are strategically placed near the adult attractions in this area (Scorpion and Phoenix), so one parent can keep the kids occupied while another rides.

Phoenix

APPEAL BY AGE	PRESCHOOL †	GRADE SCHOOL ★★★	TEENS ★★★
YOUNG ADULTS ★★½		OVER 30 ★★½	SENIORS ★

† Preschoolers are generally too short to ride.

What it is Swinging pendulum ride. **Scope and scale** Minor attraction. **When to go** Anytime. **Special comments** Riders must be at least 48 inches tall; not for those who get motion sickness. **Author's rating** Dizzying; ★★. **Duration of ride** 5 minutes.

DESCRIPTION AND COMMENTS A large wooden boat swings back and forth, starting slowly, then gaining speed before making a complete circle with passengers hanging upside down.

TOURING TIPS Remove glasses and anything in your shirt pockets to avoid losing them when the boat is suspended upside down for several seconds.

Timbuktu Theatre/ R. L. Stine's Haunted Lighthouse 4-D

APPEAL BY AGE	PRESCHOOL ½	GRADE SCHOOL ★★★½	TEENS ★★★
YOUNG ADULTS ★★★		OVER 30 ★★½	SENIORS ★★

What it is 3-D horror show with extra punch. **Scope and scale** Headliner. **When to go** Early in the morning or after crowds diminish. **Author's rating** Creative and a lot of fun; ★★★½. **Duration of show** 20 minutes.

DESCRIPTION AND COMMENTS Serving as Busch Gardens' answer to Universal's Back to the Future: The Ride and Terminator 2 3-D, as well as Disney's *It's Tough to Be a Bug!*, the revamped Timbuktu Theatre takes the place of the venerable dolphin and sea lion show. Now outfitted with state-of-the-art equipment, this theater sports 3-D visual effects and seats equipped with individual surround sound, vibrating buzzers, and nozzles for spraying water and air. All these effects are in the service of R. L. Stine's Haunted Lighthouse 4-D, a lightweight scary story dreamed up by the best-selling writer of juvenile horror. A high number of startles and creepy crawlies are guaranteed.

TOURING TIPS Three-dimensional ghosts plus sometimes-loud volume and other special effects make it this production too intense for preschoolers or younger children. Use discretion when determining what sensitive wee ones can tolerate.

CONGO

Ubanga-Banga Bumper Cars

APPEAL BY AGE	PRESCHOOL ★★★	GRADE SCHOOL ★★★	TEENS ★★★
YOUNG ADULTS ★★½		OVER 30 ★★	SENIORS ★

What it is Bumper-car ride. **Scope and scale** Minor attraction. **When to go** Anytime. **Author's rating** ★★½. **Duration of ride** Approximately 2 minutes, depending on park attendance.

DESCRIPTION AND COMMENTS Basic carnival bumper-car ride.

TOURING TIPS Don't waste time waiting in the usually very long line for this attraction if you're on the roller-coaster circuit. However, because this ride is right next to Kumba, it is a perfect place for kids and others in your group to wait for those braving the coaster.

Kumba

APPEAL BY AGE	PRESCHOOL †	GRADE SCHOOL ★★★★	TEENS ★★★★
YOUNG ADULTS ★★★★		OVER 30 ★★★★	SENIORS ★★

† *Preschoolers are generally too short to ride.*

What it is Steel super roller coaster. **Scope and scale** Super headliner. **When to go** Before 11 a.m. or after 2:30 p.m. **Special comments** Riders must be at least 54 inches tall. **Author's rating** Excellent; ★★★★. **Duration of ride** Approximately 3 minutes.

DESCRIPTION AND COMMENTS Kumba's dramatic loops rise above the treeline in the Congo area, with a trainload of screaming riders twisting skyward. Just like sister coaster Montu, Kumba is one of the best in the country. Unlike Montu, Kumba's trains sits on top of the track as it roars through 3,900 feet of twists and loops. Reaching speeds of 60 mph, Kumba is certainly fast, but it also offers an incredibly smooth ride. This is a good thing, because the coaster's intense corkscrews will churn up your insides something fierce. Thrilling elements include a diving loop, a camelback with a 360-degree spiral, and a 108-foot vertical loop.

TOURING TIPS Ride Gwazi and, depending on which track you take, either SheiKra or Montu second, then head to Kumba. Just like Montu and SheiKra, as many as 32 riders can brave Kumba at once, so even if there is a line, the wait shouldn't be unbearable.

Congo River Rapids

APPEAL BY AGE	PRESCHOOL ★★★½	GRADE SCHOOL ★★★½	TEENS
★★★½	YOUNG ADULTS ★★★	OVER 30 ★★★	SENIORS ★★½

What it is Whitewater raft ride. **Scope and scale** Headliner. **When to go** After 4 p.m. **Special comments** You will get soaked. **Author's rating** A great time, but not worth more than a 45-minute wait; ★★★. **Duration of ride** 3 minutes. **Loading speed** Slow to moderate; unloading is very slow.

DESCRIPTION AND COMMENTS Whitewater raft rides have become somewhat of a theme park standard, and this version is pretty fun and exciting. Twelve riders sit on a circular rubber raft as they float down a jungle river, jostling and spinning in the waves and rapids. Scary signs warn of dangerous crocodiles in the "river," but no beasts (robotic or otherwise) ever show themselves. It is possible to avoid getting drenched through the sheer luck of where your boat goes, but in the end, getting very wet is almost guaranteed by water jets operated by mischievous onlookers over a bridge and a final gauntlet of giant water jets that soaks almost every raft that passes through. There's nothing like the helpless feeling of watching your boat drift into the path of one of these mega firehoses.

TOURING TIPS Wear a poncho, either your own or one purchased at nearby concession huts. Stow as much clothing in the lockers as you can take off and remain decent (especially socks—nobody likes squishy feet). Also, know that long lines are inevitable for this slow-loading and -unloading attraction. We recommend you ride the roller coasters first, saving this attraction for later in the afternoon. The cute monkeys on display make waiting in the first third of the line fairly entertaining.

Claw Island Tigers

APPEAL BY AGE	PRESCHOOL ★★	GRADE SCHOOL ★★★	TEENS ★½
YOUNG ADULTS ★½		OVER 30 ★★½	SENIORS ★★½

What it is Tiger habitat. **Scope and scale** Minor attraction. **When to go** Animals are most active in the morning, but they're always visible. **Author's rating** Beautiful critters, but lame presentation; ★½.

DESCRIPTION AND COMMENTS A lush, sunken island is home to several Bengal tigers, one of which is a rare white tiger. A waterfall-fed lagoon surrounds the island. Fairly unexciting.

TOURING TIPS The animals are visible, but they're usually napping in the afternoon. On your morning walk to Kumba, stop by quickly to possibly catch them in action. Check the daily entertainment guide or a listing at the habitat for interaction times.

Python

APPEAL BY AGE	PRESCHOOL †	GRADE SCHOOL ★★★½	TEENS ★★½
YOUNG ADULTS ★★★		OVER 30 ★★★	SENIORS ★★

† Preschoolers are generally too short to ride.

What it is Roller coaster. **Scope and scale** Headliner. **When to go** After 3 p.m. **Special comments** Riders must be at least 48 inches tall. **Author's rating** A quick adrenaline rush; ★★★. **Duration of ride** 1 minute.

DESCRIPTION AND COMMENTS At less than a third the size of Kumba, the Python offers a brief thrill. Riders climb six stories before hurling through two vertical loops, exceeding speeds of 40 mph.

TOURING TIPS This one's short and doesn't have the large capacity of Kumba and Montu. Save it for the afternoon, when lines should be shorter.

Kiddie Rides

APPEAL BY AGE	PRESCHOOL ★★★	GRADE SCHOOL †	TEENS †	YOUNG
ADULTS †		OVER 30 †		SENIORS †

† Not designed for older kids and adults.

What they are Pint-sized carnival rides. **Scope and scale** Minor attraction. **When to go** Anytime. **Author's rating** Good diversion for children; ★★½.

DESCRIPTION AND COMMENTS Nothing fancy, but these attractions help kids who aren't old enough to ride the thrillers feel like they aren't being left out. Similar to the kiddie rides in Timbuktu.

TOURING TIPS These rides are strategically placed near the adult attractions in this area (Kumba and Python), so one parent can keep the kids occupied while another rides.

STANLEYVILLE

SheiKra

APPEAL BY AGE	NOT OPEN AT PRESS TIME.

What it is Quick steel-track dive coaster. **Scope and scale** Super headliner. **When to go** Before 11 a.m. or after 4 p.m. **Special comments** Riders must be at least 54 inches tall. **Author's rating** Not open at press time. **Duration of ride** 3 minutes.

DESCRIPTION AND COMMENTS This newest attraction is 200 feet tall, making it the tallest coaster in the state of Florida, as well as the tallest dive coaster in the world and one of only three dive coasters that exist anywhere. (A dive coaster means the ride has a completely vertical drop.) Also incorporated are twists, swooping turns, and a second huge plunge. The drops aren't just steep—riders hurtle down at an average of 70 miles per hour.

TOURING TIPS If you decide to take route #2, hit Gwazi when the park opens, then make SheiKra your second stop. If taking route #1, try to head to SheiKra as late in the day as possible, leaving an hour or so (just in case) to wait in line and ride before the park closes.

Tanganyika Tidal Wave

APPEAL BY AGE	PRESCHOOL †	GRADE SCHOOL ★★★	TEENS ★★★
YOUNG ADULTS ★★★		OVER 30 ★★★	SENIORS ★★

† Preschoolers are generally too short to ride.

What it is Quick, super water-flume ride. **Scope and scale** Headliner. **When to go** Before 11 a.m. or after 3 p.m. **Special comments** Riders must be at least 48 inches tall; you will get soaked. **Author's rating** A long wait for a very short thrill; ★★½. **Duration of ride** 2 minutes.

DESCRIPTION AND COMMENTS The Tanganyika Tidal Wave was king before the Orlando parks realized that a super water-flume ride should entertain you as well as get you wet. Consequently, this ride pales in comparison with Splash Mountain at Walt Disney World or Jurassic Park at Islands of Adventure. It does do a spectacular job of getting you soaked, however. Riders board a 25-passenger boat and slowly float past stilt houses before making the climb to the top of a steep drop.

The cars are specifically designed to throw the water onto the passengers, guaranteeing a soggy experience.

TOURING TIPS If you didn't get enough water on the ride, stand on the bridge crossing the splash pool. An enormous wall of water shoots from each dropping car, fully drenching onlookers. If you want the visuals without the bath, there's also a glass wall in the area that blocks the water, one of the most fun diversions in the park.

As you exit the attraction, or if you choose not to ride, visit Orchid Canyon. This gorgeous area features many varieties of orchids growing around waterfalls in artificial rocks.

Stanley Falls

APPEAL BY AGE	PRESCHOOL ★★★	GRADE SCHOOL ★★★	TEENS ★★
YOUNG ADULTS ★★		OVER 30 ★★½	SENIORS ★★½

What it is Water-flume ride. **Scope and scale** Major attraction. **When to go** After 3 p.m. **Special comments** Children not accompanied by an adult must be at least 46 inches tall. **Author's rating** Nothing too exciting; ★★. **Duration of ride** 3 minutes.

DESCRIPTION AND COMMENTS Logs drift along a winding flume before plummeting down a 40-foot drop. Because the little ones can ride with an adult, it's a good way for small children (who are ready for it) to enjoy a moderate thrill. Riders are only slightly splashed on the final big drop.

TOURING TIPS This ride is exciting without being scary or jarring. During peak season, save it for the afternoon, when lines will be shorter.

kids Land of the Dragons

APPEAL BY AGE	PRESCHOOL ★★★★½	GRADE SCHOOL ★★★	TEENS —
YOUNG ADULTS —		OVER 30 ★	SENIORS ★

What it is Kids play area. **Scope and scale** Headliner. **When to go** Anytime. **Special comments** Only those less than 56 inches tall can ride attractions in this area. **Author's rating** The best theming in Busch Gardens; ★★★.

DESCRIPTION AND COMMENTS With the height limits on its thrill rides, Busch Gardens often banishes children under the magic number of 48 inches tall to the animal exhibits. This enchanting area, however, is reason enough for families with kids to visit the park. The dragon theme is consistent throughout the area, creating some cute attractions, including a mini–Ferris wheel with dragon egg–shaped seats and a tiny dragon water flume. Kids can crawl through a huge net play area and get soaked in a fountain playground. There's also a live show featuring Dumphrey the Dragon (check the daily entertainment schedule for times).

TOURING TIPS This area is right next to Gwazi and on the same side of the park as Kumba, Python, and Scorpion. Those members of your group who don't do coasters can stay with the kids while others ride.

BIRD GARDENS

Gwazi

| APPEAL BY AGE | PRESCHOOL † | GRADE SCHOOL ★★★★ | TEENS ★★★★ |
| YOUNG ADULTS ★★★★ | | OVER 30 ★★★★ | SENIORS ★★ |

† Preschoolers are generally too short to ride.

What it is Double wooden roller coaster. **Scope and scale** Super headliner. **When to go** Before 10 a.m. or after 3 p.m. **Special comments** Riders must be at least 48 inches tall. **Author's rating** Thrilling, if a little jerky; ★★★½. **Duration of ride** 2½ minutes.

DESCRIPTION AND COMMENTS Those with a nostalgic love for the wooden roller coasters of yore will be pleased with Gwazi. And fans of steel coasters shouldn't be disappointed with the 1.25 million feet of lumber, either. Though it's not as smooth, for a wooden ride, this coaster delivers thrills typically associated with its steel cousins. It's really two roller coasters in one, with two completely different tracks—the Gwazi lion and the Gwazi tiger—intertwined to create a frenzied race, including six "fly-by" encounters where riders pass within feet of each other. It's not as intensely confrontational as Dueling Dragons at Islands of Adventure, but it's certainly neat to see a wooden coaster use such an ultramodern gimmick.

TOURING TIPS Head here first thing in the morning to avoid long waits. But if you have time, try the coaster again before leaving the park, as it takes on a new feel after dark. Both of Gwazi's tracks are thrilling; the Tiger is a little wilder on the humps, whereas the Lion is a little faster. Both tracks have separate lines for the front and back cars. The front cars offer the best view, but the back cars whip around more for a little extra thrill. Adults waiting for their party to ride can visit the nearby Hospitality House for free samples of Anheuser-Busch beers. For little ones who don't ride, Land of the Dragons is also nearby.

Bird Show Theater/Wild Wings of Africa

| APPEAL BY AGE | PRESCHOOL ★★ | GRADE SCHOOL ★★ | TEENS ★ |
| YOUNG ADULTS ★½ | | OVER 30 ★★ | SENIORS ★★★ |

What it is Show featuring exotic African birds. **Scope and scale** Minor attraction. **When to go** Check daily entertainment schedule. **Author's**

rating Beautiful birds, but a pretty ho-hum show; ★½. **Duration of show** 30 minutes.

DESCRIPTION AND COMMENTS It's not the most wildly entertaining diversion, but many of the birds are quite beautiful. A good way to rest your feet or wait for riders on Gwazi.

TOURING TIPS If you're over age 21, grab a free beer at the Anheuser-Busch Hospitality House next door and head to this performance. Watching the gorgeous birds is better than wasting time sitting at the Hospitality Center.

Lory Landing

APPEAL BY AGE	PRESCHOOL ★★★	GRADE SCHOOL ★★★	TEENS ★★★
YOUNG ADULTS ★★★	OVER 30 ★★★		SENIORS ★★★½

What it is Interactive aviary. **Scope and scale** Major attraction. **When to go** Birds are hungrier in the morning. **Author's rating** Cute; ★★★.

DESCRIPTION AND COMMENTS Many area attractions feature aviaries, but this is by far the biggest and the best. Tropical birds from around the world dot the lush landscape, fill the air in free flight, and are displayed in habitats. Purchase a nectar cup for $1, and some of these delightful creatures will be eating right out of your hand. Many will land on your hands, arms, shoulders, or even head, making this attraction a nightmare for those with bird-in-the-hair phobia. The illustrated journal of a fictitious explorer helps differentiate between the many species, including lorikeets, hornbills, parrots, and avocets.

TOURING TIPS Try to visit before lunch, because the birds usually get their fill of nectar by early afternoon.

DINING

BUSCH GARDENS OFFERS A SIMILAR SELECTION of food as sister park SeaWorld. Fast food should cost about $6–$9 per person, including drinks. Carved deli sandwiches on freshly baked bread and fajita wraps are a favorite at Zagora Café.

For a real treat, try a sit-down meal at Crown Colony House restaurant, which offers amazing views of the Serengeti Plain. The menu features salads, sandwiches, pasta, and seafood. For the best deal, go for the family-style dinner of fried chicken or fish, with a vast selection of side dishes; it's $11.95 for adults, $6.95 for kids age 12 and under. Dinner at the restaurant can be combined with an off-road tour of the Serengeti Plain for $56 adults, $42 children.

unofficial **TIP** The Desert Grill in Timbuktu could almost be considered an attraction because of its grandeur, detail, and authenticity, as well as some great entertainment.

The 1,000-seat, air-conditioned restaurant is a nice break from the outside heat. Bare wooden tables surround a stage from which dancers and singers perform a lively show several times throughout the day, but it's nothing to write home about. Baby-back ribs and Italian entrees like spaghetti and meatballs and fettuccini alfredo, as well as sandwiches and a full kids menu, are offered. Keeping in mind that the Desert Grill serves cafeteria-style and feeds thousands daily, the food is not bad and the prices are reasonable, with sandwiches for $7–$8, desserts for $3, and beer for about $4.

unofficial **TIP**
For those traveling on a budget, McDonald's is within walking distance of the main entrance. Just remember to save your admission ticket and have your hand stamped as you exit.

The Zambia Smokehouse is the newest indoor-outdoor restaurant, and it's positioned next to the brand-new SheiKra monster coaster, allowing great views of the screaming passengers and the impressive swoops and drops the ride offers. Entrees like ribs, chicken, and brisket are smoked for several hours and are reasonably priced, ranging $7.50–$11.50.

SHOPPING

THERE'S PLENTY OF BUSCH GARDENS–LOGO merchandise, but visitors looking for something more should be happy with the vast selection. Find nature-themed gifts, such as wind chimes and jewelry, at Nature's Kingdom. African gifts and crafts, including clothing, brass urns, and leather goods, can be found throughout the park. Most have reasonable prices, although some larger, intricate items can be more expensive. For that hard-to-shop-for adult, try the Anheuser-Busch Label Stable or the West African Trading Company, which features hand-crafted items from many countries, as well as a walk-in cigar humidor. Similar to SeaWorld, Busch Gardens offers a vast array of kid-pleasing stuffed animals; kids and parents should be happy with the prices.

THE PARK OPENED IN 1936 as a 16-acre, lush, landscaped garden with wandering Southern belles decked out in traditional hoop skirts, a stunt-filled water-ski show, and elaborate, flower-filled topiaries. In its day, it was a fairly popular place to spend the day. Then Disney World came.

The only "ride" at Cypress Gardens was the rotating Island in the Sky platform, which slowly glided up and down a 160-foot-tall tower, providing 360-degree views of orange groves and lakes . . . but not much else. The gardens were beautifully maintained, but for the most part it was a sleepy little park in a sleepy little corner of central Florida. Yawn.

As competition grew and appetites for ride-filled parks increased, the attendance at Cypress Gardens declined. Its ownership changed hands a few times, but no steps were taken to update the park. Though it had become somewhat of a Florida landmark, its gates were eventually closed in 2003 due to poor attendance and lack of attention-grabbing attractions.

The man who owns Wild Adventures in Valdosta, Georgia, had big plans for Cypress Gardens, and he purchased it in early 2004. The park was given a $45 million face-lift—the gardens and ski show were preserved, and new rides and shows were added to draw younger visitors and hopefully improve attendance.

The result is a small-scale amusement park that appeals to almost all ages. Older teens may be bored here, but there are rides appropriate for kids as young as three. Adults and seniors will enjoy the park's gardens and shopping; the shows will appeal to most age groups, especially the impressive water-ski act.

Cypress Gardens

1. Adventure Grill
2. Animal Encounters
3. ATM
4. Aunt Julie's Country Kitchen
5. Backwater Bill's BBQ
6. Big Daddy's Pizza
7. Bird Aviary
8. Boardwalk Carousel
9. Boardwalk Funnel Cakes
10. Cherry on Top
11. Chico's
12. Citrus Line Railroad
13. Cypress Belle
14. Cypress Cove Ferry Line
15. Cypress Gardens on Ice
16. Cypress Landing
17. Delta Kite Flyers
18. Disk'O
19. Dizzy Dragons
20. Dip-n-Dots
21. Drifter's Ski & Surf
22. Farmyard Frolics
23. Fiesta Express
24. Fire Brigade
25. First Aid
26. Fun Slide
27. Galaxy Spin
28. Garden Gondolas
29. Gator Bites
30. Gear Jammers
31. Grove Snacks
32. Guest Services
33. Hickory Hollow
34. Inverter
35. Island Traders
36. Jalopy Junction
37. Jubilee Ice Cream
38. Jubilee Marketplace
39. Jubilee Mercantile
40. Junior Rampmasters
41. Kara's Kastle
42. Kringle's Christmas Shop
43. Live Musical Performances
   (Seasonal)
44. The Living Garden
45. Lockers
46. Longwing's Emporium
47. Megabounce
48. Myrtle's Candle Company
49. Night Magic (Seasonal)
50. Nile Crocodiles
51. Okeechobee Rampage
52. Paradise Sky Wheel
53. Petting Zoo
54. Pharaoh's Fury
55. The Photo Shop
56. Pirate Ship
57. Power Surge
58. Red Baron
59. Rio Grande Train
60. Rockin' Tug
61. Sandra Dee's
62. Seafari Swings
63. Sheba, the female jaguar

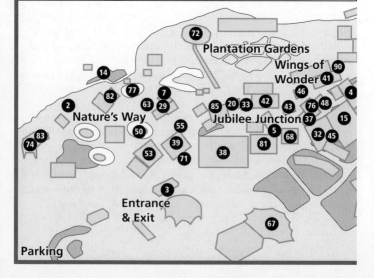

64. Sideswipers
65. Ski Show Spectacular
66. Soaring Scooters
67. Star Haven Amphitheatre
68. Star Haven Commissary
69. Stars & Stripes
70. Storm Surge
71. Strollers/Wheelchairs
72. Sunshine Sky Adventure
73. Super Trucks
74. Swamp Critters
75. Swamp Thing
76. Tan Yer Hide Leather Shop
77. Tarzan, the 75 year old alligator
78. Thunderbolt
79. Tilt-A-Whirl
80. Tiny Trotters
81. Trains, Planes & Automobiles
82. Treasure of Cypress Cove
83. Tricks of the Trade
84. Triple Hurricane
85. True Confections
86. Upsy Daisy
87. Volcano Jim's
88. Wave Runner
89. Wild West Shenaniguns
90. The Wood Works Shop
91. Yo-Yo

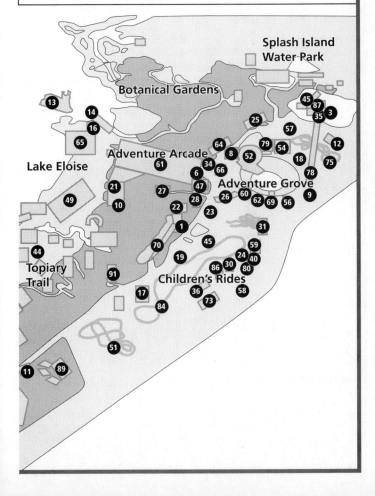

When it comes to thrill rides, it's certainly no Busch Gardens or Islands of Adventure. But what the park does, it does well. It is clean, small, and easy to navigate. The gardens are beautifully kept, and the topiaries are pretty cool, too.

unofficial **TIP**
To get the flavor of "old-school" Florida tourist attractions, head to Cypress Gardens.

Lines are short, admission is (relatively) inexpensive, and the atmosphere is cute, if not a bit contrived. All in all, it's the perfect place to go when you want to spend a day at a theme park but aren't hot on the idea of long lines, big crowds, and $8 hot dogs. It may never be on the same scale as other adventure parks, but it's not really trying to be . . . which is pretty refreshing.

GETTING THERE

CYPRESS GARDENS IS ROUGHLY 35 miles and 45 minutes west of Walt Disney World. From the Orlando area, take Interstate 4 West and exit onto US 27 South. Continue on this road about 20 miles. Turn right at FL 540/Cypress Gardens Boulevard. The park is 4 miles on the left. At press time, the turnoff was not very well marked, so keep an eye out for green mileage signs that point the way. Parking is $7 for cars and $9 for RVs. A yearlong parking pass is available for $25.

ADMISSION PRICES

One-Day Admission

REGULAR ADMISSION INCLUDES a second day free, within six days of original visit. Tickets include all areas of the park, as well as any concerts or special events.

Adults $34.95 + tax
Children ages 3–9 $29.95 + tax
Seniors age 55+ $29.95 + tax

Annual Passports

PASSPORTS PROVIDE UNLIMITED ADMISSION to Cypress Gardens, including all concerts and special events; and admission to its sister park, Wild Adventures, in Valdosta, Georgia.

All ages $64.95 plus tax

ARRIVING

CYPRESS GARDENS OPENS at 10 a.m. daily. Closing time depends on the time of year and whether there are special events like concerts or shows going on, but generally is around 6 or 7 p.m. on weekdays and 10 p.m. on weekends.

Depending on the amount of things you try to do and see, touring the park probably will not take an entire day. Plan on about four to six hours to see the park fully, ride most rides, and see a show or two. Because the attractions range from small-scale roller coasters to shows to a topiary garden, the time you take to see or do all of them totally depends on what kind of mood your family is in.

unofficial **TIP**
To get your chance to ride the thrill rides, head to the back of the park first.

Do you have pint-size thrill seekers on your hands? Head straight to the back of the park where the new adventure rides are located. The lines will be shortest in the morning, though on the day we were there, the longest we had to wait for any ride all day was about 10 minutes. The trick for avoiding long lines (or any lines at all, really) is getting to the park when it opens and heading to the rides first. The majority of the adventure rides are carnival-type attractions, complete with the requisite tilt-a-whirl, carousel, and Ferris wheel. Unlike Busch Gardens or Islands of Adventure, this self-dubbed adventure park is on a much smaller scale, both size-wise and ride-wise.

The three main roller coasters are fun, if not a bit rinky-dink. There are two steel-track coasters and one wooden coaster, and all three combined will take about 20 minutes to ride, including the time it takes to walk from one to the other. Other thrill rides include a giant waterslide you ride down in a raft, spinning and sloshing all the way; a ride that zips you to the top, then plummets you down; and a contraption that lifts you up, spins you around, then lets you dangle upside-down for a moment before spinning and swinging you back to the ground. Ideally, you should put these rides on your agenda before lunch.

After you spend the first part of your day on the rides, make your way back to the front of the park—stop for some lunch and to watch the famous water ski show, stroll through the topiary and botanical gardens, peek into the butterfly arboretum, and wander through the shops in Jubilee Junction.

CONTACTING CYPRESS GARDENS

FOR MORE INFORMATION, call Cypress Gardens at ☎ 863-324-2111 or visit the Web site at **www.cypressgardens.com**.

ATTRACTIONS

ADVENTURE GROVE

Triple Hurricane

APPEAL BY AGE	PRESCHOOL ★★	GRADE SCHOOL ★★★★	TEENS ★★★½
YOUNG ADULTS ★★★★		OVER 30 ★★★½	SENIORS ★★

What it is Wooden roller coaster. **Scope and scale** Super headliner. **When to go** Before 11 a.m. **Special comments** Must be 36 inches tall to ride with an adult, 42 inches to ride alone. **Author's rating** Our choice for the most fun ride in the park; ★★★★. **Duration of ride** 1 minute. **Loading speed** Moderate.

DESCRIPTION AND COMMENTS It's a short ride, but an enjoyable one. Even small children may enjoy the dips, turns and mini drops on this old-fashioned "woody." When we were there, many of the riders were quite small but enjoyed the mini thrills on this coaster. A camera snaps your picture on the first drop of the ride, and you can check out your lovely roller coaster face at the end.

TOURING TIPS Along with the Okeechobee Rampage and the Swamp Thing, this is one of the park's major rides. Head to these coasters first, as the line grows as the day goes on. If you liked it and the line is still short, loop back around for one more spin before heading to the next ride.

Okeechobee Rampage

APPEAL BY AGE	PRESCHOOL ★★★½		GRADE SCHOOL ★★★★
TEENS ★★★	YOUNG ADULTS ★★★	OVER 30 ★★	SENIORS ★★

What it is Roller coaster. **Scope and scale** Headliner. **When to go** Before 11 a.m. **Special comments** Must be 36 inches tall to ride with an adult, 42 inches to ride alone. **Author's rating** ★★★. **Duration of ride** 45 seconds. **Loading speed** Fast.

DESCRIPTION AND COMMENTS This coaster is the shortest, but if the crowds are small (which they often are), the attendants will let riders have a second run. It's not exactly comparable to the bigger coasters at Islands of Adventure or Busch Gardens, so don't go in expecting a ride of the monstrous proportions those parks have. Taken for what it is—a small-scale, fun-for-the-whole-family kind of adventure—it's pretty darn enjoyable. There are no big hills or steep drops on this one, so even the coaster-shy may enjoy the fast but relatively easy ride.

TOURING TIPS Again, this is one of the park's major attractions, so the earlier you ride this one, the better. If you are okay with saving the gardens and lake for the end of the day, you can bypass the scenic route and take a left behind the locker station. Walk past the concert stage, and the first thing you'll see is the twisting track.

Thunderbolt

APPEAL BY AGE	PRESCHOOL ½	GRADE SCHOOL ★★	TEENS ★★★
YOUNG ADULTS ★★★		OVER 30 ★★	SENIORS ★½

What it is Tummy tumbler. **Scope and scale** Headliner. **When to go** Before you eat lunch. **Special comments** Must be 42 inches to ride. **Author's rating** ★★★. **Duration of ride** 1 minute, 30 seconds. **Loading speed** Fast.

DESCRIPTION AND COMMENTS Strap in and hang on! Sitting strapped into a car, feet dangling, the most distressing part of the whole experience is the sl-o-o-o-w ascent to the top of the 120-foot tower. Enjoy the view while you can—the plunge down was so fast it left many of us screamless. It's an exhilarating free fall, not for the faint of stomach

TOURING TIPS This is another big draw at the park—the line usually isn't very long, but it's worth scoping out before you head to any other rides after the coasters. Chances are the line will grow as the day goes on.

Pharaoh's Fury

APPEAL BY AGE	PRESCHOOL ½	GRADE SCHOOL ★★★½	TEENS ★★★½
YOUNG ADULTS ★★		OVER 30 ★½	SENIORS ½

What it is A sailor's worst nightmare. **Scope and scale** Major attraction. **When to go** Anytime. **Special comments** Must be 48 inches tall to ride. **Author's rating** Not for the easily nauseated; ★½. **Duration of ride** 1 minute, 45 seconds. **Loading speed** Slow; the ride can accommodate between 40 and 60 people at a time—if there's no line, you may have to wait as the ride fills up.

DESCRIPTION AND COMMENTS A giant pendulum-like wooden boat swings riders to and fro, reaching speeds of close to 80 miles per hour. The boat gains speed throughout the ride, and the last two tick-tocks are a doozie.

TOURING TIPS This is one attraction where a larger crowd waiting to ride is usually a good thing. The attendants generally won't run it if there are fewer than 20 people in line, so hold out for this one until the park fills up. You may have to wait in a bit of a line, but it's better than sitting on the actual ride waiting for more people. Be aware that people often lose pocket contents on this ride. Secure them in advance.

Storm Surge

APPEAL BY AGE	PRESCHOOL ★★★½	GRADE SCHOOL ★★★½	TEENS ★★
YOUNG ADULTS ★★		OVER 30 ★★★	SENIORS ★★½

What it is A drier-than-normal waterslide. **Scope and scale** Major attraction. **When to go** Anytime. **Special comments** Must be 42 inches tall to ride. **Author's rating** ★★½. **Duration of ride** 2 minutes, 30 seconds. **Loading speed** Fast.

DESCRIPTION AND COMMENTS   This hybrid of a waterslide and a rapids course provides a pretty fun jaunt, but if spinning rides are not your cup of tea, so to speak, then take note: you will spin the whole way down. Up to six people can ride in the raft, so the whole family can ride together, which adds to the fun. For the most part it's a pretty dry experience except for a line of misters at the bottom who shower you with a spritz of water—just enough to cool you off, but not so much that it soaks your socks.

TOURING TIPS   Younger kids enjoy this raft ride, teens and young adults may find it too slow—and dizzying—to keep them very interested.

Swamp Thing

APPEAL BY AGE	PRESCHOOL ★	GRADE SCHOOL ★★★★½	TEENS ★★★½
YOUNG ADULTS ★★½		OVER 30 ★★	SENIORS

What it is An inverted, steel-track roller coaster. **Scope and scale** Headliner. **When to go** Before noon. **Special comments** Must be 44 inches tall to ride. **Author's rating** Fast and fun; ★★★½. **Duration of ride** 45 seconds. **Loading speed** Moderate.

DESCRIPTION AND COMMENTS   This ride ties with the Triple Hurricane as the most fun. Your legs dangle as you zip around corners and up and down smooth drops. Some of the turns are sharp and fast—paired with the two twists in the track, this ride left us feeling a little dizzy. Try sitting in the front: because the track is over your head, it feels a little like flying.

TOURING TIPS   This orange and blue coaster sits on the opposite end of the park from the two other coasters, which keeps its lines the shortest of the three. Still, because it's one of the more popular attractions, try to head for this one before lunch.

The Inverter

APPEAL BY AGE	PRESCHOOL †	GRADE SCHOOL ★★½	TEENS ★★★
YOUNG ADULTS ★★★		OVER 30 ★	SENIORS ★½

† Preschoolers are generally too short to ride.

What it is Lunch-tosser. **Scope and scale** Major attraction. **When to go** Before lunch. **Special comments** Must be 48 inches to ride. **Author's rating** ★★½. **Duration of ride** 1 minutes, 45 seconds. **Loading speed** Average.

DESCRIPTION AND COMMENTS   A set of seats at the bottom of an upside-down T-shaped pendulum flips upside down as the giant pendulum swings back and forth. A little too dizzying for us, but the teens we rode with couldn't get enough.

TOURING TIPS   If you're skipping the Thunderbolt, skip this, too, as they're closely related on the stomach-tossing scale. Remove anything in shirt pockets so they won't go flying when the car is upside down.

Power Surge

APPEAL BY AGE	PRESCHOOL †	GRADE SCHOOL ★★★½	TEENS ★★★
YOUNG ADULTS ★★★		OVER 30 ★★	SENIORS ½

† Preschoolers are generally too short to ride.

What it is A rotating, spinning ride. **Scope and scale** Major attraction. **When to go** Anytime. **Special comments** Must be 52 inches tall to ride. **Author's rating** ★★½. **Duration of ride** 2 minutes. **Loading speed** Fast.

DESCRIPTION AND COMMENTS Cars on the ends of arms of a windmill-like contraption spin as the windmill rotates.

TOURING TIPS Although it's not too wild, this is another one to try before lunch or a few hours after.

Disk'O

APPEAL BY AGE	PRESCHOOL †	GRADE SCHOOL ★★★½	TEENS ★★★
YOUNG ADULTS ★★★		OVER 30 ★★	SENIORS ½

† Preschoolers are generally too short to ride.

What it is Carnival-type wild ride. **Scope and scale** Major attraction. **When to go** Anytime. **Special comments** Must be 48 inches tall to ride. **Author's rating** ★★★. **Duration of ride** 2 minutes. **Loading speed** Fast.

DESCRIPTION AND COMMENTS Round cars with motorcycle-shaped seats spin around while they slide back and forth along an oblique U-shaped track.

TOURING TIPS Fitting into the theme of stomach-stirring rides, this is one of the best, but another one to be wary of if motion sickness is a problem for you or your family members.

kids Paradise Sky Wheel

APPEAL BY AGE	PRESCHOOL ★★★★	GRADE SCHOOL ★★★★	TEENS ★★
YOUNG ADULTS ★★		OVER 30 ★★★★	SENIORS ★★★★

What it is Old-fashioned Ferris wheel. **Scope and scale** Minor attraction. **When to go** Anytime. **Special comments** You must be 42 inches or taller if not accompanied by an adult to ride. **Author's rating** ★★★. **Duration of ride** 1 minute, 45 seconds; if there's no line, you can ride several times. **Loading speed** Moderate.

DESCRIPTION AND COMMENTS A throwback to the early days of amusement parks, this Ferris wheel might look more in place toward the front of the park, away from its flashy, fast-moving neighbors. But it's a nice break from all the tummy-churning rides, and a fun way to see the whole park, as you probably won't notice much at the top of the Thunderbolt. It might be a little too slow-moving for older kids, but preschoolers especially enjoy the graceful ride.

TOURING TIPS Head to the Sky Wheel when your feet are tired or you need a moment to settle your stomach. The line is generally pretty short no matter what time of day, because the wheel is almost constantly in motion.

Wild West Shenaniguns

APPEAL BY AGE	PRESCHOOL ★★½	GRADE SCHOOL ★★★	TEENS ★½
YOUNG ADULTS ★★		OVER 30 ★★★	SENIORS ★★★

What it is Melodramatic Western-themed show. **Scope and scale** Diversion. **When to go** Check schedule for daily show times. **Author's rating** Eye-rollingly hokey; ★★. **Duration of show** 10 minutes.

DESCRIPTION AND COMMENTS This "shoot-'em-up" melodrama is cheesy at best; painful at worst. Performed in a flimsy makeshift stage with wooden benches for seats, it reminds us of a group of summer camp counselors trying to amuse their charges. It's the classic good guy/bad guy struggle, with bad acting and even worse Southern accents—but that's the whole point. The show includes lots of tripping, falling, chasing, and silly puns, which is why children seem to love it and adults can't help but chuckle at the effort put forth for this over-the-top show.

TOURING TIPS The gun-wielding cowboys are harmless enough, and any hint of violence is clearly all in good fun; however, the guns do emit loud shots several times throughout the performance that may scare young children.

ADDITIONAL ADVENTURE GROVE RIDES

Wave Runner
What it is Twisting waterslides you slip down on a two-person raft. Easy to stay dry. Must be 36 inches tall to ride with an adult, 42 inches to ride alone. **Who will enjoy it** Ages 3+.

Delta Kite Flyers
What it is Lie flat on your back or stomach on individual platforms at the end of long arms that bob up and down and rotate around a central tower. **Who will enjoy it** Ages 4+.

Rockin' Tug
What it is Kiddie version of the Pirate Ship and Pharaoh's Fury. **Who will enjoy it** Ages 5–10.

kids Soaring Scooters
What it is Similar to the flying swings, little cars situated at the ends of long arms swing up and out as the ride rotates. **Who will enjoy it** Ages 4–10.

Cypress Cove Ferry Line

What it is Boat ride along the shoreline of Lake Eloise from one end of the park to the other while a narrator tells the history of Cypress Gardens. Must be 42 inches tall to ride without an adult. **Who will enjoy it** All ages.

kids Garden Gondolas

What it is Gondolas slide up a 35-foot tower and can be spun independently; must be 42 inches tall to ride alone. **Who will enjoy it** Ages 2–10.

Citrus Line Railroad

What it is Similar to the Ferry Line, a train chugs throughout a section of the park; a narrator tells the history of Cypress Gardens. Must be 42 inches tall to ride without an adult. **Who will enjoy it** All ages.

Yo-Yo

What it is A circular set of swings on arms that rotate and move up and out to make the swings fly; must be 42 inches tall to ride. **Who will enjoy it** Ages 6+.

Tilt-a-Whirl

What it is Two-person carts that tilt, spin, and slide around a circular track. Must be 32 inches tall to ride; must be at least 46 inches tall to ride without an adult. **Who will enjoy it** Ages 3+.

Mega Bounce

What it is Two-person carts that bounce up and down and spin around a center tower; must be 42 inches tall to ride. **Who will enjoy it** Ages 6+.

Fun Slide

What it is Slide that you slip down on a mat bouncing through slaloms; a classic. Must be over 42 inches tall to ride alone. **Who will enjoy it** Ages 5+.

Side Swipers

What it is Bumper cars. Must be 50 inches tall and at least 8 years old to ride with an adult; must be 60 inches tall to ride alone. **Who will enjoy it** Ages 8+.

kids CHILDREN'S RIDES

Boardwalk Carousel

What it is Double-decker carousel; must be 42 inches tall to ride unless accompanied by an adult. **Who will enjoy it** Ages 3–10.

Pirate Ship

What it is A mini version of Pharaoh's Fury. Under 36 inches tall must be accompanied by a rider 48 inches or taller. **Who will enjoy it** Ages 3–10.

Seafari Swing
What it is A mini version of the Yo-Yo. Must be 32 inches tall to ride.
Who will enjoy it Ages 3–7.

Stars and Stripes
What it is A slower, miniature version of the Thunderbolt. Must be 42 inches tall to ride. **Who will enjoy it** Ages 5–9.

Fire Brigade
What it is Cross between a carnival game and a carnival ride. Miniature fire trucks rotate around "burning" buildings; aim the water squirting from your truck onto the faux flames to determine how the truck moves. Must be 36 inches tall to ride. **Who will enjoy it** Ages 2–7.

Jalopy Junction
What it is Pint-size, old-fashioned cars that run on a small, circular track. Must be 36 inches tall to ride unless accompanied by an adult. **Who will enjoy it** Ages 2–6.

Fiesta Express
What it is Mini roller coaster. Must be 36 inches tall to ride. **Who will enjoy it** Ages 3+.

Dizzy Dragons
What it is Riders sit in the belly of a dragon that travels along on a circular track; passengers can spin the dragon itself as it travels around. Must be 36 inches tall to ride unless accompanied by an adult. **Who will enjoy it** Ages 3–7.

Gear Jammers
What it is Mini cars and trucks on a track. Must be between 42 inches and 52 inches tall to ride. **Who will enjoy it** Ages 4–6.

Red Baron
What it is Little red prop planes "fly" in circles; riders can control the up-and-down movements. Must be between 42 inches and 52 inches tall to ride. **Who will enjoy it** Ages 3–6.

Rio Grande Train
What it is Four-car mini train on a small track; must be 42 inches tall to ride alone. **Who will enjoy it** Ages 3–7.

Super Truckers
What it is Kid-sized semi-tractor trailers on a track; must be at least 3 years old to ride; must be at least age 6 to ride without an adult. **Who will enjoy it** Ages 3–7.

Junior Rampmasters

What it is Miniature speedboats float on a track through a circular water-filled canal; must be between 42 inches and 56 inches tall to ride. **Who will enjoy it** Ages 4–7.

Upsy Daisy

What it is A mini version of the Delta Kite Flyers; Minimum 42 inches tall, maximum 52 inches tall to ride. **Who will enjoy it** Ages 4–8.

Tiny Trotters

What it is Horses that slide around a track; must be 42 inches tall to ride. **Who will enjoy it** Ages 4–6.

When Radios Were Radios Display

What it is A collection of historic radios. **Who will enjoy it** Ages 50+; it only borders on being interesting, unless you happen to be into radios, so this is one stop not really worth making.

MANGO BAY

Mango Bay Water Ski Show

APPEAL BY AGE	PRESCHOOL ★★★	GRADE SCHOOL ★★★½	TEENS ★★★
YOUNG ADULTS ★★★½		OVER 30 ★★★★	SENIORS ★★★½

What it is A stunt show on the lake including impressive feats. **Scope and scale** Major attraction. **When to go** Check schedule for performance times. **Author's rating** ★★★★. **Duration of show** 25 minutes.

DESCRIPTION AND COMMENTS Whizzing speed boats, tricky water skiers, wakeboarders, and more put on an exciting show. There's not a real plot; the whole point is to admire the performers as they zip by. Among the impressive feats are kite boarding, barefoot skiing, jumping, doubles skiing, and other remarkable stunts.

TOURING TIPS Scope out your seats early; this is a popular attraction. There's not a bad seat in the house, but about halfway up the stadium-like bleachers is the best vantage point.

Pirates of Mango Bay

APPEAL BY AGE	NOT OPEN AT PRESS TIME

What it is Melodramatic pirate-themed show. **Scope and scale** Diversion. **When to go** Check schedule for daily show times. **Author's rating** Not open at press time.

DESCRIPTION AND COMMENTS Though we didn't see it, we know that it will be produced to be much like the Western show, only on the lake and involving pirates.

TOURING TIPS Our guess is that you could choose either the Pirate show or the Western show for a similar experience.

Night Magic

APPEAL BY AGE   NOT OPEN AT PRESS TIME.

What it is Fireworks and laser show. **Scope and scale** Headliner. **When to go** 1 show nightly. **Author's rating** Not open at press time. **Duration of show** Unknown at press time.

DESCRIPTION AND COMMENTS A combination of lasers and fireworks set to music will illuminate the sky over Mango Bay, the park's central lake.

TOURING TIPS Come early to grab seats on the grass lawn in front of the lake or inside the water ski show stadium.

JUBILEE JUNCTION

Royal Palm Theater/Figure Skating Show

APPEAL BY AGE	PRESCHOOL ★★	GRADE SCHOOL ★★★	TEENS ★½
YOUNG ADULTS ★★		OVER 30 ★★★	SENIORS ★★★

What it is Figure skating show. **Scope and scale** Headliner. **When to go** Anytime; check daily performance schedule. **Author's rating** Fairly unexciting; ★★½. **Duration of show** 25 minutes.

DESCRIPTION AND COMMENTS The talented skaters and a few impressive moves do little to save the pretty average show; cheesy music and costumes don't help much either. Figure skating enthusiasts will enjoy it, and it's a cool respite from the heat if you need a break.

TOURING TIPS Save this for the end of the day when feet are tired and everybody's hot and ready for a rest.

Wings of Wonder Butterfly Arboretum

APPEAL BY AGE	PRESCHOOL ★★★	GRADE SCHOOL ★★★½	TEENS ★½
YOUNG ADULTS ★★		OVER 30 ★★★	SENIORS ★★★

What it is Greenhouse that is home to more than 20 species of butterflies. **Scope and scale** Diversion. **When to go** Anytime. **Author's rating** ★★½.

DESCRIPTION AND COMMENTS This small, humid greenhouse is slated to be home to about 20 species of butterflies, but the day we were there, we only spotted 2 types. As the park grows, there probably will be several more kinds of butterflies added.

TOURING TIPS Swing through here on your way to lunch or out of the park; there's never a line and rarely a crowd, and it only takes about five minutes to see the exhibit fully.

Snively Plantation Gardens

APPEAL BY AGE	PRESCHOOL ★★	GRADE SCHOOL ★★	TEENS ★
YOUNG ADULTS ★★★	OVER 30 ★★★½	SENIORS ★★★½	

What it is Manicured grass dotted with beds of beautiful flowers, from azaleas to pansies to roses. **Scope and scale** Major attraction. **When to go** Anytime. **Author's rating** ★★★.

DESCRIPTION AND COMMENTS At its inception, this was a park about flowers and trees. This and the topiary trail (below) are the major areas that set this park apart from the rest in Orlando. The plants and trees don't just soften the concrete landscape; they're actually an *attraction*. If you want to get a feel for what Cypress Gardens was originally meant to be, this is a stop worth making.

TOURING TIPS The gardens are rarely crowded, but on very warm days, head here as early as possible, as the flowers often droop in the summer heat.

Topiary Trail

APPEAL BY AGE	PRESCHOOL ★★★★	GRADE SCHOOL ★★★½	TEENS ★★
YOUNG ADULTS ★★★	OVER 30 ★★★½	SENIORS ★★★½	

What it is Collection of bushes carved into the likenesses of animals, bugs, and other shapes. **Scope and scale** Headliner. **When to go** Anytime. **Author's rating** Cute and nostalgic; ★★★½.

DESCRIPTION AND COMMENTS Another throwback to the classic Cypress Gardens, this collection is pretty fun to see. It may be hokey, but this is one of our favorite spots in the park—take a moment to enjoy the manicured grass lawn and breeze from the lake. And don't forget your cameras: nothing says "wish you were here" like a picture with an octopus-shaped bush.

TOURING TIPS Stop by on your way out of the park; early in the day, as people make their way from the front gates to the rides in the back, many end up stopping here, clogging the walkways and packing the space. Save this stop for the afternoon.

Sunshine Sky Adventure

APPEAL BY AGE	PRESCHOOL ★	GRADE SCHOOL ★★★	TEENS ★★
YOUNG ADULTS ★★★	OVER 30 ★★★½	SENIORS ★★★	

What it is Remember the mention of the only ride in the Cypress Gardens of years past? This is it. A platform glides up almost 160 feet and slowly rotates to reveal panoramic views of the area. This is definitely not for anyone with a fear of heights. **Scope and scale** Headliner. **When to go** At the end of your visit. **Special comments** Must be 48 inches tall to ride without an adult. **Author's rating** Great view, but not too exciting; ★★★. **Duration of ride** 6 minutes. **Loading speed** Fast.

DESCRIPTION AND COMMENTS Although there still isn't much else besides orange groves, houses and lakes, it's pretty stunning.

TOURING TIPS Stop here on your way out of the park, as it's located near the entrance and everyone will enjoy a slower-paced attraction after the tosses and turns of the other rides.

ANIMALS

IN MAY 2005, CYPRESS GARDENS OPENED the animal section of the park. Though not open at press time, the menagerie is slated to include alligators, snakes, small monkeys, and several species of birds, reptiles, and small mammals.

DINING

CYPRESS GARDENS OFFERS a few more choices beyond the standard burger and fries. For the most part, food is not spectacular, but it's less expensive than their theme park counterparts.

For a sit-down meal of traditional Southern fixins, like chicken and dumplings, macaroni and cheese, biscuits, and cobblers, Aunt Julie's Country Kitchen is the place.

Backwater Bill's serves up some pretty lame barbecue. Actually, the chicken is the only thing worth ordering—the pulled-pork sandwiches are little more than sloppy joes, and the sides were bland and cafeteria-like. We recommend you try another restaurant.

Jubilee Marketplace is more like it; it has an all-American counter with decent hamburgers, hot dogs, and the like; an Italian counter with pizzas and pastas; and a bakery serving pastries and coffee.

Cherry on Top features delicious sundaes, soft serve, and regular ice cream; Orange Blossom Confections has hand-made candies, caramel apples, and such.

SHOPPING

SHOPPING IS AN ATTRACTION IN ITSELF in Jubilee Junction. Stores mostly offer country-kitsch merchandise, and it's generally pretty cute. Keep in mind, though, that if you shop first thing in the morning, you'll be toting your purchases throughout the park, so it's best to save these shops for the end of the day.

The Wood Works Shop has hand-carved statues, name plaques, and so on, all made of—you guessed it—wood. Tan Yer Hide stocks a similarly generic collection of all things leather.

Kara's Kastle features sparkly, frilly, and frou-frou offerings like tiaras, dresses, and tutus. If your little girl loves to shop, you may want to steer clear or you may end up with a bagful of girly goodies.

Christmas fanatics will enjoy Kringles, which sells Christmas decorations like Nutcrackers, villages, and tree ornaments.

Longwing's Emporium sells garden-related goodies just outside of the Wings of Wonder butterfly arboretum.

Wax Myrtle Candle Company sells candles made in a traditional way, using the berries of the wax myrtle tree, many of which are found on the Cypress Gardens grounds. You can try your hand at making a candle, which is the main draw for this store.

If it has wings or four wheels, chances are you'll find a model of it for sale at Planes, Trains, and Automobiles. The best thing to see here is the model train—one of the most elaborate we've ever seen.

SPLASH ISLAND

IN MAY 2005, CYPRESS GARDENS OPENED an adjoining water park called Splash Island. It wasn't open at press time, but our guess is that it will lessen the crowds even further in the main park and create a nice, cool way to end a morning or afternoon on the rides. Tickets to Cypress Gardens include admission to Splash Island. If your family is into water rides, bring along a bathing suit and tack on a couple extra hours to explore the slides, lazy river, and wave pool.

GATORLAND

IN THESE DAYS OF THE GENIAL Crocodile Hunter, it's hard to imagine a man like Florida showman Owen Godwin, who established Gatorland way back in 1949. More of a reptile-fixated P. T. Barnum than an environmental enthusiast, Godwin traveled the world collecting toothy critters for his zoo collection of gators and "jungle crocs." But the days of aggressive collecting are gone. Most of the alligators are born right in the Gatorland swamp, and Gatorland natural-ists will earnestly tell you of their efforts to rehabilitate a variety of injured or displaced animals brought to them from all over Florida.

For more than 50 years, Gatorland has existed as a road-side wonder. Before the days of magic castles and studio back lots, visitors flocked to the Sunshine State for its beaches and wildlife. Sprin-kled along the highways that linked the state's natural attractions were tiny out-posts of tourism—"must-see" roadside stops meant to break up the monotony of travel. Gatorland fell brilliantly into this category. The park was ripe with tourist appeal—who can resist a park that hawks Florida's most infamous resident, the alligator?

unofficial **TIP**
For those who want variety in their sightseeing itinerary, this is the place for a real change of pace.

Today, Gatorland seems to disappear in the clutter of touristy Orlando. But rather than fall victim to its own kitsch or wither in the Disney glare, Gatorland has adapted enough to proudly call itself "Orlando's best half-day attrac-tion." It doesn't try to be one of the high-falutin' theme parks in its back yard. Although the attraction has grown to

Gatorland

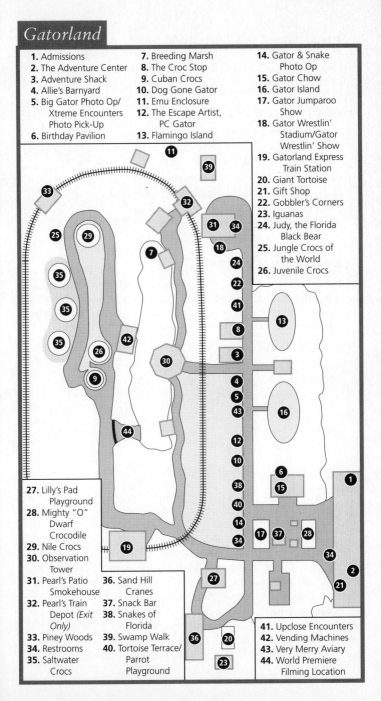

1. Admissions
2. The Adventure Center
3. Adventure Shack
4. Allie's Barnyard
5. Big Gator Photo Op/ Xtreme Encounters Photo Pick-Up
6. Birthday Pavilion
7. Breeding Marsh
8. The Croc Stop
9. Cuban Crocs
10. Dog Gone Gator
11. Emu Enclosure
12. The Escape Artist, PC Gator
13. Flamingo Island
14. Gator & Snake Photo Op
15. Gator Chow
16. Gator Island
17. Gator Jumparoo Show
18. Gator Wrestlin' Stadium/Gator Wrestlin' Show
19. Gatorland Express Train Station
20. Giant Tortoise
21. Gift Shop
22. Gobbler's Corners
23. Iguanas
24. Judy, the Florida Black Bear
25. Jungle Crocs of the World
26. Juvenile Crocs

27. Lilly's Pad Playground
28. Mighty "O" Dwarf Crocodile
29. Nile Crocs
30. Observation Tower
31. Pearl's Patio Smokehouse
32. Pearl's Train Depot *(Exit Only)*
33. Piney Woods
34. Restrooms
35. Saltwater Crocs
36. Sand Hill Cranes
37. Snack Bar
38. Snakes of Florida
39. Swamp Walk
40. Tortoise Terrace/ Parrot Playground
41. Upclose Encounters
42. Vending Machines
43. Very Merry Aviary
44. World Premiere Filming Location

more than 100 acres, the whole place is barely big enough for a good-sized Walt Disney World parking lot. But nowhere else will you see this many gators and crocs, and nowhere else are they celebrated with such abandon. In short, Gatorland is a hallmark of old Florida made good.

GETTING THERE

FROM DISNEY Take FL 192 (or the Osceola Parkway, if you don't mind paying a few bucks in tolls) to FL 441 (Orange Blossom Trail). Turn left. Gatorland is on your right.

FROM ORLANDO Take Interstate 4 to FL 528 (Beeline Highway). Exit at Consulate and turn right. Make a right on FL 441 (Orange Blossom Trail). Gatorland is about 7 miles south, between the Osceola Parkway and FL 417 (the Central Florida Greeneway). Parking is free.

ADMISSION PRICES

FOLLOWING ARE THE FULL-PRICE ADMISSION PRICES at press time. Coupons are available in Gatorland brochures (found at kiosks throughout Orlando) and at **www.gator land.com**. The park offers AAA and AARP discounts.

One-Day Pass

Adults $19.95 + tax
Children ages 3–12 $9.95
Children under age 3 Free

Annual Pass

Adults $32.95 + tax
Children ages 3–12 $19.98

ARRIVING

GATORLAND IS OPEN DAILY from 9 a.m. to 5 p.m. Gators don't mind rain (and most observation walkways have canopies), so the attraction is open rain or shine.

Gatorland bills itself as a half-day attraction, which makes it the perfect alternative when you don't have a full day to spend at Walt Disney World, SeaWorld, or the Kennedy Space Center Visitor Complex. Plan to spend about three to four hours to see it well. However, the park lends itself to any type of schedule. With nearby parking and the park's manageable size, it is easy to come and go. A small-

unofficial **TIP**
Colder temperatures will make the alligators sluggish and less likely to jump for food.

gauge railroad ride traverses part of the park and passes by local flora and fauna in their natural swampy habitat.

unofficial **TIP**
Plan your visit to this park around the shows.

Shows and feeding times are scheduled throughout the day, with performances shortly after opening, after lunch, and mid-afternoon. Performances are scheduled for easy back-to-back viewing.

Check the show schedule when you arrive. Because the shows are "can't-miss" attractions, plan your schedule around them. There are plenty of diversions near each show area. The Jungle Crocs of the World feeding "show" is the farthest away, requiring about a 12-minute walk, so keep that in mind when heading for this area of the park.

CONTACTING GATORLAND

FOR MORE INFORMATION, contact Gatorland at ☎ 800-393-JAWS or **www.gatorland.com.**

ATTRACTIONS
Gator Jumparoo Show

APPEAL BY AGE	PRESCHOOL ★★★		GRADE SCHOOL ★★★★
TEENS ★★★½	YOUNG ADULTS ★★★	OVER 30 ★★★	SENIORS ★★★

What it is It's gators: they jump, you watch—from a distance. **Scope and scale** Super headliner. **When to go** Check entertainment schedule. **Author's rating** Yikes! ★★★★. **Duration of show** 15 minutes.

DESCRIPTION AND COMMENTS This is, as they say, the money shot. Visitors gather around a square pond, framed by wooden boardwalks (thankfully with high railings). A trainer ventures out to an all-too-fragile-looking cupola on the water, and then the fun begins. Everyone is encouraged to stamp their feet on the boards, which lets the alligators know that supper's ready. The reptiles come gliding in from adjacent ponds, and the trainer yells and waves to attract them. Plucked chickens are strung up on wires over the water, and them gators commence to jumpin'. Trainers also dangle treats over the water and gators snatch the food right from their hands. After you see a 10-foot-long 300-pounder leap head-high out of the water to crunch some poultry, you'll spend the rest of your time at Gatorland nervously skirting the railings. Visit the nonthreatening lorikeet aviary to calm down if necessary.

TOURING TIPS There's no seating here, so be sure to arrive at least 10 minutes before show time to stake your claim along the railing.

Gatorland Train

APPEAL BY AGE	PRESCHOOL ★★★	GRADE SCHOOL ★★★	TEENS ★
YOUNG ADULTS ★½		OVER 30 ★★	SENIORS ★★½

What it is A circling train. **Scope and scale** Diversion. **When to go** Anytime for a quick rest of your feet. **Author's rating** Can a gator hijack a train? ★★. **Duration of ride** 6 minutes.

DESCRIPTION AND COMMENTS Given the park's small size, the train isn't really necessary as transportation. But it's good for a break and a different view of the natural areas. Chances are, the nutty guy who narrates your ride will turn up again later in the gator wrestling or Jumparoo shows.

TOURING TIPS It costs an extra $2, but it's a good way to see the park and rest your feet. Skip it if you don't need the break.

Jungle Crocs of the World

APPEAL BY AGE	PRESCHOOL ★★	GRADE SCHOOL ★★★½	TEENS ★★★
YOUNG ADULTS ★★★		OVER 30 ★★★½	SENIORS ★★★½

What it is A rare collection of international crocodiles. **Scope and scale** Headliner. **When to go** Around feeding time. **Author's rating** Insidiously catchy theme song; ★★★. **Duration of show** 10 minutes (feeding show).

DESCRIPTION AND COMMENTS As you step onto the boardwalk, leading you to Gatorland's newest animal exhibit, you'll soon notice how the park revels in its own cheese factor. Speakers lining the walkway play a song devoted entirely to Owen Godwin and his many adventures to claim this collection of "jungle crocs." This song, a close relative to the theme from *The Beverly Hillbillies*, will not leave your brain for at least an hour after departing Gatorland. But eventually, you come to the crocodile habitats. There are four total, featuring crocodiles from North and South America, Cuba, Asia, and Africa's Nile River. This exhibit features a rare collection of crocodiles, such as the Cuban crocodile. The smallest and most dangerous of breeds, Cuban crocs can leap from the water like dolphins to catch birds in flight. This area includes plenty of sight gags, including downed planes and pup tents that mysteriously lack any human beings.

TOURING TIPS Be sure to stick around for a feeding session, listed on the show schedule.

Gator Wrestling Stadium/Gator Wrestlin' Show

APPEAL BY AGE	PRESCHOOL ★★	GRADE SCHOOL ★★★★
TEENS ★★★★	YOUNG ADULTS ★★★ OVER 30 ★★★½	SENIORS ★★★

What it is Where man (especially his head) was not meant to go. **Scope and scale** Super headliner. **When to go** Check entertainment schedule; usually 3 shows daily. **Author's rating** Not to be missed; ★★★★. **Duration of show** 15 minutes.

DESCRIPTION AND COMMENTS There are no bad views in the 800-seat stadium. There is one seat, however, that most audience members would rather not have. That's the perch on the back of an alligator in a sandy pit in the middle of the theater. Here, a wise-cracking fool keeps the audience spellbound with his courage—or reckless disregard for bodily integrity—for 15 minutes. The show features two "crackers," the nickname for Florida ranchers who often cracked their whips to get their animals to move. In their best Southern accents, the two play off of one another while one unfortunate soul wrestles the gator, opens its mouth, and even (gulp!) places his chin under its snout.

TOURING TIPS Arrive a bit early to see the "wrestlers" warming up. Although every side offers a good view, the red bleachers typically have the best vantage.

Gatorland Zoo

| APPEAL BY AGE | PRESCHOOL ★★★ | GRADE SCHOOL ★★★ | TEENS ★★ |
| YOUNG ADULTS ★★½ | | OVER 30 ★★ | SENIORS ★★ |

What it is A collection of animal displays. **Scope and scale** Diversion. **When to go** Between shows. **Author's rating** Fun, but not as cool as gators; ★★.

DESCRIPTION AND COMMENTS Dozens of animal exhibits line the 150-foot main walkway, including a bear, Florida white-tailed deer, emus, llamas, snakes, turtles, tortoises, iguanas, and birds. Allie's Barnyard petting zoo—always a favorite among young children—contains the usual collection of goats and sheep. The walk-through Very Merry Aviary is stocked with lorikeets, tiny multicolored birds that are trained to land on visitors' shoulders to drink nectar from a cup (available for $1). Baby alligators are sometimes on display here, and there's a special Snakes of Florida exhibit highlighting local serpents.

TOURING TIPS Zoo exhibits are near both main show areas and are perfect filler between other shows. Bring along a handful of quarters to buy animal food. It's a minimal cost for a big thrill.

Up Close Encounters/Snake Show

| APPEAL BY AGE | PRESCHOOL ★★ | GRADE SCHOOL ★★★ | TEENS ★★ |
| YOUNG ADULTS ★★★ | | OVER 30 ★★½ | SENIORS ★★ |

What it is Educational hands-on animal show. **Scope and scale** Minor attraction. **When to go** When not at the other 3 shows. **Author's rating** Creepy and fun; ★★★.

DESCRIPTION AND COMMENTS This small stadium hosts a show-and-tell of whatever creatures—mostly snakes—the keepers might have in Gatorland's bag of tricks that day. The keepers hold the venomous critters aloft, but visitors can actually handle some of the other creatures. Gatorland provides a home for lots of captured or injured wildlife, including animals confiscated from illegal pet traders. One keeper offered to let us hold some friendly snakes and the most recent arrival: a giant emperor scorpion, creepy-crawly as can be. We respectfully declined.

TOURING TIPS Our bad example aside, the best way to enjoy the show is get close to the creatures and interact. Though the knowledgeable Gatorland naturalists can tell you a lot about the snakes and other animals, the real thrill comes from holding them yourself.

kids   Lilly's Pad and Alligator Alley

APPEAL BY AGE	PRESCHOOL ★★★		GRADE SCHOOL ★★★★
TEENS ★★½	YOUNG ADULTS ★★★	OVER 30 ★★	SENIORS ★

What it is A wet and dry playground for kids. **Scope and scale** Major attraction. **When to go** When the temperature kicks up a notch. **Author's rating** A welcome way to cool down; ★★★.

DESCRIPTION AND COMMENTS Small children will go berserk when they see this water playground. Gatorland really shines here, with an area that rivals the children's play fountains at other Orlando parks. You'll find several interactive fountains and other water-soaking games. Nearby, a dry playground is available for those who don't want to get wet.

TOURING TIPS Let the kids loose at Lilly's Pad *after* the shows, so they won't have to walk around wet for the rest of the day.

Alligator Breeding Marsh and Bird Sanctuary

APPEAL BY AGE	PRESCHOOL ★★	GRADE SCHOOL ★★	TEENS ★★
YOUNG ADULTS ★★★	OVER 30 ★★★		SENIORS ★★★

What it is A breeding ground for gators in a picturesque setting. **Scope and scale** Diversion. **When to go** At the warmer part of the day. **Author's rating** The quiet heart of Gatorland; ★★★½.

DESCRIPTION AND COMMENTS The alligator breeding marsh is one of Gatorland's most unexpected attractions. Set in the middle of a park of zoolike cages and enclosures, this large body of water is home to nearly 200 alligators in their natural setting. Once you consider the somewhat grim fact that the park also doubles as an alligator farm selling meat and hides, you realize that you're looking at the real "ranch" behind all the wrestlin' and jumpin'. Despite the eco-unfriendly downer, a flotilla of a couple dozen gators hovering placidly by your feet is enough to make you reconsider leaning over the railing for a better photo. Try out each floor of the three-story observation tower for different (and safely distant) perspectives.

The marsh is also a haven for bird-watchers. Every year, more than 4,000 birds make their home at Gatorland, including green, blue, and tricolored herons; cattle egrets; and cormorants. At feeding time, the trees along the boardwalk marsh fill with waterbirds, including several rare and protected species.

TOURING TIPS For the best view, bring binoculars. It is truly spectacular to feed the gators here (a bag of fish is $5). There is a smaller feeding area elsewhere, but you'll get more of a show if you take the goodies here. On one visit, a family brought several loaves of bread to feed the gators. It was a fascinating sight, and it attracted what seemed like hundreds of creatures. Check the trees on your right as you walk toward the petting farm, with the marsh behind you. On our June visit, there were hundreds of nesting herons, with the accompanying chirps of their young. Because the second level of the observation tower is above the trees, it provides a rare look at these birds.

Swamp Walk

APPEAL BY AGE	PRESCHOOL ★	GRADE SCHOOL ★	TEENS ★
YOUNG ADULTS ★★½		OVER 30 ★★★	SENIORS ★★★

What it is Boardwalk through undisturbed nature. **Scope and scale** Diversion. **When to go** When you need some quiet time. **Author's rating** Natural Florida; ★★★.

DESCRIPTION AND COMMENTS Cross the swinging bridge that leads to a boardwalk trail through a beautiful natural swamp. So far removed from the rest of the attractions that many visitors fail to discover it, the walk is easily one of the most exotic and unusual promenades to be found in all of Florida. The swamp is actually part of the headwaters for the Florida Everglades, the critically important south Florida swampland hundreds of miles away. Winding gracefully with no apparent impact on the environment, the walk, flanked by towering cypress and draped with Spanish moss, disappears deep into the lush, green swamp. Simultaneously tranquil and serene yet bursting with life, the swamp radiates a primeval loveliness.

TOURING TIPS Visit the Swamp Walk before sunset, when the mosquitoes come out to feast on unsuspecting Gatorland tourists.

DINING

DINING AT GATORLAND can be either an adventure or a nonevent. It's a letdown if you come to sample its regular

unofficial **TIP**
Ever try a gator rib? This could be your chance, and you may be pleasantly surprised.

menu items. They are nothing spectacular, but then again they are also fairly inexpensive by Orlando theme-park standards. A hamburger is $2.25, and a kids' meal is $3.99. The menu is varied, however, and includes chicken breast and a fish 'n chips basket.

But who comes to Gatorland to eat a hot dog? No true individual can visit without trying at least a bite of gator meat. Pearl's Smokehouse features two such items, including gator nuggets and gator ribs. In humanity's never-ending quest to reduce all animals to nugget form, this is one of the less impressive examples. Yes, the gator nuggets do taste like chicken, but spicier and much tougher. They come with barbecue dipping sauces to mask any unfamiliar tastes. The ribs are a bit more intimidating, but quite good. They are also quite small and, consequently, contain small bones, so be careful. Try the sampler platter, which gives you a taste of both treats. If you see a nearby gator eyeing you accusingly, console yourself with the thought that he'd do the same to you—only with less barbecue sauce and a lot more screaming.

SHOPPING

IF YOU ARE LOOKING FOR A TACKY FLORIDA SOUVENIR for that prized spot on your mantel, Gatorland is the place. Similar to shops that line US 192, the park hawks everything gator-related that you could ever imagine—and even a few things you would, in a sane world, never even consider. There are also several merchandise carts throughout the park and two unique photo locations.

THE HOLY LAND EXPERIENCE

AN ENTIRELY NEW KIND OF THEME PARK opened in Orlando in early 2001. The Holy Land Experience is a re-creation of biblical-era Israel by way of evangelical Christianity. Don't expect a Jehovah Coaster or Red Sea Flume, though—this park is only for thrills of the spiritual kind. The Holy Land Experience has more in common with passive attractions like Gatorland than with places like Walt Disney World or Universal Studios.

unofficial **TIP**
Not built in a day: you'll notice a similar attention to detail here as in some Disney parks.

At 15 acres, this park is tiny by local standards. It's packed with a half-dozen exhibits and re-creations of structures dating from 1450 BC to the first century AD. Elaborately crafted by the same company that built parts of Walt Disney World and Universal Islands of Adventure, the theming and detail are meticulous and impressive. Costumed performers roam the park and interact with guests, sometimes assembling for performances or impromptu congregations.

Which brings up a big caveat: though the historical recreations might interest period enthusiasts, straight history is not really the focus here. Some Jewish groups have expressed concern about the appropriation of Jewish history and ritual for a Christian-themed park. Because it's ministry-operated, the park is very open about its evangelical mission. Every exhibit, show, performance, and shop is geared toward the Christian faith—essentially the Protestant version. No one will treat you rudely or force you to participate

unofficial **TIP**
Goes without saying: come to Holy Land only if you're interested in all things Christian.

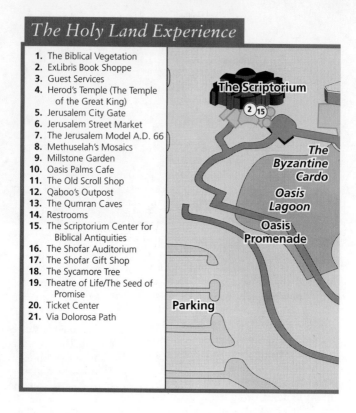

The Holy Land Experience

1. The Biblical Vegetation
2. ExLibris Book Shoppe
3. Guest Services
4. Herod's Temple (The Temple of the Great King)
5. Jerusalem City Gate
6. Jerusalem Street Market
7. The Jerusalem Model A.D. 66
8. Methuselah's Mosaics
9. Millstone Garden
10. Oasis Palms Cafe
11. The Old Scroll Shop
12. Qaboo's Outpost
13. The Qumran Caves
14. Restrooms
15. The Scriptorium Center for Biblical Antiquities
16. The Shofar Auditorium
17. The Shofar Gift Shop
18. The Sycamore Tree
19. Theatre of Life/The Seed of Promise
20. Ticket Center
21. Via Dolorosa Path

The Scriptorium

2 15

The Byzantine Cardo

Oasis Lagoon

Oasis Promenade

Parking

in anything that makes you uncomfortable, but you can no more escape Christianity at the Holy Land Experience than you could escape Mickey Mouse at Walt Disney World. If that's not your cup of tea, then this place is not for you.

If Christian-oriented touring suits you and your family, The Holy Land Experience is a singular attraction. Tremendous press coverage and high initial attendance proved that its creators have hit on something unique. However, a general tourism slump and declining crowds led to a huge increase in ticket prices (not to mention an end to free parking), making the Holy Land Experience less of a deal than it once was. The park's small size makes it a manageable outing though, and the needs of the elderly, disabled, or foreign tourist get special attention here. In fact, most guests tend to

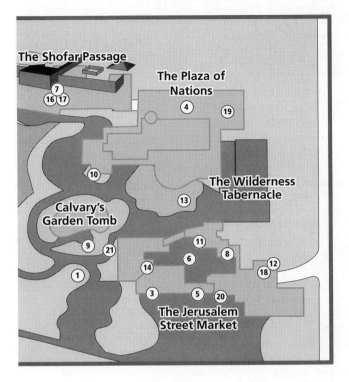

The Shofar Passage

7
16 17

The Plaza of Nations

4

19

10

The Wilderness Tabernacle

13

Calvary's Garden Tomb

9   21

11

6

8

12

18

14

1

3

5   20

The Jerusalem Street Market

be adults or seniors. Despite the often cutting-edge theming and production values, children are likely to get bored after more than a few hours here (though they may be distracted for a while by the cute baby goats).

GETTING THERE

THE HOLY LAND EXPERIENCE is very easy to find because it's located right off Interstate 4 near Universal Studios Florida. From Disney World or points south, take I-4 East to Exit 78 (just past Universal Studios Florida and the Florida Turnpike). The Holy Land Experience is just off the exit ramp, on the west side of I-4. From Orlando, take I-4 West for five miles to Exit 78.

ADMISSION PRICES

ONE-DAY PASS
Adults $29.99 + tax
Children ages 6–12 $19.99 + tax
Children under age 6 Free

Multiday and Annual Passes

JERUSALEM GOLD ANNUAL PASSES cost $69.75. For groups of 20 or more (six-week advance reservation and three-week advance payment required), admission is $25.75 for adults and $17.75 for children ages 6–12. Package deals including a meal inside the park (lunch or dinner) are available for groups of 35 or more (again, advance reservation and payment required). Parking is $5.

ARRIVING

THE HOLY LAND EXPERIENCE IS OPEN DAILY, with special programs during holidays (call ahead for details). Hours are Monday–Thursday, 10 a.m.–7 p.m.; Friday and Saturday, 10 a.m.–10 p.m.; and Sunday, noon–7 p.m. Tickets are purchased at the Ticket Center near the front entrance. If there's a substantial line at the ticket windows, check the Guest Services desk, found through the large double doors to the left of the main entrance; tickets are sometimes sold there as well.

Most of this small park is meant to be enjoyed on a walk-through basis at your own pace, but there are several shows and presentations to see. All but the Scriptorium are less than 30 minutes long, and all run throughout the day. A thorough tour of the Holy Land Experience takes just over half a day, assuming you want to experience every single thing. Our advice is to check the daily schedule and make a point of seeing the featured exhibits, using the various live performances and presentations as filler.

CONTACTING THE HOLY LAND EXPERIENCE

FOR INFORMATION ABOUT TICKETS, hours, or special presentations, contact the Holy Land Experience at ☎ 866-USA HOLYLAND or 407-367-2065, or **www.holylandexperience.com.**

ATTRACTIONS

The Wilderness Tabernacle

APPEAL BY AGE	PRESCHOOL ★★	GRADE SCHOOL ★★★	TEENS ★★
YOUNG ADULTS ★★		OVER 30 ★★★	SENIORS ★★★

What it is Historical demonstration of Jewish ritual. **Scope and scale** Headliner. **When to go** Later in the day, when crowds have thinned out. **Author's rating** Interesting history; ★★½. **Duration of show** 25 minutes; shows every 30 minutes.

DESCRIPTION AND COMMENTS Visitors enter a preshow area where they learn about the struggles of the 12 tribes of Israel on their journey to the Promised Land. They then move into an indoor exhibition hall with bleacher seats; the lighting creates the illusion of being outdoors at dusk, and a narrator introduces himself as a Levitican priest and a descendent of Aaron, the brother of Moses. He then reenacts various rituals of the priesthood practiced during the Israelites' 40 years in the desert. Portentous rumbling, fog, and lighting effects accompany prophetic narration broadcast over the loudspeakers. The details of ritual are explained plainly enough, even though part of the scenario takes place in an enclosed tent.

TOURING TIPS All seats have good eyelines in this small space. Moving to the far left will guarantee the best vantage to see the final portion of the presentation, as well as allowing for an easy exit.

Calvary's Garden Tomb

APPEAL BY AGE	PRESCHOOL ★	GRADE SCHOOL ★	TEENS ★
YOUNG ADULTS ★★		OVER 30 ★★	SENIORS ★★½

What it is Re-creation of Christ's empty tomb and setting for dramatic and historical presentations. **Scope and scale** Minor attraction. **When to go** During one of the presentations. **Author's rating** Not much to see; ★★. **Duration of show** 15–20 minutes; check presentation schedule.

DESCRIPTION AND COMMENTS Visitors wind their way along a highly attenuated version of the Via Dolorosa ("way of suffering"), which Jesus walked on his way to Calvary to be crucified. Eventually, you end up in a garden with Jesus' tomb as its centerpiece, the door stone rolled away to reveal its emptiness. Regular dramatic and historical presentations of the life of Jesus are held in, around, and above the tomb.

TOURING TIPS This is an especially similar re-creation of the Garden Tomb in Israel—serene and poignant. Try to plan your visit during one of the presentations.

Theater of Life/The Seed of Promise

APPEAL BY AGE	PRESCHOOL ★½	GRADE SCHOOL ★★	TEENS ★½
YOUNG ADULTS ★★		OVER 30 ★★½	SENIORS ★★★

What it is Bible high points in movie form. **Scope and scale** Headliner.
When to go After experiencing the Scriptorium and Jerusalem Model.
Author's rating Surprisingly chintzy; ★½. **Duration of show** 25 minutes; shows every half hour.

DESCRIPTION AND COMMENTS The Theater of Life is set in the behemoth Temple of the Great King, a half-scale replica of Herod's temple from first-century Jerusalem. The ornate temple is the gleaming centerpiece of the Holy Land Experience, so you can't miss it. Pass through the Corinthian columns of the Plaza of the Nations to enter the right side of the temple, where the theater is located. *The Seed of Promise* film is a sort of biblical *Cliffs Notes,* covering the highlights of both Old and New Testaments—everything from Genesis all the way to the Second Coming. Shot on location in Jerusalem, the film is projected onto a six-story-high screen. The film aims to be an "emotionally immersive" retelling of these Bible stories, with special effects thrown in for extra punch.

TOURING TIPS *The Seed of Promise* is oddly disjointed and fairly boring, with historical sets and computer-generated effects that already appear dated. A lot of money was poorly spent here. Our advice: rent *The Ten Commandments* when you get home.

The Jerusalem Model A.D. 66

APPEAL BY AGE	PRESCHOOL ★	GRADE SCHOOL ★★	TEENS ★★★
YOUNG ADULTS ★★★		OVER 30 ★★★½	SENIORS ★★★½

What it is Elaborate replica of ancient Jerusalem. **Scope and scale** Headliner. **When to go** After experiencing the Scriptorium. **Author's rating** Very cool; ★★★½. **Duration of show** 30 minutes; check daily schedule for presentation times.

DESCRIPTION AND COMMENTS This is touted as "the world's largest indoor model of first-century Jerusalem." The 25-foot-wide model is meant to represent Jerusalem circa AD 66, including the Temple of Jerusalem as rebuilt by Herod while the Romans ruled the city. You must wait for one of the guided tours to enter the building (no examining the model at your leisure, unfortunately). The tours cover what everything in the model is, the history of the era, where Jesus went during the last week of his life, and more.

TOURING TIPS Because this is the only headliner attraction with only a few scheduled openings (as opposed to constant, regular openings on the half-hour or hour), make sure to consult the daily schedule to fit a visit into your plans. Try to make it to the first opening of the morning to ensure touring flexibility later on.

The Scriptorium Center for Biblical Antiquities

APPEAL BY AGE	PRESCHOOL ★	GRADE SCHOOL ★★½	TEENS ★★½
YOUNG ADULTS ★★★		OVER 30 ★★★	SENIORS ★★★½

What it is Walk-through exhibit detailing the history of the Bible itself. **Scope and scale** Super headliner. **When to go** Immediately on entering the park. **Author's rating** World-class collection; ★★★. **Duration of show** 55 minutes; presentations every hour.

DESCRIPTION AND COMMENTS This museum showcases a fascinating collection of biblical antiquities, some dating from thousands of years ago. Exhibits include ancient cuneiform, scrolls, Gutenberg and Tyndale Bibles, manuscripts, and more. Narration guides visitors from room to room; spotlights shine on particular objects while the narration explains their historical and religious significance. Theming and attention to detail are the best of anywhere in the park, and the Holy Land Experience's overriding evangelism is also front and center. The walk-through ends in a modern home setting that is conspicuously Bible-free, which is meant to inspire reflection on how we can bring the Good Book back into our collective lives. (We first thought we'd mistakenly wandered into someone's living quarters, until a man in monk's robes appeared and assured us that it was all part of the program.)

TOURING TIPS Most guests initially visit the attractions near the park entrance. Proceeding immediately to the Scriptorium will get you through it with the first batch of guests (there were only three people in our group) and free you up for other attractions and shows.

DINING

THE ONLY RESTAURANT is an American/Middle Eastern–themed restaurant, the Oasis Springs Café. The menu includes fast-food fare suited to the period and geography, such as hummus, falafel, and gyros. American choices include the endearingly named Goliath-burger. Also, wandering vendors sell snacks and drinks throughout the park.

SHOPPING

THE JERUSALEM STREET MARKET at the park's entrance is the main shopping venue here. Various costumed craftspeople hawk their wares, and a cluster of stores sell a variety of souvenirs. Typical gifts like Bibles and crosses are available, but there are also more exotic choices like mosaics, horn shofars, olive-wood crèches, or plush-toy camels and lambs. Another small gift shop geared toward books and the history of Bible-making can be found in the Scriptorium.

KENNEDY SPACE CENTER VISITOR COMPLEX

YOU MAY BE OLD ENOUGH TO REMEMBER the excitement and anticipation of the early days of space exploration. If not, you've probably seen the movies. Regardless, the pioneer spirit of the space program—sparked when President John F. Kennedy promised to land a man on the moon—is contagious.

Kennedy Space Center has been the training area and launch site for most major U.S. space programs, including Project Mercury's manned orbital missions, Project Apollo's voyages to the moon, and the Space Shuttle program. In addition, weather and communications satellites are regularly put into orbit from here.

After a $100-million expansion in 1999, the Kennedy Space Center Visitor Complex is thoroughly modern and offers all the attractions and amenities of a contemporary theme park. The complex does a wonderful job of capturing the spirit of adventure—and the uncertainty—of the early days of America's space program. It also offers a unique glimpse into the latest NASA advancements and some interesting visions of where the future of space exploration may lead. Aware of the sometimes wide gulf of interests between the average tourist and the hard-core space junkie, the Visitor Complex is much more engaging and kid-friendly than in the past. Serious space cadets can still visit all the authentic installations and buildings they like, and others can marvel at gee-whiz exhibits, IMAX movies, and really giant rockets. Even so, be sensitive to your group's likes and dis-

likes, especially when it comes to the specialty tours—some of which are hours long
and involve lengthy bus rides.

After the terrorist attacks of September
11, 2001, security at Kennedy Space Center
increased dramatically. Some of the tours
have been drastically altered, with visits to
various secure areas reduced or eliminated
entirely. If you're considering a tour, we advise you to find
out exactly what sights you'll be seeing and from how far
away. Check out the individual tour profiles here for guidance, but be advised that all of this can change if security
conditions dictate.

We can't stress enough that the tours at Kennedy Space
Center are most enjoyable for those with a serious interest in
the space program and a high tolerance for "touring at a distance"—and even then, you may not be happy. With stars
quite literally in their eyes, visitors can be disappointed by
security restrictions and the less-than-thrilling visual impact
of bunker-style buildings seen from a mile away (or more).
As a reader from Cherry Hill, New Jersey, writes:

> The tours are a waste of time (and money). In particular, the
> NASA Up Close tour is anything but. [Like our tour guide
> said,] "There's a space shuttle inside that building, over there
> . . . but you can't see it . . . and there's another shuttle on the
> launch pad over yonder . . . but you can't see that either."

If you really want to stay up close with the space stuff, it
takes less time, money, and hassle to just explore the Visitor
Complex proper. This is especially true for visitors with children, who would likely have little tolerance for a few hours
on a bus.

GETTING THERE

KENNEDY SPACE CENTER VISITOR COMPLEX is an easy
day trip from most central Florida attractions. From
Orlando, visitors can take FL 528 (Beeline Highway toll
road) east. (A round-trip on the Beeline will cost about $5 in
tolls, so have some cash handy.) Turn onto FL 407 North,
then FL 405 East, and follow to the Kennedy Space Center
Visitor Complex. You can also take Colonial Drive (FL 50),
and travel east to FL 405, but the Beeline is definitely the
quickest and easiest route. Parking is free.

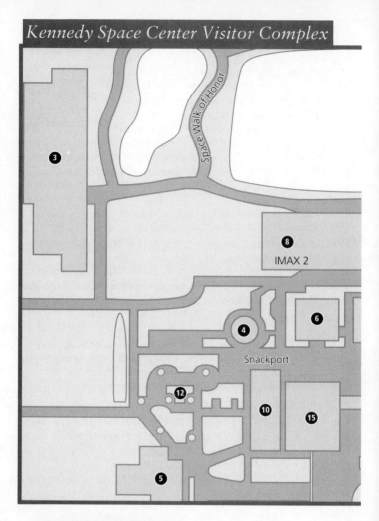

Kennedy Space Center Visitor Complex

ADMISSION PRICES

Standard Admission

THE STANDARD ADMISSION BADGE includes the Kennedy Space Center Tour, both IMAX films, and all attractions and exhibits.

STANDARD ADMISSION	
Adults $30 + tax	
Children ages 3–11 $20 + tax	*Children under age 3* Free

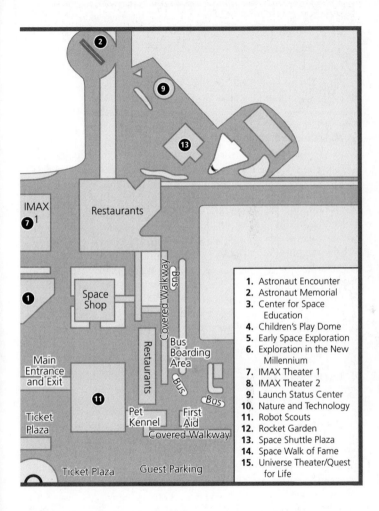

1. Astronaut Encounter
2. Astronaut Memorial
3. Center for Space Education
4. Children's Play Dome
5. Early Space Exploration
6. Exploration in the New Millennium
7. IMAX Theater 1
8. IMAX Theater 2
9. Launch Status Center
10. Nature and Technology
11. Robot Scouts
12. Rocket Garden
13. Space Shuttle Plaza
14. Space Walk of Fame
15. Universe Theater/Quest for Life

Maximum Access Admission

THE MAXIMUM ACCESS ADMISSION includes everything the Standard Admission does, plus access to the Astronaut Hall of Fame and interactive space flight simulators.

MAXIMUM ACCESS ADMISSION
Adults $37 + tax
Children ages 3–11 $27 + tax

SPECIAL INTEREST TOURS
Adults $59 + tax *Children ages 3–11* $43 + tax

ANNUAL PASS
Adults $46 + tax *Children ages 3–11* $30 + tax

Astronaut Training Experience

IF YOU'RE REALLY INTO THE ASTRONAUT THING, the Astronaut Training Experience (or ATX as it's called) takes visitors ages 14 and up (children under age 18 must be accompanied by an adult) through the training real astronauts use to get them ready for a launch. Zero-gravity simulators; mock mission control access; a guided, behind-the-scenes tour of Kennedy Space Center; lunch; and a final simulated launch and orbit are included in the steep price. This is for true space enthusiasts only. Call ☎ 321-449-4400 for more information or to make reservations. You can also reserve a spot via the Web site: **www.kennedyspacecenter.com.**

unofficial **TIP**
To infinity and beyond: take kids with a real interest in becoming an astronaut on the ATX.

AGES 14+ $225 + tax

ARRIVING

KENNEDY SPACE CENTER VISITOR COMPLEX is open from 9 a.m. to 5:30 p.m. Unlike other area attractions, the Space Center is closed on Christmas Day and may close for certain shuttle launches. Call ahead before making the drive. Also note that even though the Visitor Complex may be open during shuttle launches, the Launch Complex 39 Observation Gantry may be closed to tourists when there's "a bird on the pad." Bus tour guides will try to make it up with some other sights around the Space Center, but if you can't see LC 39, you're missing one of the highlights of the tour.

unofficial **TIP**
This facility's tour can take an entire day, so be sure everyone in your group is truly interested in seeing everything there is to see before you board the bus.

Each of the IMAX movies is about 40 minutes long, and the bus tour alone can take more than 3 hours. If this leaves you feeling overwhelmed, you're right—there's a lot of ground to cover here. The wrong approach is to race from attraction to attraction in one day. Instead, take it slow and soak in some of the better attractions, leaving the others behind.

Most visitors should start their day with some of the exhibits at the hub, which provide an informative background on space history. Then, if you've found one that really meets your interests, head for the bus tour. Buses come frequently (every 15 minutes), but if your timing is off, you can stand a full 15 minutes before boarding, then sit on the bus for a few minutes before taking off. Buses visit LC 39, the Apollo/Saturn V Center, and other locales as the tour's emphasis (or security restrictions) demand. Each of the stops involves movies and displays that are very text-heavy but usually interesting. The movies are wonderful and are of documentary quality, but after a while some may begin to grow tired of the movie-bus-movie-bus shuffle.

After the bus tour, see at least one of the IMAX movies. The five-and-a-half-story screens provide amazing views, and the sound systems are excellent. You can choose from peeking at the future in 3-D or witnessing the thrilling sensation of space flight.

CONTACTING KENNEDY SPACE CENTER

FOR MORE INFORMATION about Kennedy Space Center, call ☎ 321-449-4444. You can also try ☎ 800-KSC-INFO, but this is a quick, recorded message of basic information that doesn't allow you to transfer to an actual person. The Space Center will mail you a brochure about tours, as well as launch schedule information.

kids You can also visit **www.kennedyspacecenter.com,** which has a page just for kids.

ATTRACTIONS

VISITOR CENTER COMPLEX HUB

Robot Scouts

APPEAL BY AGE	PRESCHOOL ★★	GRADE SCHOOL ★★★	TEENS ★★
YOUNG ADULTS ★★		OVER 30 ★★	SENIORS ★★

What it is Walk-through exhibit featuring robots. **Scope and scale** Minor attraction. **When to go** At the end of the day, if there's time. **Author's rating** Somewhat hokey; ★★.

DESCRIPTION AND COMMENTS Robot Starquester 2000 will take you through this exhibition of NASA's past, present, and future robotic space explorers. Starquester 2000 interacts with other space probes, like the Viking Mars Lander and the Hubble Space Telescope, to explain how robotic space exploration aids human exploration.

TOURING TIPS You can hit this exhibit on entering the center, before the bus tours.

Astronaut Encounter

APPEAL BY AGE	PRESCHOOL ★	GRADE SCHOOL ★★★	TEENS ★½
YOUNG ADULTS ★★★	OVER 30 ★★★		SENIORS ★★★½

What it is Talk with a real live astronaut. **Scope and scale** Diversion. **When to go** Anytime. **Author's rating** Somewhat forced; ★½.

DESCRIPTION AND COMMENTS At scheduled times throughout the day, a NASA astronaut appears in the central food court area for a meet-and-greet. The astronaut's "opening act" is a Visitor Complex MC who warms up the crowd with some fun space facts and nutty science tomfoolery, assisted by a kid volunteer from the audience. Then the astronaut is introduced, talks for a while, and takes questions. It's kind of interesting, but once the slight thrill of seeing an astronaut wears off, the whole thing feels like one of those desperate attempts by a schoolteacher to make science fun and exciting. "OK, kids! Do you know how cold the vacuum of space is? Brrrr! Well, it's so cold that. . ." Children do seem moderately intrigued, but they don't appear to go for the astronaut hero worship more popular with preceding generations.

For an even more intimate astronaut encounter, sign up for Lunch with an Astronaut. As the name implies, this involves sharing a meal with an astronaut, who first shows a video about life on the Space Shuttle, then gives a personalized presentation about his or her own space experiences. A Q&A follows, as well as a chance to take photos (a signed souvenir photo is included). The meal (served at 12:30 p.m. daily) consists of rotisserie chicken, salad, sides, dessert, and beverage, with kid-friendly options available for children. Cost is $19.99 adults, $12.99 for kids ages 3–11. Park admission is required; call ☎ 321-449-4444 for advance reservations or purchase online at **www.kennedyspacecenter. com.** Tickets for Lunch with an Astronaut can also be purchased at the Visitor Complex, but same-day tickets may already be sold out.

unofficial **TIP**
To get up close and personal with an astronaut, have lunch with them—make reservations in advance

TOURING TIPS Check the daily entertainment schedule for times. If kids get bored, the spread-out seats make it easy to tactfully get up and wander off to another attraction.

Exploration in the New Millennium

APPEAL BY AGE	PRESCHOOL ★★★	GRADE SCHOOL ★★★½	TEENS ★★
YOUNG ADULTS ★★★		OVER 30 ★★½	SENIORS ★★

What it is Exhibits about the future of space travel. **Scope and scale** Diversion. **When to go** While waiting for the bus or IMAX films. **Author's rating** Future funky; ★★½.

DESCRIPTION AND COMMENTS A collection of hands-on exhibits that speculate on where our space travelers will go and how they will get there. Some exhibits are educational and straightforward, like many dealing with the various Mars landers and the Pathfinder mission (you can even sign up to send your signature to the Red Planet on the next mission). Other exhibits go on flights of fancy about how futuristic spacecraft will work and what colonizing other planets would be like. A live-action show called Mad Mission to Mars 2025 uses special effects and "splatter cannons" to teach the audience about the physics involved in space travel.

TOURING TIPS An easy walk-through, with nothing too surprising. Kids will like the touching-encouraged exhibits. Hit this one as filler when needed.

IMAX Films

APPEAL BY AGE	PRESCHOOL ★★★	GRADE SCHOOL ★★★★	TEENS ★★
YOUNG ADULTS ★★★		OVER 30 ★★★½	SENIORS ★★★½

What it is Large-format films projected onto huge screens with incredible sound systems. **Scope and scale** Headliner. **When to go** Check daily entertainment schedule; perfect during rain. **Author's rating** Excellent; ★★★½. **Duration of shows** About 40 minutes.

DESCRIPTION AND COMMENTS Kennedy Space Center offers two excellent IMAX films:

The Dream Is Alive. Get inside the cabin with amazing in-flight footage shot by astronauts in space. You'll enjoy the beauty that astronauts experience firsthand and learn about the challenges of living in space.

Space Station 3-D. Narrated by Tom Cruise, this film includes footage shot by 25 astronauts and cosmonauts as they lifted off from Earth and visited the International Space Station. Various effects and 3-D models create the illusion that the audience is actually flying in the Space Shuttle and visiting the station themselves.

TOURING TIPS *The Dream Is Alive* is the oldest film here and the nostalgic favorite. *Space Station 3-D* is a good bet, too, as it's both the newest film and also the most complete look at the space station available at the Visitor Complex (since the International Space Station Center is usually closed to visitors nowadays). Regardless of which movie you choose, we recommend sitting toward the back of the theater for the best view and to fully experience the awesome sound system. You will need to arrive early because these theaters are fairly small. As in most theaters, popcorn, candy, and sodas are available in the lobby.

Universe Theater/Quest for Life

| APPEAL BY AGE | PRESCHOOL ★ | GRADE SCHOOL ★★ | TEENS ★★½ |
| YOUNG ADULTS ★★ | | OVER 30 ★★ | SENIORS ★★ |

What it is Film about life on other planets. **Scope and scale** Minor attraction. **When to go** Anytime. **Author's rating** Amusingly similar to preride film at Universal's Men in Black: Alien Attack; ★★½. **Duration of show** 15 minutes.

DESCRIPTION AND COMMENTS Does life exist on other planets? Leading scientists lend evidence that there may have been life on Mars. The film addresses the likelihood of other planets sustaining life and NASA's plans to determine if life exists in other parts of the universe. It's a bit too earnest in this *X-Files* world of ours, but still interesting.

TOURING TIPS Make this your final stop before leaving the Visitor Complex proper.

Nature and Technology: Merritt Island National Wildlife Refuge

| APPEAL BY AGE | PRESCHOOL ★ | GRADE SCHOOL ★½ | TEENS ★½ |
| YOUNG ADULTS ★★ | | OVER 30 ★★ | SENIORS ★★ |

What it is Small exhibit on the coexistence of local wildlife and high technology. **Scope and scale** Diversion. **When to go** Anytime. **Author's rating** Unremarkable; ★½.

DESCRIPTION AND COMMENTS Though it's harmless enough, this walk-through exhibit is largely uninspired. Small displays catalog the lives and habits of various wild animals in the refuge as well as Cape Canaveral National Seashore, including bald eagles, alligators, otters, sea turtles, manatees, and so on.

TOURING TIPS Skip this one unless you're killing time while someone else is on the bus or in the movie theater.

kids Children's Play Dome

| APPEAL BY AGE | PRESCHOOL ★★★ | GRADE SCHOOL ★★ |
| TEENS – | YOUNG ADULTS – | OVER 30 – | SENIORS – |

What it is Kiddie playground. **Scope and scale** Diversion. **When to go** If your older kids are looking at the Rocket Garden, supervise the young ones here. **Author's rating** Small but cute; ★★.

DESCRIPTION AND COMMENTS This little playground, under cover from the hot sun, is a nice diversion for kids. It's similar to the kids areas at other attractions, but a space theme prevails.

TOURING TIPS One adult can take the older kids to an IMAX movie or on a stroll through the Rocket Garden, while another supervises the little ones here.

Rocket Garden

APPEAL BY AGE	PRESCHOOL ★	GRADE SCHOOL ★★	TEENS ★
YOUNG ADULTS ★		OVER 30 ★★	SENIORS ★★

What it is Outdoor rocket display. **Scope and scale** Diversion. **When to go** Before you head home. **Author's rating** Unique; ★★.

DESCRIPTION AND COMMENTS Rockets, spacecraft, and antennae dot a vast lawn. The big rockets take center stage and are the perfect backdrop for group photos. If you're wondering what Old Scratch has been up to lately, consult the SATAN Tracking Antenna. The Rocket Garden underwent a massive renovation and refurbishment in 2002, with new landscaping, shade, and fresh coats of paint all around, giving the attraction a much-needed face-lift. Space enthusiasts and grade schoolers may enjoy the climb-in replicas of Mercury, Gemini, and Apollo capsules.

TOURING TIPS Morning and afternoon guided tours are offered. Check the sign near the garden entrance for times.

Early Space Exploration

APPEAL BY AGE	PRESCHOOL ★	GRADE SCHOOL ★½	TEENS ★★
YOUNG ADULTS ★★★		OVER 30 ★★★½	SENIORS ★★★★

What it is Relics from the birth of spaceflight. **Scope and scale** Diversion. **When to go** While waiting for the bus or IMAX films. **Author's rating** Very informative and nostalgic; ★★★.

DESCRIPTION AND COMMENTS This well-presented series of exhibits documents the birth and maturation of human space exploration. Space suits, lunar landers, and capsules are all on display, mostly highlighting the Mercury and Gemini space programs. Newspaper clippings and other ephemera give historical context to the items on display. There's also a good deal of information on how the Russian space program evolved in competition with that of the United States, but the space race is framed as having been ultimately beneficial to both nations.

TOURING TIPS Another pleasant walk-through exhibit. Kids will have less patience with all this "old" stuff, so be prepared for some eye rolling and heavy sighs if you tarry too long.

Astronaut Memorial

APPEAL BY AGE	PRESCHOOL ★	GRADE SCHOOL ★	TEENS ★★
YOUNG ADULTS ★★		OVER 30 ★★★	SENIORS ★★★

What it is Memorial to those who died for space exploration. **Scope and scale** Minor attraction. **When to go** At the end of the tour. **Author's rating** Touching tribute; ★★★.

DESCRIPTION AND COMMENTS The entire memorial tilts and swivels to follow the sun, while mirrors direct the sun's rays onto glass names etched in a black marble slab. Probably won't want to spend a great deal of time here, but it's a poignant thing to see.

TOURING TIPS Visit the kiosk on the side of the Gallery Center Building. There you'll find computers that offer background information on the astronauts on the memorial.

Launch Status Center

APPEAL BY AGE	PRESCHOOL ★	GRADE SCHOOL ★½	TEENS ★★
YOUNG ADULTS ★★½		OVER 30 ★★★	SENIORS ★★★

What it is Live launch briefings and artifacts on display. **Scope and scale** Major attraction. **When to go** After visiting the Shuttle Plaza. **Author's rating** Cool to see the real deal; ★★★.

DESCRIPTION AND COMMENTS The artifacts are neat, but most enjoyable are the live briefings that take place on the hour between 11 a.m. and 5 p.m. Space Center communicators and live footage from throughout the complex give a glimpse into what is happening at the Space Center the day of your visit.

TOURING TIPS Visit just days before a launch and you'll catch the real action, which could include live video from the shuttle. If you visit when LC 39 is closed for a launch, this will probably be as close as you get.

Space Shuttle Plaza

APPEAL BY AGE	PRESCHOOL ★	GRADE SCHOOL ★★★	TEENS ★★
YOUNG ADULTS ★★		OVER 30 ★★	SENIORS ★★

What it is View a Space Shuttle model. **Scope and scale** Minor attraction. **When to go** Immediately before or after bus tour. **Author's rating** Impressive up close; ★★.

DESCRIPTION AND COMMENTS The Explorer, a full-size replica of the space shuttle, gives you a glimpse of what it's like to be an astronaut working and living in space. You'll see the flight deck, where astronauts fly the orbiter during launch and landing, and the mid-deck, where shuttle crews work on experiments, sleep, and eat.

TOURING TIPS This exhibit is easy to miss if you're racing to the bus tour because it's off the beaten path. Nevertheless, there may be a long line. We suggest trying back later in the afternoon rather than waiting for this interesting but uneventful tour.

U.S. Astronaut Hall of Fame

APPEAL BY AGE	PRESCHOOL ★★	GRADE SCHOOL ★★★	TEENS ★★½
YOUNG ADULTS ★★½		OVER 30 ★★½	SENIORS ★★

What it is Complex of exhibits and astronaut honor roll. **Scope and scale** Major attraction. **When to go** Anytime. **Author's rating** Worth a look if you're skipping the bus tours; ★★½.

DESCRIPTION AND COMMENTS This building, which is separate from the main Visitor Complex and set outside the guard gate, houses a collection of astronaut memorabilia and mementos, including equipment and small spacecraft, flight patches, and personal items. The Astronaut Hall of Fame itself takes up one room, listing those honored and inducted so far. Another room sports an array of simulators that will be of the most interest to kids, allowing them to land a shuttle, dock with the space station, walk on the moon, and engage in other spacely pursuits. The inevitable gift shop rounds out the proceedings.

TOURING TIPS You must purchase the Maximum Access Admission to view the Hall of Fame (simulators and all). This is a good last stop before heading to the hotel.

KENNEDY SPACE CENTER BUS TOUR

BUSES RUN EVERY 15 MINUTES and make three stops around the complex. Tour at your own pace, but the entire trip, making all the stops, should average about three and a half hours. In transit, there's no staring into "space." Television monitors show informative segments on space exploration to prepare you for the next destination. Think of this time as cramming for an exam. If possible, sit near the front of the bus, on the right side, for a better view of buildings in the area. Also, if you're lucky, an alert bus driver will point out signs of wildlife—which include an impressive bald eagle nest—along the way to the following stops:

LC 39 Observation Gantry

APPEAL BY AGE	PRESCHOOL ★★	GRADE SCHOOL ★★★	TEENS ★★
YOUNG ADULTS ★★★	OVER 30 ★★★★		SENIORS ★★★★

What it is Observation area that focuses on the Space Shuttle. **Scope and scale** Major attraction. **When to go** Anytime. **Author's rating** Get up close and personal with shuttle launch pads; ★★★★.

DESCRIPTION AND COMMENTS The LC 39 exhibits celebrate the Space Shuttle—the first spacecraft designed to be reusable. A seven-minute film at the LC 39 Theater, narrated by shuttle astronaut Marsha Ivins, explains how NASA engineers and technicians service the shuttle before launch. After the film, the doors open to dump you into a room with model displays. From here, head to the observation gantry, which puts you less than a mile away from Launch Pads 39A and 39B, the only sites for launching the space shuttle. These are also the pads from which the Saturn V rockets blasted off to the moon during the Apollo program.

TOURING TIPS You'll be tempted to race to the observation gantry, but watching the film first definitely provides for a better appreciation of the views offered here. Once at the observation gantry, look for the Crawlerway path, a road nearly as wide as an eight-lane highway and more than three miles long. It was specially constructed to bear the weight of the Crawler-Transporter (6 million pounds), which moves the Space Shuttle from the Vehicle Assembly Building to the launch pad.

Apollo/Saturn V Center

APPEAL BY AGE	PRESCHOOL ★★★		GRADE SCHOOL ★★★★
TEENS ★★★	YOUNG ADULTS ★★★	OVER 30 ★★★★	SENIORS ★★★★

What it is Exhibit celebrating the race to the moon. **Scope and scale** Super headliner. **When to go** Anytime. **Author's rating** Where else can you touch a moon rock?; ★★★★.

DESCRIPTION AND COMMENTS The Apollo/Saturn V Center is a gigantic building (actually constructed around the enormous Saturn V!) with several displays. All guests enter a "holding area," where you'll see a nine-minute film on the race to the moon. This film is good, but things only get better.

The next stop is the Firing Room Theater, which catapults you back in time to December 1, 1968, for the launch of the first successful manned mission to the moon. Actual remnants of the original 1960s Firing Room set the mood, including countdown clocks and launch consoles. Once the show is under way, three large screens take you back to that day with original footage from the Space Center. During this 10-minute presentation, you'll sense the stress of the launch commanders and feel like you're experiencing the actual launch through some fun special effects.

This is a pride-inducing presentation that prepares you for the real meat and potatoes of the Apollo/Saturn V Center—the actual 363-foot Saturn V moon rocket. When the doors of the Firing Room Theater open, guests are instantly overwhelmed by the size of the rocket. The amount of power the rocket produced on blast-off (7.5 million pounds of thrust) could light up New York City for an hour and 15 minutes. In addition, this room is filled with space artifacts, including the van used to transport astronauts to the launch pad, a lunar module, and Jim Lovell's Apollo 13 space suit. But there are more than just dusty relics here. Kennedy Space Center does a great job of telling the history of the era with storyboards along the walls to document the highlights of each Apollo mission.

If you're up for another movie, visit the Lunar Theater. Neil Armstrong leads you through his lunar landing during this suspenseful documentary on Apollo 11. The 12-minute film is nearly perfect, with the exception of the lame effects at the end—a lunar module lands and a wax Armstrong pops up from the "moon."

TOURING TIPS If you're traveling with kids, they may well be restless by now. Check out the interactive exhibits or maybe step outside. There is a patio near the dining area where your family can get some fresh air.

OTHER TOURS

Cape Canaveral: Then and Now

APPEAL BY AGE	PRESCHOOL ★★	GRADE SCHOOL ★★½	TEENS ★★½
YOUNG ADULTS ★★★½	OVER 30 ★★★★		SENIORS ★★★★

What it is Bus tour to Cape Canaveral. **Scope and scale** Headliner. **When to go** Check the daily schedule. **Special comments** Tour is sometimes canceled or altered due to launch activity; photo ID required. **Author's rating** A piece of NASA history; ★★★½. **Duration of tour** About 2 hours, plus parts of the main bus tour.

DESCRIPTION AND COMMENTS Situated about 15 miles from Kennedy Space Center, Cape Canaveral Air Station is an active launch facility where unmanned rockets are sent into space on NASA, military, and commercial missions. Even more interesting, though, is Cape Canaveral's place in history as the original home of the U.S. space program. It is here that the early Mercury missions, as well as the first Americans, were launched into space. And unlike the main bus excursion, with its faraway viewing, this tour allows you to actually explore these historical locations firsthand. Elements of the main KSC Bus Tour are included in this tour as well.

A highlight of the tour is the Air Force Space and Mission Museum, home of the world's largest outdoor collection of missiles on display.

TOURING TIPS Unfortunately, you are not allowed to tour at your own pace and must depart with the same group on the same bus. This tour costs an extra $22 for adults and $16 extra for children ages 3–11 on top of the regular admission and is for true space aficionados only.

NASA Up Close Tour

APPEAL BY AGE	PRESCHOOL ★	GRADE SCHOOL ★	TEENS ★
YOUNG ADULTS ★★	OVER 30 ★★½		SENIORS ★★★

What it is Bus tour of sights not on main tour. **Scope and scale** Headliner. **When to go** Check the daily schedule. **Special comments** Tour is sometimes canceled or altered due to launch activity. **Author's rating** Fairly tedious; ★½. **Duration of tour** About 2 hours, plus parts of the main tour.

DESCRIPTION AND COMMENTS This tour takes visitors out for photo ops at Launch Pads 39A and 39B, the Vehicle Assembly Building (where the shuttle is "stacked" and loaded prior to rolling over to the pads), and likely views of the massive Crawler-Transporter (the goliath vehicle that actually moves the shuttle around). Various other sundry sites may be visited depending on launches and the whims of your tour guide.

Fair warning: if you are not a down-to-the-bones space program maniac, this tour has the potential to bore you to tears. Despite the tour's name, many buildings are viewed at a distance. And many more that are viewed up close turn out to be one unprepossessing gray bunker after another.

TOURING TIPS Unfortunately, you are not allowed to tour at your own pace and must depart with the same group on the same bus. This tour costs an extra $22 for adults and $16 extra for children ages 3–11 on top of the regular admission and is for true space aficionados only.

kids VIEWING A LAUNCH

DOES YOUR CHILD DREAM of becoming an astronaut? Maybe you remember the exact day Neil Armstrong set foot on the moon. If so, seeing a live launch is truly awe-inspiring and will leave you with a memory you'll never forget.

Kennedy Space Center offers a bus trip to a viewing site about six miles from the launch area plus maximum access admission to the Visitor Complex, priced at $50 for adults and $40 for children ages 3–11. Tickets are generally available up to six weeks in advance of launches and sell out quickly. For more information, call ☎ 321-449-4444.

Launches can also be seen outside of Kennedy Space Center along US 1 in Titusville, Florida, and along US A1A in Cape Canaveral and Cocoa Beach. All of these locations can be reached from FL 528 (Beeline Highway toll road) East. You should arrive early (about three hours in advance) however, as many locals line the streets for launches.

Be aware that some of the attractions at the Kennedy Space Center Visitor Complex may be closed the day of a launch for safety reasons. Also, traffic can be unbearable after a launch, so plan to visit one of the many nearby beaches until roads are clear.

SHOPPING

THERE ARE GIFT SHOPS at each of the
stops on the bus tour, and a jumbo gift
shop at the Visitor Center hub. Don't be
shy—try the freeze-dried ice-cream sand-
wich or strawberries. You can also find snow globes, Space
Shuttle gummy candy, T-shirts, and more. Prices vary from
$2 for candy to $30 for T-shirts.

unofficial **TIP**
Let your kids try
astronaut ice cream
in the gift shop.

DINING

DON'T PLAN TO GRAB BREAKFAST (or any other meal) in
the vicinity of Kennedy Space Center. It is very isolated, and
there simply are not any restaurants within 20 miles. There are
food locations on site, but they're nothing to cheer about.
However, if you must eat, you'll find pizza and such at Plane-
tary Pizza and a wider selection in a food court at Orbit
Restaurant. Mila's offers more of a sit-down, full-service experience. There are also many food stands throughout the entire Kennedy Space Center Visitor Complex for a quick bite.

SEAWORLD

A WORLD-CLASS MARINE-LIFE THEME PARK, SeaWorld is the odd middle child of central Florida's megaparks—without the allure of Mickey Mouse or the glitz of the movie studio attractions. For years, this park succeeded by appealing to those who appreciated the wonder of sea creatures like killer whales and dolphins. Walt Disney World may have cornered the market on make-believe, but SeaWorld offered the unique opportunity of watching people interact with live animals.

As competition for tourists' time increased and Disney ventured into the wild-animal business with its Animal Kingdom, SeaWorld created new interactive encounters that can't be found at any other area park. SeaWorld also added thrill rides, including a flight simulator, a roller coaster, and a hybrid flume-coaster. Combined with the charm of the animals, these attractions and several entertaining shows have created a whole new SeaWorld that isn't just for the fish-and-whale crowd. Many *Unofficial Guide* readers consider the park to be a favorite part of an Orlando vacation.

unofficial **TIP**
If you and yes, even your kids, tire of imitation animals the likes of Minnie and Mickey, try a day at SeaWorld.

A family from England writes:

> The best organized park [is] Sea World. The computer print-out we got on arrival had a very useful show schedule, told us which areas were temporarily closed due to construction, and had a readily understandable map. Best of all, there was almost no queuing. Overall, we rated this day so highly that it is the park we would most like to visit again.

A woman from Alberta, Canada, gives her opinion:

We chose SeaWorld as our fifth day at "The World." What a pleasant surprise! It was every bit as good (and in some ways better) than WDW itself. Well worth the admission, an excellent entertainment value, educational, well run, and better value for the dollar in food services. Perhaps expand your coverage to give them their due!

A father of two from Winnipeg, Manitoba, gives SeaWorld's nighttime laser show top marks, commenting:

But the absolute topper is the closing laser show, which beats out IllumiNations at Epcot for extravaganza. The SeaWorld show combines fireworks, lasers, and moving holographic images back-projected on a curtain of water. In the word of our older daughter: awesome! And you watch the whole thing seated in the lakeside arena, instead of jostling for a standing view around the Epcot lagoon.

A reader from Sylvania, Georgia, believes Disney could learn a thing or two from SeaWorld:

Disney ought to take a look at how well this place is run. I know they don't have the same crowds or the exciting rides, but there is still a lot of entertainment here and never a wait. This allows you to set your pace without worrying about what you'll have to miss. You'll see it all no matter how you do it, you'll come away feeling you got better value for your dollars, you won't feel as tired as a Disney day, and you will probably learn more, too. Only downside is you'll probably be hungry. Food is not one of the park's assets.

On top of its accumulated charms, SeaWorld recently opened a new aquatic sub-park, Discovery Cove. Here, you can swim with live dolphins—an attraction offered nowhere else in central Florida. All of this makes SeaWorld a great way to shift gears from the Mouse race, while still enjoying the big production values of a major theme-park destination.

unofficial **TIP**
There's more than just marine life at this well-organized park to keep everyone entertained.

GETTING THERE

SEAWORLD IS ABOUT 10 MILES EAST of Walt Disney World. Take Interstate 4 to FL 528 (Beeline Highway East). Exit at the first ramp, which is International Drive. Turn left off the exit ramp. Turn right at Central Florida Parkway. The entrance to

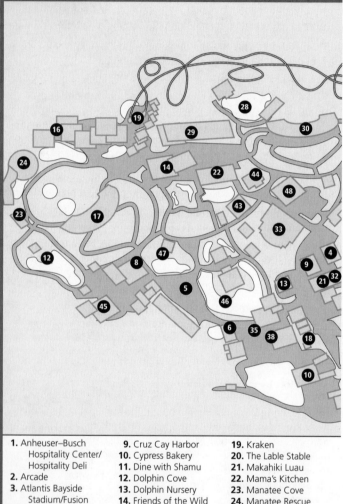

SeaWorld

1. Anheuser–Busch
   Hospitality Center/
   Hospitality Deli
2. Arcade
3. Atlantis Bayside
   Stadium/Fusion
4. Beach Stage
5. Bud's Brands
6. Children's Store
7. Clydesdale Hamlet
8. Coconut Bay
   Trader

9. Cruz Cay Harbor
10. Cypress Bakery
11. Dine with Shamu
12. Dolphin Cove
13. Dolphin Nursery
14. Friends of the Wild
15. Games Area
16. Journey to Atlantis
17. Key West Dolphin
    Stadium/
    Blue Horizons
18. Keyhole Photo

19. Kraken
20. The Lable Stable
21. Makahiki Luau
22. Mama's Kitchen
23. Manatee Cove
24. Manatee Rescue
25. Mango Joe's Café
26. Mistify
27. Nautilus Theatre/
    Odyssea
28. Pacific Point Preserve
29. Penguin Encounter

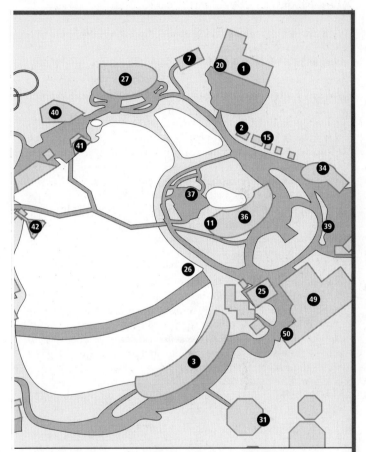

SeaWorld is on the right just prior to a large SeaWorld sculpture. Parking costs $6 per car, $7 per RV or camper.

Discovery Cove is directly across the Central Florida Parkway from SeaWorld. Parking at the Discovery Cove lot is free.

ADMISSION PRICES

EXCEPT UNDER THE MOST CROWDED CONDITIONS, a typical visitor can see most (if not all) of SeaWorld in one solid day of touring, so a standard One-Day Pass makes sense. In fact, SeaWorld has discontinued most of its multi-day tickets in favor of package deals and annual passes. However, SeaWorld really wants your business, and there are several options that will get you a lot more time in the park for not much more money than a one-day ticket. In fact, if you schedule it right, you can use the SeaWorld Fun Card for park admission almost all year long for an extra $5. If you're planning to spend time at other local theme parks, consider the money-saving Orlando FlexTicket. Several deals are also available combining SeaWorld admission with tickets for Busch Gardens and the water park Adventure Island, both in Tampa (and both also owned by SeaWorld corporate parent Anheuser-Busch). Discounts are available for AAA members, disabled visitors, senior citizens, and military personnel. All tickets, even the FlexTicket, can be purchased on the park's Web site (**www.seaworld.com**). It's convenient and a time-saver to have tickets in hand before you even reach the park.

ONE DAY PASS

Adults $59.75 + tax
Children ages 3–9 $48   *Children under age 3* Free

SeaWorld Fun Card

THIS PASS IS BY FAR THE BEST DEAL for admission to SeaWorld, but there are a few catches. For $5 more than the One-Day Pass, you get unlimited admission to SeaWorld for one calendar year, except blackout dates of Easter weekend and December 27–31. There's also a Fun Card that allows admission to Busch Gardens (with the same restrictions).

FUN CARD

Adults $64.75 + tax
Children ages 3–9 $53 + tax

FUN CARD PLUS BUSCH GARDENS
Adults $119.95 + tax
Children ages 3–9 $109.95 + tax

SeaWorld/Busch Gardens Value Ticket

THIS PASS ALLOWS ONE-DAY ADMISSION to SeaWorld and one-day admission to Busch Gardens.

Adults $94.95 + tax
Children ages 3–9 $84.95 + tax

Annual Passports

THESE ALLOW UNLIMITED ADMISSION to either SeaWorld alone or SeaWorld plus Busch Gardens for one or two years.

SEAWORLD SILVER PASSPORT (ONE YEAR)
Adults $94.95 + tax
Children ages 3–9 and seniors $84.95 + tax

SEAWORLD GOLD PASSPORT (TWO YEARS)
Adults $144.95 + tax
Children ages 3–9 and seniors $134.95 + tax

SEAWORLD/BUSCH GARDENS SILVER PASSPORT (ONE YEAR)
Adults $144.95 + tax
Children ages 3–9 and seniors $134.95 + tax

SEAWORLD/BUSCH GARDENS GOLD PASSPORT (TWO YEARS)
Adults $219.95 + tax
Children ages 3–9 and seniors $209.95 + tax

Orlando FlexTicket

THIS PASS IS GOOD FOR UP TO 14 CONSECUTIVE DAYS at five parks: Busch Gardens Universal Studios Florida, Universal Islands of Adventure, SeaWorld, and Wet 'n' Wild. There's also a version that excludes Busch Gardens, so be sure to get the one you want.

FLEXTICKET
Adults $224.95 + tax
Children ages 3–9 and seniors ages 50+ $189.95 + tax

FLEXTICKET WITHOUT BUSCH GARDENS
Adults $184.95 + tax
Children ages 3–9 and seniors ages 50+ $150.95 + tax

ARRIVING

SEAWORLD OFFICIALLY OPENS AT 9 A.M. Ropes to a smaller section on the north side drop at 10 a.m., except during the busiest times of the year, when the entire park opens all at once. Closing time fluctuates from 6 or 7 p.m. in late fall and winter to 10 p.m. in the summer and on holidays.

Exploring SeaWorld takes a full day. Because the majority of attractions are shows, it won't be a mad rush to avoid lines like at other theme parks. However, seeing the few attractions with long waits and large crowds requires getting there early during busy times of the year. Like other area parks, SeaWorld turnstiles often open at either 8:30 a.m. or 8:45 a.m. depending on the season, which means you can enter the park before the scheduled 9 a.m. opening. You can only wander around a limited area with a bakery and a few shops, however. Nonetheless, during peak season, we suggest you arrive no later than 8:20 a.m., allowing time to park and purchase tickets. At other times, arriving at 8:40 a.m. should give you a jump on the crowds.

While a member of your party purchases tickets, have another track down a SeaWorld map. Map-toting employees are usually positioned in front of the ticket booth. While waiting for the park to open, plan your attack.

During peak season, if you're a fan of water thrill rides, locate the quickest route to Journey to Atlantis, which combines elements of a water ride and dry roller coaster. When the ropes drop, head straight there. You'll be tempted to stop at animal exhibits along the route, but save those for later. The line for Journey to Atlantis will be most manageable early in the day.

unofficial **TIP**
If you plan on getting wet on the water rides, head for them first.

Right next to Journey to Atlantis is Kraken, SeaWorld's super roller coaster. Lines for this ride will also get longer as the day progresses, so make it an early priority—either right before or right after Journey to Atlantis.

When attendance isn't at its highest, the lines for Journey to Atlantis and Kraken can be quite short. At those times of the year, or if you don't like water rides or coasters, plan to hurry to Dolphin Cove in the Key West area when the park opens. In addition to beating the bulk of the crowd, you'll get to see the animals at their most active in the morning. You can stand along the edge of this gorgeous two-acre pool teeming with dolphins to get a close-up view. But if the dolphins are one of your main reasons for visiting SeaWorld, use your morning visit to get the feeding schedule for the day, which is posted at the mint-green fish house on the left side of the pool. There is usually a feeding scheduled at 9:15 a.m., and you can get in line to purchase fish right away.

unofficial **TIP**
Animals at Sea-World and other parks are most active early in the morning.

Arrange the remainder of your day around the show schedule. Attractions encircle a large lagoon, and the best strategy to see it all is to travel clockwise, especially because the opposite side does not open until 10 a.m. (We've ordered the attractions listings in the clockwise order.) This tactic depends on the entertainment schedule, of course, but at the very least, allow time to see the attractions in the area surrounding each show. You will save time and energy by not roaming aimlessly, and there's not much point in rushing—the entertainment schedule is not designed for immediate back-to-back viewing of shows.

Walt Disney World might be known for its friendly, informative cast members, but they certainly haven't cornered the market. At each animal exhibit in SeaWorld, you can find pleasant and extremely knowledgeable employees who will share interesting information and answer any questions.

SeaWorld also allows visitors to view training sessions that occur at many of the show stadiums. A schedule for these sessions isn't published, but if you're near any of the stadiums between shows, pop in. You can also hang out a bit after a show to possibly catch some unscripted action.

CONTACTING SEAWORLD

FOR MORE INFORMATION, call ☎ 800-327-2424, or visit the SeaWorld Web site at **www.seaworld.com.** If you or your children are interested in learning more about the park's animals before visiting, SeaWorld also maintains a Web site designed for students and teachers at **www.seaworld.org.**

▌ ATTRACTIONS

Turtle Point

APPEAL BY AGE	PRESCHOOL ★★	GRADE SCHOOL ★★★	TEENS ★★
YOUNG ADULTS ★★		OVER 30 ★★	SENIORS ★★

What it is Outdoor turtle habitat. **Scope and scale** Diversion. **When to go** Anytime; most informative when an educator is present. **Author's rating** Just turtles; ★★.

DESCRIPTION AND COMMENTS A white-sand beach and palm trees surround a small pool at this exhibit. Several large turtles can be seen swimming or sunning themselves. Most of them have been rescued by SeaWorld, and many of their injuries are evident, such as missing flippers (caused by discarded fishing line or shark attacks) or cracked shells (from boat propellers).

TOURING TIPS Because the turtles are not terribly active, this attraction is only worth a quick peek. A visit becomes more interesting if an educator is present to talk about the animals and the ways humans can help protect them in the wild.

Stingray Lagoon

APPEAL BY AGE   **PRESCHOOL** ★★   **GRADE SCHOOL** ★★★½   **TEENS** ★★★
YOUNG ADULTS ★★★   **OVER 30** ★★★   **SENIORS** ★★½

What it is Stingray pool. **Scope and scale** Minor attraction. **When to go** Feeding times. **Author's rating** Ray-riffic; ★★★.

DESCRIPTION AND COMMENTS The shallow water in this waist-high pool is filled with dozens of undulating stingrays. They may seem menacing, but they are actually quite mellow, and you shouldn't be afraid to stick in your fingers to gently feel their silky skin.

TOURING TIPS Although a small tray of fish costs $3, don't miss feeding these graceful creatures. (Feedings are scheduled throughout the day.) The fish are slimy, and the tail end must be carefully placed between two fingers, but even the most squeamish in our group enjoyed the stingrays swimming over their hands and lightly sucking the food into their mouths.

Dolphin Cove

APPEAL BY AGE   **PRESCHOOL** ★★★   **GRADE SCHOOL** ★★★★
TEENS ★★★★   **YOUNG ADULTS** ★★★★   **OVER 30** ★★★★   **SENIORS** ★★★★

What it is Outdoor dolphin habitat. **Scope and scale** Major attraction. **When to go** In the morning; for scheduled feedings. **Author's rating** Impressive; ★★★★.

DESCRIPTION AND COMMENTS This sprawling, two-acre habitat is filled with a community of swimming and leaping dolphins. You can stand along one side of the pool and touch or feed the dolphins. A path along the opposite side of the pool leads to an overlook area that provides excellent views and a great photo location. If you can live without touching the dolphins, this area is also much less crowded. Next to the overlook is a walkway to an underwater viewing area that provides the best glimpse of these delightful mammals in action.

TOURING TIPS Feedings take place at scheduled times throughout the day, usually immediately following the dolphin show at nearby Key West Dolphin Stadium. Feedings provide the best opportunity to interact with the dolphins, but also generate large crowds. Check the schedule at the fish house to the left of the pool. A small tray of fish costs $3. Feedings provide the best opportunity to touch these amazing creatures, but the times may not fit into your plan to view the park. They are also incredibly crowded.

There is a chance to touch the dolphins at other times. Sea-World employees say the key is to simply keep your hands still under the water and patiently wait for the animals to brush into you. You may see SeaWorld trainers slapping the water to get the dolphins' attention, but this doesn't seem to work for guests. Apparently, the dolphins know and trust the trainers, but they are frightened by strange hands hitting the water.

With the opening of Discovery Cove, SeaWorld's swim-with-the-dolphins subpark, the pool of available dolphins has been stretched a little thin. Some of the park's dolphins might be away at Discovery Cove when you visit, although SeaWorld claims all bases will be covered.

Key West Dolphin Stadium/Blue Horizons

APPEAL BY AGE   NOT OPEN AT PRESS TIME.

What it is Dolphin and false killer whale show. **Scope and scale** Headliner. **When to go** Check daily entertainment schedule. **Author's rating** Not open at press time.

DESCRIPTION AND COMMENTS A whimsical show involving people, dolphins, killer whales, and several species of birds performing to music; the show was developed by a renowned Broadway producer and combines imaginative choreography and animal stunts above and under the water.

TOURING TIPS The middle of the bleachers provide the best view; higher up is best so the whole set can be seen.

Manatee Rescue

APPEAL BY AGE	PRESCHOOL ★★½	GRADE SCHOOL ★★½	TEENS ★★★
YOUNG ADULTS ★★★		OVER 30 ★★★	SENIORS ★★★

What it is Outdoor manatee habitat and underwater viewing. **Scope and scale** Minor attraction. **When to go** Anytime. **Author's rating** Remarkable animals in a creative habitat; ★★★.

DESCRIPTION AND COMMENTS Manatees, which are on the endangered species list, are still disappearing at a rapid rate. All of the docile creatures in this exhibit were injured in the wild and have been rescued by SeaWorld. The area resembles an inland canal, a favorite spot of these gentle giants. For most of the rescued animals, this is the last part of their rehabilitation, and many will be returned to their natural environment.

TOURING TIPS Be sure to visit the underwater viewing area. It offers an excellent view of the huge creatures. Along the way, you'll see a short video about the plight of these endangered animals.

On occasion, SeaWorld rescues orphaned baby manatees. Check with an educator in the area to find out if there are any in the exhibit, if they might be bottle-fed, and at what time. It's pure, distilled cuteness.

kids Journey to Atlantis

APPEAL BY AGE	PRESCHOOL †	GRADE SCHOOL ★★★	TEENS ★★★
YOUNG ADULTS ★★½		OVER 30 ★★	SENIORS ★★

†Preschoolers are generally too short to ride.

What it is Water ride and roller coaster combo. **Scope and scale** Headliner. **When to go** Before 10 a.m. or after 4 p.m. during peak season; avoid visiting immediately after a Key West Dolphin Fest show. **Special comments** Riders must be 42 inches tall; pregnant women or people with heart, back, or neck problems should not ride. **Author's rating** Fun, if not cheesy; ★★½. **Duration of ride** 6 minutes. **Loading speed** Moderate.

DESCRIPTION AND COMMENTS Riders board eight-passenger boats and plunge down a nearly vertical 60-foot waterfall before careening through a mini–roller coaster. Though housed in a truly impressive edifice that spouts fire and water, the payoff inside is pretty meager. The attraction supposedly takes guests on a voyage through Atlantis as they try to avoid an evil spirit, but even after several trips, we still didn't have a good grasp on this story line (what's up with that goldfish, or seahorse, or whatever it was?). For that reason, and because of an "it's over before you know it" feeling, we have to give the ride lower marks than those of Disney's Splash Mountain. However, Journey to Atlantis definitely provides the bigger thrill.

TOURING TIPS Closer to sunset, the special effects in this attraction are more intense because the darker evening sky helps keep light from leaking into the ride when the boats travel outdoors. However, during peak seasons the wait in line can be an hour or longer, and we don't think Journey to Atlantis is worth that much of your time. For best results, arrive early and dash to this attraction when the park opens at 9 a.m. to minimize the wait. Then, stop by in the evening and ride again if the line isn't too long. You can always hit the Kraken roller coaster next door if lines are a problem here; of course, we're prejudiced, because we feel if we must stand in line, it may as well be for a coaster.

Journey to Atlantis will get you wet, especially in the front seats. If you want to minimize the drenching, bring along a poncho or purchase one at the gift shop at the attraction. Place any items that you don't want to get soaked, such as cameras, in the pay lockers near the entrance to the queue. Free bins are available at the loading dock, but they are not secured.

kids Kraken

† Preschoolers are generally too short to ride.

What it is Roller coaster. **Scope and scale** Super headliner. **When to go** Immediately following a ride on Journey to Atlantis. **Special comments** Riders must be 42 inches tall; pregnant women or people with heart, back, or neck problems should not ride. **Author's rating** A real brain rattler; ★★★★. **Duration of ride** 3 minutes. **Loading speed** Quick.

DESCRIPTION AND COMMENTS The roller coaster war has reached epic proportions in central Florida. SeaWorld enters the battle with Kraken, named after the mythological underwater beast. At a top speed of 65 miles per hour, a length of more than 4,000 feet, and with a first drop of 144 feet, it is Orlando's fastest, longest, and tallest roller coaster. How long will it reign? If history is any indication, it's only a matter of time before Disney or Universal ups the ante yet again.

This "floorless" coaster puts riders in 32 open-sided seats, in eight rows, riding on a pedestal above the track. It's a sort of combination of the newer inverted coasters (where riders dangle in seats, rather than sit in cars) with the open ceiling of a traditional coaster. The net effect is that nothing up, down, or sideways blocks your view, an especially amazing effect on that first big drop—when it seems like you're about to plunge right into a lake.

Despite its overall great fun, be warned that this coaster does not offer the smoothest ride. You will be jerked around a bit, and repeated rides may lead to woozy crab-walking.

TOURING TIPS This extremely popular coaster draws the crowds, but it can move them, too. Even large lines will move at a good clip, but you can still cut down your wait by riding before 10 a.m. or after 4 p.m. During peak season, we suggest you arrive when the park opens, ride Journey to Atlantis, and immediately head to Kraken. After getting drenched on Journey, the high-speed coaster trip will help dry you off.

kids Penguin Encounter

What it is Indoor penguin habitat. **Scope and scale** Major attraction. **When to go** Anytime. **Author's rating** Adorable tuxedo models; ★★★.

DESCRIPTION AND COMMENTS The first section of this exhibit features an icy habitat behind a glass wall, providing an excellent view of the penguins' antics in several feet of water. Step on the people mover to the right for a close-up view of these critters as they congregate, waddle, and dive into the frigid water. Then circle back behind the people mover to an elevated section where you can take a longer look at the large king penguins. A learning area is just past the habitat, where interactive kiosks provide information about the animals and their environment. The walkway then leads to a smaller exhibit, which is home to puffins and other species that prefer a warmer climate.

TOURING TIPS The pungent penguin odor will hit you before you step through the door, but after a couple minutes you'll get used to it. During summer, SeaWorld darkens the exhibit to simulate the Antarctic environment, where it is actually winter. The birds are still active and visible, but you may need to spend more time on the stationary upper level to get a good look. During this season, you will not be allowed to shoot any photos of the habitat because the flash negates the effect of the darkened room for the animals.

Pacific Point Preserve

APPEAL BY AGE	PRESCHOOL ★★★½		GRADE SCHOOL ★★★½
TEENS ★★★	YOUNG ADULTS ★★★	OVER 30 ★★★	SENIORS ★★★

What it is Outdoor sea lion habitat. **Scope and scale** Major attraction. **When to go** Feeding times (scattered throughout the day). **Author's rating** Fun and startling; ★★★.

DESCRIPTION AND COMMENTS Let the sound of more than 50 barking sea lions and harbor seals lead you to this nifty area tucked behind Sea Lion and Otter Stadium. An elevated walkway behind a glass partition surrounds the sunken habitat. The animals can be found sunning themselves on the rocky terrain or lounging in the shallow waves. More often, though, they'll be barking impatiently—perhaps very impatiently—for a snack. Although these animals aren't trained, a few of the sea lions will improvise cute antics for food, such as mimicking you sticking out your tongue. Sometimes, they get so excited about a possible meal that their barking reaches amazing, ear-splitting levels.

TOURING TIPS If you participate in a feeding, which costs $3 for one tray of fish (or $5 for two), watch out for the large, aggressive birds that lurk in this area. They are poised to steal the fish right out of your hand, snatch one in midair as you toss it to the sea lions, or even land on your head or shoulders to make a grab for the goods (we saw this happen twice).

Look closely at the animals, and you might spot some adorable sea lion or harbor seal pups—especially if you visit during the spring or summer.

kids Sea Lion and Otter Stadium/ Clyde and Seamore Take Pirate Island

APPEAL BY AGE   **PRESCHOOL** ★★★★   **GRADE SCHOOL** ★★★★
TEENS ★★★   **YOUNG ADULTS** ★★★   **OVER 30** ★★★   **SENIORS** ★★★

What it is Show featuring sea lions, otters, and a walrus. **Scope and scale** Major attraction. **When to go** Check daily entertainment schedule. **Author's rating** Unabashed cornball comedy; ★★★½. **Duration of show** 25 minutes.

DESCRIPTION AND COMMENTS   SeaWorld's famous sea lion duo, Clyde and Seamore, are the stars of this eminently dorky but funny show. The plot has the pair looking for a treasure map that's been swiped by a mischievous otter. During the search, the sea lions' antics are quite entertaining, as they mimic their trainers and leap, flip, and swan dive into the narrow pool in front of the stage. The trainers get in on the act with slapstick humor, especially when the animals don't quite cooperate (the why-me routine begins to look rehearsed, but who's quibbling?). For the finale, an enormous walrus makes an appearance. Look out if you're in the front center rows because this guy spits mouthfuls of water, and his aim and projection are excellent.

TOURING TIPS   Arrive early, not only to get a good seat, but also to enjoy a preshow that's almost as much fun as the actual performance. A ruthless mime pokes fun at unsuspecting visitors entering the stadium. During one visit, the mime created an elaborately panicked chase scene with a guest, who happily joined in the act in his fast-moving electric wheelchair. The chase ended in mock-epic showdown of mime versus man.

Sea Lion and Otter Stadium/ Clyde and Seamore Present Sea Lions Tonight

APPEAL BY AGE   **NOT OPEN AT PRESS TIME.**

What it is Nighttime version of the regular show, featuring sea lions, otters, and a walrus. **Scope and scale** Major attraction. **When to go** Check daily entertainment schedule. **Author's rating** Not open at press time. **Duration of show** 25 minutes.

DESCRIPTION AND COMMENTS   Probably somewhat similar to the daytime show, so if you happen to miss it, seeing this one will have the same effect.

SeaWorld Theater/Pets Ahoy!

APPEAL BY AGE   **PRESCHOOL** ★★★   **GRADE SCHOOL** ★★★   **TEENS** ★★½
YOUNG ADULTS ★★★   **OVER 30** ★★★   **SENIORS** ★★★

What it is Show featuring trained pets. **Scope and scale** Major attraction. **When to go** Check daily entertainment schedule. **Author's rating** The truth about cats and dogs?; ★★★. **Duration of show** 20 minutes.

DESCRIPTION AND COMMENTS Most people don't immediately think of trained dogs and cats when they think of SeaWorld, but this show holds the charm of the rest of the park sans the water. *Pets Ahoy!* stars a menagerie of trained animals from frisky felines to a precocious pig. You'll be amazed at what these animals can do, though it makes your own pet's game of fetch seem less impressive. Even more amazing, most of these animals were rescued from an uncertain fate at local animal shelters.

TOURING TIPS Be sure to arrive early. Because many of the animals perform throughout the theater, doors close promptly at show time. Stick around afterward to meet a few of the star performers at the foot of the stage.

Sky Tower

APPEAL BY AGE	PRESCHOOL ★★	GRADE SCHOOL ★★	TEENS ★★
YOUNG ADULTS ★★½		OVER 30 ★★½	SENIORS ★★★

What it is Scenic aerial ride. **Scope and scale** Minor attraction. **When to go** Anytime, although it's quite beautiful at night. **Special comments** Costs $3. **Author's rating** ★★. **Duration of ride** Nearly 7 minutes. **Loading speed** Slow.

DESCRIPTION AND COMMENTS This attraction forces visitors to make a philosophical decision. Should a theme park charge an additional fee for one of its rides? Although the answer is probably "no," a ride to the top of the tower is somewhat calming. The tower has two levels of enclosed seats that rotate as they rise to the top for great views of the park. It's amazing how serene the park looks—and how tiny the killer whales appear—from the top. On a clear day, you can see many other interesting sites, including downtown Orlando, the top of Spaceship Earth at Epcot, and the unmistakable toaster shape of Disney's Contemporary Resort.

TOURING TIPS This attraction closes if lightning or high winds pop up, and both are frequent in central Florida. It also doesn't run during the peak season's nighttime fireworks display. The Sand Bar Lounge at the bottom of the tower serves a variety of refreshments.

Shark Encounter

APPEAL BY AGE	PRESCHOOL ★★★	GRADE SCHOOL ★★★½	TEENS ★★★★
YOUNG ADULTS ★★★½		OVER 30 ★★★½	SENIORS ★★★½

What it is Exhibit of sharks, eels, and other dangerous sea creatures. **Scope and scale** Major attraction. **When to go** Anytime. **Author's rating** Pleasantly creepy; ★★★½.

DESCRIPTION AND COMMENTS This walk-through exhibit immerses you (almost literally) in the frightening world of dangerous marine life. First, you are surrounded by moray eels as you walk through an acrylic tube at the bottom of a large aquarium. These eels peer out from lairs in an artificial tropical reef or undulate through the water. Next are several large aquariums housing poisonous fish, including the beautiful but lethal scorpion fish and the puffer fish, one of the world's most deadly. Then get ready for the grand finale—a 600,000-gallon tank filled with six different species of sharks, including bull sharks, nurse sharks, and lemon sharks, as well as dozens of enormous grouper and other smaller fish. An entire wall of a large room gives an overall view of this beautifully lit tank. Then these amazing creatures will glide next to you and directly overhead as you pass through an acrylic tunnel. As you exit the tunnel, you'll learn that it supports 500 tons of salt water, but if necessary, it could handle nearly five times that weight—the equivalent of more than 370 elephants. A reassuring thought.

TOURING TIPS The crowd usually bottlenecks at the eel habitat. If possible, worm your way through the initial backup. The tube is fairly long, and you'll find the same great view with a smaller crowd near the other end.

If you visit SeaWorld on a Tuesday or Thursday, don't miss the feeding frenzy when the sharks in the main habitat feast at 11 a.m. (call beforehand to verify the schedule).

You can get in on the feeding yourself on select days at a small pool at the entrance to the exhibit. Purchase a tray of fish for $3 (two for $5) and toss them cheerfully to small hammerhead and nurse sharks. If that's still not enough all-shark action for you, consider the Sharks Deep Dive, in which guests don scuba or snorkel gear and plunge directly into the shark tank (in a shark cage). Cost is $150 for scuba, $125 for snorkeling. Call ☎ 800-406-2244 for reservations and information.

Nautilus Theatre/Odyssea

APPEAL BY AGE	PRESCHOOL ★★	GRADE SCHOOL ★★½	TEENS ★★
YOUNG ADULTS ★★★	OVER 30 ★★★		SENIORS ★★★

What it is New-school circus acts. **Scope and scale** Major attraction. **When to go** Check daily entertainment schedule. **Author's rating** Funny and entertaining; ★★★. **Duration of show** 30 minutes.

DESCRIPTION AND COMMENTS The performance features an amazing group of variety acts, including a contortionist who twists and bends into crazy poses balanced on a small platform. Another scene showcases a couple who fly and twist suspended high above the stage, while goofy "penguins" bounce on trampolines. Although it's hard to compare a theme-park show with the full-scale production of Cirque du Soleil at Downtown Disney, this show does capture the element of circus-as-theater for those who balk at the steep price tag at Walt Disney World.

TOURING TIPS This indoor, air-conditioned theater rarely fills up, but we suggest you arrive early to enjoy the preshow and a pleasant break from the Florida heat. Also, once your group gets settled, use the time for a bathroom break. Restrooms are conveniently located at the back of the theater. In addition, this show is not performed two days of the week. If it's a priority, call to verify.

Clydesdale Hamlet/Hospitality Center

APPEAL BY AGE	PRESCHOOL ★★½	GRADE SCHOOL ★★★	TEENS ★½
YOUNG ADULTS ★★½		OVER 30 ★★½	SENIORS ★★½

What it is Stable and free beer. **Scope and scale** Diversion. **When to go** Avoid visiting immediately following *Odyssea* or a Shamu show. **Author's rating** Most kids will enjoy the horses, most adults will enjoy the beer; ★★.

DESCRIPTION AND COMMENTS An Anheuser-Busch theme park, Sea-World features a white stable that is home to several Clydesdales, the huge and beautiful draft horses that are the beer company's trademark. Walk through the stable on the way to the Hospitality House. Here, if you're age 21 or older, you can partake in two free samples of Anheuser-Busch beer. You can also sign up for Budweiser Beer School, a free 40-minute class on beer making, which includes a variety of samples. Repeating the class to get more beer samples is discouraged.

TOURING TIPS The Clydesdales are incredibly beautiful animals, but skip this area if you're in a hurry. Also, check the entertainment schedule for appearances of the Clydesdales in the park. The Hospitality House also features The Deli. Save time by combining lunch with your free beer sample.

kids Shamu Stadium/The Shamu Adventure

APPEAL BY AGE	PRESCHOOL ★★★★	GRADE SCHOOL ★★★★½
TEENS ★★★★	YOUNG ADULTS ★★★★½	OVER 30 ★★★★½

What it is Killer whale show. **Scope and scale** Super headliner. **When to go** Check daily entertainment schedule; first show is sometimes more crowded. **Author's rating** Truly amazing, not to be missed; ★★★★½. **Duration of show** 25 minutes.

DESCRIPTION AND COMMENTS Fog rolls over the pool and ominous music fills the stadium as this show begins. Beyond a 6-foot-high clear wall, an immense killer whale circles in a 5-million-gallon pool. Jack Hanna, appearing via videotape on a large screen elevated above the water, introduces the whales and keeps the show flowing with information about their environment and feeding habits. The real stars of this show are a family of orcas, commonly known as killer whales. Like most celebrities, they're known by stage names—most notably, Shamu and Baby Shamu.

Of course, the trainers and whales work closely and jointly provide the most spectacular sight of the show—a trainer perched on the nose of a whale shooting nearly 30 feet out of the water. The absolute trust and bond of friendship between trainer and whale allows plenty of other maneuvers, including surfing on a whale's back, riding through the water on a whale's nose, or zipping across the water's surface while holding on to a whale's flipper.

If these huge creatures' leaps and arcs are the most spectacular portion of the show, a display of their incredible power is the most stunning. This is when gallons and gallons of 55°F salt water are flung into the first 14 rows by the flukes of a large whale. The audience is warned, but most folks must not realize how much water will head their way or how cold it really is. Nevertheless, some, especially the under-age-12 set, make it a point to be in the water's path.

Now, this sight is incredible, but the most astonishing scene is yet to come . . . when a five-ton whale, the largest in captivity, makes his splashing rounds. Not only do the folks in the first 14 rows get soaked, but the water actually travels an extra 15–20 feet to reach the second tier of this large stadium. Suckers are routinely picked from the audience to participate in little contests or stunts, and—what do you know?—they always seem to end up soaked to the bone. Trainers do give them T-shirts as consolation prizes—even as those same trainers whip up handy umbrellas to shield themselves from the same deluge that drenches the volunteers.

TOURING TIPS We're not kidding when we say gallons of chilly salt water. You will get soaked in the first few rows. If you or the kids think you're up for it, you might want to bring along some extra clothes to change into after the cold shower. You should leave your cameras with someone out of the range of the corrosive salt water.

Although this is a large stadium, you must arrive early to get a seat. Jack Hanna will keep you entertained with a video pop quiz. Audience members are amusingly caught off-guard by their image on the screen and must answer a multiple-choice question.

 kids Shamu Stadium/Shamu Rocks America

APPEAL BY AGE	PRESCHOOL ★★★★		GRADE SCHOOL ★★★★
TEENS ★★★★	YOUNG ADULTS ★★★★	OVER 30 ★★★½	SENIORS ★★★

What it is Nighttime killer whale show. **Scope and scale** Headliner. **When to go** Check daily entertainment schedule. **Author's rating** Orca MTV; ★★★½. **Duration of show** 25 minutes.

DESCRIPTION AND COMMENTS The whales take center stage for this night show—no narration or audience participation to interfere with the all-whale action. It's essentially a few of the most exciting stunts from *The Shamu Adventure* set to rockin' tunes. This show also has a more footloose feel than the daytime shows—if Shamu had hair, this is when he'd let it down. A comical blooper clip is shown on the video screen, and Shamu does some cute "dance" moves as he bobs and shakes to the music.

TOURING TIPS This is a fun counterpart to *The Shamu Adventure* and a nice conclusion to your day. However, if you're pinched for time and can't see both shows, choose the daytime performance for maximum whaleness. An exception might be during peak times when the park is open later and *Shamu Rocks America* is performed after sunset. Then the show is magic, with a spotlight on Shamu, colored lights scanning the audience, and the pool glowing aqua and green.

Just as with *The Shamu Adventure,* you will get soaked with chilly salt water in the first 14 rows of the stadium.

Shamu Underwater Viewing

APPEAL BY AGE	PRESCHOOL ★★	GRADE SCHOOL ★★★	TEENS ★★½
YOUNG ADULTS ★★★		OVER 30 ★★★	SENIORS ★★★

What it is Whale viewing area. **Scope and scale** Minor attraction. **When to go** Avoid visiting immediately before or after a Shamu show. **Author's rating** Good look at these incredible animals; ★★½.

DESCRIPTION AND COMMENTS Go behind the scenes at Shamu Stadium for a peek at the stars of the show in their 1.5-million-gallon pool. Check the above-water viewing area for a training session or a veterinary visit. When standing "next to" these animals in the underwater viewing area, be prepared to be awestruck by their enormous size.

TOURING TIPS When the animals are not active, or not even present, this area is not worth visiting. Check with the SeaWorld employee usually stationed nearby for the best times to visit on a particular day.

Have your camera ready at the underwater viewing area. The whales usually slowly circle the pool, offering an amazing backdrop for a group photo.

Shamu's Happy Harbor

| APPEAL BY AGE | PRESCHOOL ★★★ | GRADE SCHOOL ★★★ | TEENS ★ |
| YOUNG ADULTS ★ | | OVER 30 ★ | SENIORS ★ |

What it is Children's play area. **Scope and scale** Minor attraction. **When to go** Avoid visiting after a Shamu show. **Special comments** Open from 10 a.m. until an hour before the park closes. **Author's rating** A nice oversized playground; ★★★.

DESCRIPTION AND COMMENTS Four stories of net span this three-acre children's play area. Children and brave adults can climb, crawl, and weave through this net jungle. Other activities include an air bubble where kids under 54 inches tall can bounce and play and an interactive submarine with several water cannons and fountains. There is also an area for smaller kids (they must be under 42 inches tall) with a standard ball-filled room and several playground contraptions.

TOURING TIPS Parents can grab a cool drink and relax at Coconut Cove while watching their children play. Most adults should stay clear of the patience-testing, headache-causing steel-drum area, where kids are allowed to bang to their hearts' content.

kids Wild Arctic

| APPEAL BY AGE | PRESCHOOL ★★★ | GRADE SCHOOL ★★★★ | TEENS ★★★ |
| YOUNG ADULTS ★★★ | | OVER 30 ★★½ | SENIORS ★★★ |

What it is Simulator ride and animal exhibit. **Scope and scale** Major attraction. **When to go** Avoid going immediately following a Shamu show; wait will be shorter before 11 a.m. and after 4 p.m. **Author's rating** Animal exhibit is better than hokey simulator; ★★½. **Duration of ride** 5 minutes for simulator; at your own pace for exhibit. **Loading speed** Moderate.

DESCRIPTION AND COMMENTS Wild Arctic combines a mediocre simulator ride with a spectacular animal habitat, featuring huge polar bears, blubbery walruses, and sweet-faced beluga whales. The usually long line gives you the option of not riding the simulator and heading straight to the animal habitat—a great idea if you're in a hurry, prone to motion sickness, or have experienced the superior simulators at Disney and Universal.

The simulator provides a bumpy ride aboard a specially designed 59-passenger "helicopter." Once passengers are safely strapped in, the ride ostensibly takes visitors to a remote Arctic research station (the wildlife habitat). On the way, riders fly over polar bear and walrus, but, of course, Things Go Horribly Wrong. A storm blows through, the engine inconveniently fails during an avalanche, and there is much wailing and gnashing of teeth. The loud hullabaloo and dated effects amount to nothing in particular, and in the end you make it to the station unscathed.

As you step off the simulator, or if you bypass it, you'll enter a cavernous, fog-filled room. A walkway on the far side overlooks a large pool that is home to a few beluga whales, and if you're lucky, some cute harbor seals. This room establishes the Arctic theme, but unless it's feeding time, the animals rarely surface here.

Proceed down a wooden ramp and you may come face to face with an enormous polar bear. The most famous inhabitants of this exhibit are twins, Klondike and Snow. The duo received tons of media coverage after they were abandoned by their mother and hand-raised at the Denver Zoo. SeaWorld uses toys and enrichment devices to keep the bears occupied. Variations in their schedule help keep them on their toes, so feeding times change frequently. Next to the bears are the gigantic walruses. These animals are often lounging near the glass or swimming lazily by.

As you descend farther into the exhibit, you'll discover a deep, underwater viewing area. Swarms of fish circle in the polar bear exhibit. If you're lucky, you'll spot a bear diving for fish. In addition, the underwater view gives you a real sense of the walruses' immense size. If it's quiet you can also hear the deep, reverberating vocalizations of these large beasts. This is also the best location to catch a glimpse of the beluga whales. Looking like puffy, bulbous dolphins, these gentle creatures glide through the water. On occasion, a few playful harbor seals will join them. These crazy critters will come right up to the glass for a staring match with you.

TOURING TIPS Wild Arctic has two queues: "By Air," which is for the simulator, and "By Land," which goes right to the animal exhibit. Given the so-so quality of the simulator ride, we recommend skipping it if there's a significant line. The animals are definitely worth seeing, though. As in all animal exhibits, several SeaWorld educators are scattered around to answer any questions. Here, they are easy to spot in bright red parkas.

The simulator holds nearly 60 riders, who flood the animal area after each trip. If you do ride it, hang back behind the crowd for a few minutes when the simulator offloads, waiting for the masses to clear. Then you can have the area mostly to yourself until the next group dumps off the ride.

Atlantis Bayside Stadium/Fusion

APPEAL BY AGE   NOT OPEN AT PRESS TIME

What it is Water sports stunt show. **Scope and scale** Headliner. **When to go** Check daily entertainment schedule. **Author's rating** Not open at press time. **Duration of show** 30 minutes.

DESCRIPTION AND COMMENTS Trick kites, cool water sports (like barefoot skiing, wakeboarding, and knee-boarding) and more, all set to music.

TOURING TIPS This stadium is huge, and all seats, even in the second tier, provide great views. If you do take the stairs to the balcony, be aware that you cannot walk freely from one section to the next in this level. We suggest you go up the stairs near the middle of the stadium to find a center-stage seat.

Dolphin Nursery

APPEAL BY AGE	PRESCHOOL ★	GRADE SCHOOL ★★	TEENS ★
YOUNG ADULTS ★★		OVER 30 ★★	SENIORS ★★

What it is Outdoor pool for expectant dolphins or mothers and calves. **Scope and scale** Diversion. **When to go** Anytime. **Author's rating** Only worth a quick glimpse unless a baby is present; ★★.

DESCRIPTION AND COMMENTS Seeing this tiny pool that used to be the sole dolphin experience at SeaWorld should make you appreciate Dolphin Cove and Discovery Cove all the more. But the small size is perfect for its current purpose—providing a separate area for pregnant dolphins and new moms and calves. Stop by for a quick glance if it's an expectant dolphin. Stay longer if there's a baby in the pool.

TOURING TIPS This area will be roped off and guests understandably kept away when a dolphin goes into labor. Because it's near the park entrance, swing by on your way out to see if the area has reopened, and you might be able to view mom and baby.

Hiding next to the Dolphin Nursery is one of the most beautiful and secluded areas of SeaWorld. Find the path next to the nursery and enter a lush tropical rain forest. A large banyan tree and 30-foot-tall bamboo trees shade the entire area. Large fish swim in a small pond, and two beautiful macaws perch on a branch.

There is also an aviary featuring blue dacnis and red-legged honeycreepers, both adorably tiny birds. There are no formal benches, but a few stone ledges provide the perfect place to get away from the sun and the theme-park hustle and bustle.

Tropical Reef

APPEAL BY AGE	PRESCHOOL ★½	GRADE SCHOOL ★★	TEENS ★
YOUNG ADULTS ★½		OVER 30 ★½	SENIORS ★★

What it is Indoor aquariums/outdoor tide pool. **Scope and scale** Diversion. **When to go** Anytime; skip if in a hurry. **Author's rating** Easy to miss; ★½.

DESCRIPTION AND COMMENTS A small outdoor tide pool is home to several sea urchins, sea cucumbers, and spiny lobsters. It's not much to look at, but visitors are encouraged to stick their hands in and touch the urchins—a unique experience. Inside, hundreds of tropical fish swim in numerous aquariums. The aquariums are set into the walls, so the colorful fish are only visible through the front pane of glass. Information and factoids can be found on lighted signs near each aquarium.

TOURING TIPS True fish fanatics only. Others will find their time better spent at the more elaborate exhibits.

Mistify

APPEAL BY AGE	PRESCHOOL ★★★	GRADE SCHOOL ★★★	TEENS ★★★
YOUNG ADULTS ★★★		OVER 30 ...	SENIORS ★★★

What it is Laser and fireworks show. **Scope and scale** Major attraction. **When to go** Check daily entertainment schedule. **Special comments** Only displayed during peak seasons. **Author's rating** Good big booms; ★★★. **Duration of show** 1 hour.

DESCRIPTION AND COMMENTS Presented over the lagoon in the Waterfront Village. The theme of the show changes frequently, but common elements include fireworks, lasers, and movies projected on a water curtain in the lagoon—all set to music. Although the show might not be quite as spectacular as Disney's *IllumiNations,* it is a great fireworks display and the projections on the water screen are unique.

TOURING TIPS As a pleasant change from Disney's nighttime shows, there's no need to stake out a spot hours in advance. We recommend arriving about 15 minutes early. In addition, you won't be stuck standing up or with tree-blocked views, because the action is easily seen from the Village's shore.

Behind-the-Scenes Tours

APPEAL BY AGE	PRESCHOOL ★★½	GRADE SCHOOL ★★★½	TEENS ★★½
YOUNG ADULTS ★★★		OVER 30 ★★★½	SENIORS ★★★★

What it is Just what the name implies. **Scope and scale** Major attraction. **When to go** Check education counter for schedule. **Special comments** Cost $16 for adults, $12 for children ages 3–9. **Author's rating** A great deal; ★★★.

DESCRIPTION AND COMMENTS These 60-minute tours are extremely informative and entertaining, and well worth the additional charge. A variety of subjects and areas are covered, and the tours and times vary according to the park's (and the animals') schedules. The three different tours include a look at the animal rescue program, the shark tank at Terrors of the Deep, and the penguins at Penguin Encounter at Wild Arctic.

TOURING TIPS Advance reservations are not accepted for these tours. You must stop by the guided-tour counter at the front of the park on the day of your visit or reserve a spot on the park's Web site (**www.seaworld.com**). If you know you'll want to take one of the tours, we recommend making reservations online because the spots fill quickly and reservations are on a first-come, first-served basis.

Taking an hour out of your SeaWorld visit for these tours will require careful planning, but for sea-life enthusiasts, it's a neat experience.

Marine Mammal Keeper Experience

APPEAL BY AGE	PRESCHOOL †	GRADE SCHOOL †	TEENS ★★★★
YOUNG ADULTS ★★★★		OVER 30 ★★★	SENIORS ★★½

†Preschoolers and grade-school kids are not old enough.

What it is Chance to shadow a SeaWorld trainer for a day. **Scope and scale** Major attraction. **When to go** Program begins at 7 a.m. **Special comments** Costs $399 (admission is included); participants must be at least 13 years old and 52 inches tall; passport holders receive a $29 discount. **Author's rating** Extremely expensive, but worth it for enthusiasts; ★★★.

DESCRIPTION AND COMMENTS Shadow a genuine SeaWorld trainer during this eight-hour program. Learn through hands-on experience how SeaWorld staff members care for and train their animals, from stuffing vitamins into a slimy fish to positive-reinforcement training techniques. The fee includes lunch, a T-shirt, souvenir photo, and a seven-day pass to SeaWorld.

TOURING TIPS Attendance for this program is limited to four people per day. Calling up to six months ahead is best, but cancellations do occur. For information and reservations, call ☎ 800-423-1178. Participants must be in good physical condition and at least 13 years old.

DINING

SEAWORLD OFFERS MUCH MORE than the usual theme-park fare of burgers and fries. The food for the most part is very good, and prices are a bit lower than at Disney World.

Your feasting can begin at Cypress Bakery, which opens at 8:30 a.m. during the busy season and at 8:45 a.m. otherwise. Choose from a dizzying array of wonderful pastries, cakes, and muffins to enjoy while you plan your day.

Also offered in the morning is a SeaWorld character breakfast, held from 8:45 to 10 a.m. at the Seafire Inn in the new Waterfront area.

*un*official **TIP** Cypress Bakery opens early and offers fantastic breakfast breads and pastries.

A buffet with classic offerings like scrambled eggs, pancakes, muffins, and fruit is served for $14.95 (adults) and $9.95 (children ages 3–9); children under age 3 eat free with reservations. Speaking of reservations, they are recommended, though walk-ups will be seated on availability. Reservations can be made by calling ☎ 800-327-2420. Usually only one character is present, often Shamu.

For a more toothsome experience, try Sharks Underwater Grill at the Shark Encounter attraction, which offers "Floribbean" cuisine served next to floor-to-ceiling windows into the shark tank. A typical meal will run $20 per person at this ostensibly upscale eatery.

For quick service, try Mango Joe's Cafe for fajitas, salads, and sandwiches; Mama's Kitchen for BBQ sandwiches, po'boys, and more; or Smoky Creek Grill for barbecue. Another favorite: the hand-carved sandwiches at The Deli in the Hospitality House.

Another unique option is the Dine with Shamu program, which allows guests to enjoy a buffet-style meal alongside the killer-whale tanks, all the while mingling with trainers and observing behind-the-scenes training exercises. Cost is $34 for adults and $18 for kids ages 3–9 in addition to park admission.

unofficial **TIP**
Want to eat alongside Shamu? Try the Dine with Shamu program.

Along the Waterfront there are several options, including the Spice Mill, a walk-up cafe with selections like jerk chicken, jambalaya, and a saffron chef salad. There's also Voyagers Wood Fired Pizza, where the pizza is strangely served on top of a bed of waffle fries. Other dishes include pasta dishes and the tasty Mediterranean foccacia club sandwich.

SHOPPING

UNLIKE AT DISNEY, shopping at SeaWorld isn't an attraction in and of itself. There is, of course, a huge selection of SeaWorld merchandise. Some of it is unique, and prices are relatively reasonable. Fans of ocean wildlife can find a vast array of marine merchandise, ranging from high-quality, expensive sculptures to T-shirts, beach towels, and knick-knacks. Children will be overwhelmed by the huge selection of stuffed animals, and parents will be pleased by their low prices—many small- to medium-sized toys are priced under $10. Budweiser enthusiasts will enjoy the large selection of Anheuser-Busch merchandise, including beer mugs, caps, and nice golf shirts.

Along the Waterfront area, there are more shopping selections, like the Tropica Trading Shop with goods from Africa, Bali, and Indonesia, among others, and a do-it-yourself shops like a bead store and a doll factory.

DISCOVERY COVE

INSPIRED BY A LARGE NUMBER OF REQUESTS for dolphin swims as well as the success of the original Dolphin Interaction Program, SeaWorld created Discovery Cove. This intimate subpark is a welcome departure from the hustle and bustle of other Orlando parks; the relaxed pace here could be the overstimulated family's ticket back to mental health. With a focus on personal service and one-on-one animal encounters, Discovery Cove admits only 1,000 guests per day. The tranquil setting and unobtrusive theming make this park unique for central Florida. Why, there's only one gift shop! And you don't even have to walk through it to get out!

The main draw at Discovery Cove is the chance to swim with a troupe of 25 Atlantic bottlenose dolphins. The 90-minute dolphin swim experience is open to visitors ages 6 and up who are comfortable in the water. The experience begins with an orientation led by trainers and an opportunity for participants to ask questions before entering the dolphin lagoon. Next, small groups wade into shallow water for an introduction to the dolphins in their habitat. The experience culminates with one, two, or

unofficial **TIP**
Swimming with the fishes: spend a relaxing day at Discovery Cove, surrounded by a pod of dolphins!

three guests and a trainer swimming into deeper water for closer interaction with the dolphins. Afterward, swimmers are invited to discuss their interaction with the trainers, and of course, purchase photographs of themselves with the dolphins. Though this is not an inexpensive endeavor, the singular nature of the experience cannot be overstated. The dolphins are playful, friendly, and frankly amazing to be around. This is as hands-on as it gets. Be aware that you're dealing with a powerful mischievous animal in its element, so don't be surprised if you get splashed, squirted, or even affectionately bonked with a flipper or fluke. The trainers are always in control, though, so there is nothing to fear. Overall, if this is to your taste at all, it's not to be missed. Author's rating? Five stars.

Be careful about planning who does what at Discovery Cove. The perils of being left out are illustrated by this letter sent in by a mother of three from Croydon, England:

> *Only two of the five [in our group] swam with the dol-*
> *phins because that is the only booking we could get. We*
> *would recommend that all people in the party swim with*
> *the dolphins to avoid the awful, sad feeling of being left*
> *out that three of us had. The two children refused to look*
> *at their brother, and Dad just wanted to go home. Dad felt*
> *guilty, and what was supposed to be the highlight of the*
> *trip turned into a downer.*

Not an ideal situation. If you're visiting Discovery Cove as a group, try to time your visit so everyone who wants to swim with the dolphins can.

Other exhibit areas at Discovery Cove include the Coral Reef, the Aviary, the Ray Pool, and the Freshwater Lagoon. You can snorkel or swim in the Coral Reef, which houses thousands of exotic fish and dozens of manta rays as well as an underwater shipwreck and hidden grottos. In the Aviary, you can touch and feed gorgeous tropical birds. Stingrays occupy the small Ray Pool next to the Coral Reef; you can wade in among them, under the guidance of a lifeguard. The Freshwater Lagoon is just a salt-free rocky pond, empty of aquatic life. The park is threaded by the freshwater Tropical River, in which you can float or swim to all these areas. Pleasant beaches serve as pathways connecting the attractions.

Guests at Discovery Cove need not be exceptional swimmers—the water is shallow and so heavily salted that it's very difficult not to float. Watchful lifeguards are omnipresent. You'll need to wear your bathing suit and pool shoes as well as a cover-up. On rare days when it's too cold to swim in Orlando, guests are provided with free wetsuits. The park also supplies masks and snorkels, and you get to keep the snorkel (after all, nobody wants to reuse those). Discovery Cove provides fish-friendly sunscreen: guests may not use their own sunscreen. You must also remove all watches and jewelry (except wedding bands), as they might end up getting swallowed by the animals if you lose them. Free lockers enable you to stow everything you need to put away, all day. Comfortable, clean, well-appointed bathrooms and showers are also provided.

GETTING THERE

DISCOVERY COVE IS LOCATED DIRECTLY across the Central Florida Parkway from SeaWorld. Parking is free.

PRICES AND RESERVATIONS

DISCOVERY COVE IS OPEN 9 a.m.–5:30 p.m. every day of the year. Because admission is limited to 1,000 guests per

Discovery Cove

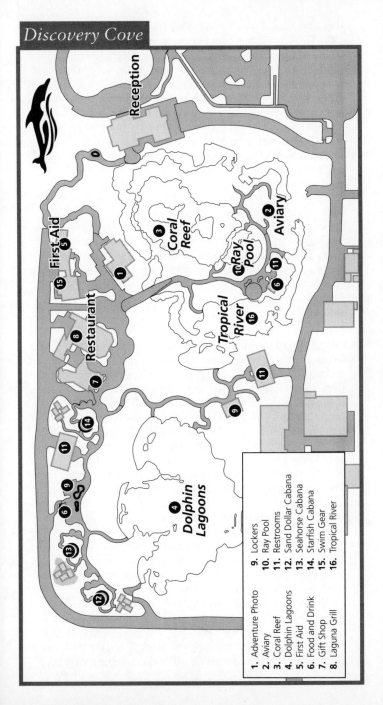

Reception

Coral Reef

Aviary

First Aid

Ray Pool

Restaurant

Tropical River

Dolphin Lagoons

1. Adventure Photo
2. Aviary
3. Coral Reef
4. Dolphin Lagoons
5. First Aid
6. Food and Drink
7. Gift Shop
8. Laguna Grill

9. Lockers
10. Ray Pool
11. Restrooms
12. Sand Dollar Cabana
13. Seahorse Cabana
14. Starfish Cabana
15. Swim Gear
16. Tropical River

day, you should purchase tickets well in advance by calling (☎ 877-4-DISCOVERY or visiting **www.discoverycove.com.** There are two admission options. The all-inclusive package is $243–$275, tax included, (depending on season) per person and includes the dolphin swim, one meal at the Laguna Grill restaurant, unlimited access to the Ray Lagoon, Coral Reef, aviary, pool, and tropical river; use of beach umbrellas, lounge chairs, towels, lockers, and swim and snorkel gear.

If you're not interested in the dolphin swim, the Non-Dolphin Swim Package is $137–$164 (depending on season) per person for the day and includes everything but the dolphin encounter. Discovery Cove admission also includes a seven-day pass to SeaWorld or Busch Gardens, making the high price tag a bit easier to swallow.

The Trainer for a Day package is similar to the program at SeaWorld, and includes everything the all-inclusive package does, along with a dolphin behavioral class and backstage tours of the Coral Reef and Ray Lagoon. Admission to be trainer for a day is $399–$459 depending on season.

ARRIVING

THOUGH THE PARK PROPER doesn't open until 9 a.m., the entrance hall usually opens about 8 a.m. It's not a bad idea to get there a little early, because if you do, you can be among the first guests to register for your dolphin interaction. Guests are assigned time slots for the dolphin swims throughout the day, but you're not assigned your time slot until you show up on the day of your reservation. The later you register, the later in the day your dolphin swim will be. Dolphins are generally more active in the morning, and once you do the interaction, you can spend the rest of your day on lazy snorkeling or snoozing on the beach (without worrying about missing your appointment with Flipper).

On registering, you'll be asked to provide a credit card number. You'll then be issued a lanyard card with your picture on it. This card corresponds to the credit card you just gave, so it can be used for purchases anywhere in Discovery Cove. This means you can stow your wallet or purse in a locker for your whole stay. The locker key is also on a lanyard, so it's very easy to keep up with everything.

You'll be assigned one of three cabanas as your meeting place for the dolphin interaction. These are easy to find, because Discovery Cove is really not that large. Show up about five minutes before your assigned time. A trainer will give a short orientation, and then it's off to the dolphin swim. Enjoy.

UNIVERSAL ORLANDO

UNIVERSAL ORLANDO HAS TRANSFORMED into a complete destination resort, with two theme parks, three hotels, and a shopping, dining, and entertainment complex. The second theme park, Islands of Adventure, opened in 1999 with five theme areas.

A system of roads and two multistory parking facilities are connected by moving sidewalks to CityWalk, a shopping, dining, and nighttime entertainment complex that also serves as a gateway to both the Universal Studios Florida and Islands of Adventure theme parks. CityWalk includes the world's largest Hard Rock Café, complete with its own concert facility; an Emeril's restaurant; a NASCAR Café, with an auto-racing theme; a Pat O'Brien's New Orleans nightclub, with dueling pianos; a Bob Marley restaurant and museum; a multifaceted Jazz Center; Jimmy Buffett's Margaritaville; a 16-screen cinema complex, and more.

LODGING AT UNIVERSAL ORLANDO

UNIVERSAL CURRENTLY HAS THREE OPERATING resort hotels. The 750-room Portofino Bay Hotel is a gorgeous property set on an artificial bay and themed like an Italian coastal town. The 650-room Hard Rock Hotel is an ultra-cool "Hotel California" replica with slick contemporary design and a hip, friendly attitude. The 1,000-room Polynesian-themed Royal Pacific Resort is sumptuously decorated and richly appointed. All three are excellent hotels; the Portofino and the Hard Rock are on the pricey side, and the Royal Pacific ain't exactly cheap.

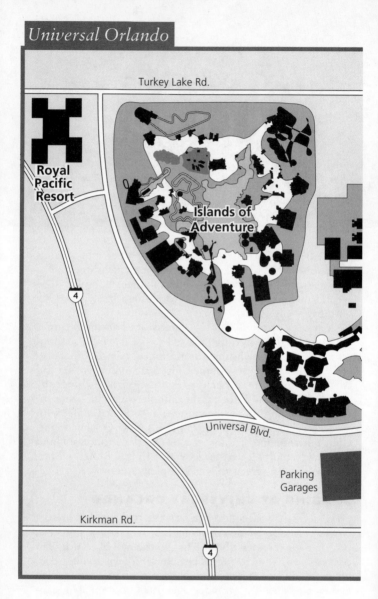

Universal Orlando

Turkey Lake Rd.

Royal Pacific Resort

Islands of Adventure

Universal Blvd.

Parking Garages

Kirkman Rd.

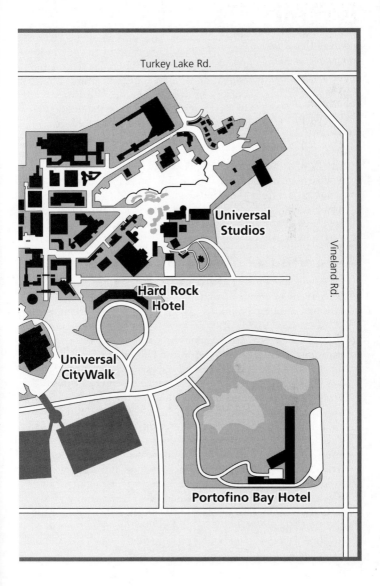

Turkey Lake Rd.

Universal Studios

Vineland Rd.

Hard Rock Hotel

Universal CityWalk

Portofino Bay Hotel

unofficial **TIP**
Staying at one of the three Universal resorts allows you special privileges such as free rides to and from the Universal parks, all day long.

Like Disney, Universal offers a number of incentives to stay at their hotels. Perks available that mirror those offered by the Mouse include free parking, delivery to your room of purchases made in the parks, tickets and reservation information from hotel concierges, priority dining reservations at Universal restaurants, and the ability to charge purchases to your room account.

Otherwise, Universal offers complementary transportation by bus or water taxi to Universal Studios, Islands of Adventure, CityWalk, SeaWorld, and Wet 'n' Wild. Hotel guests may use the Universal Express program with impunity all day long (see "Universal Express" on page 137). Universal lodging guests are also eligible for "next available" table privileges at CityWalk restaurants and similar priority admission to Universal Orlando theme park shows.

ARRIVING AT UNIVERSAL ORLANDO

THE UNIVERSAL ORLANDO COMPLEX can be accessed directly from Interstate 4. Once on site, you will be directed to park in one of two multitiered parking garages. Parking runs $8 for cars and $10 for RVs. Be sure to write down the location of your car before heading for the parks. From the garages, moving sidewalks deliver you to the Universal CityWalk dining, shopping, and entertainment venue described above. From CityWalk, you can access the main entrances of both Universal Studios Florida and Islands of Adventure theme parks. Even with the moving walkways, it takes about 10–12 minutes to commute from the garages to the entrances of the theme parks.

Universal offers One-Day, Two-Day, Three-Day, and Annual Passes. Multiday passes allow you to visit both Universal theme parks on the same day, and unused days are good forever. Multiday passes also allow for early entry on select days. Passes can be obtained in advance on the phone with your credit card at ☎ 800-711-0080. All prices are the same whether you buy your admission at the gate or in advance. Prices shown below include tax.

	ADULTS	CHILDREN (3–9)
One-Day, One-Park Pass	$64	$51
Two-Day, Two-Park Bonus Pass	$106	All guests
Two-Park Annual Preferred Pass	$191	All guests
Two Park Annual Power Pass	$127	All guests

Be sure to check Universal's Web site (**www.universal orlando.com**) for seasonal deals and specials.

If you want to visit more than one park on a given day, have your park pass and hand stamped when exiting your first park. At the second park use the re-admission turnstile, showing your stamped pass and hand.

Combination passes are available: A four-park, 14-day pass allows unlimited entry to Universal Studios, Universal's Islands of Adventure, SeaWorld, and Wet 'n' Wild and costs about $196 for adults and $160 for children (ages 3 to 9). A five-park, 14-day pass provides unlimited entry to Universal Studios, Universal's Islands of Adventure, SeaWorld, Wet 'n' Wild, and Busch Gardens and costs about $239 for adults and $201 for children.

The main Universal Orlando information number is ☎ 407-363-8000. Reach Guest Services at ☎ 407-224-4233, schedule a character lunch at **www.universalorlando.com,** and order tickets by mail at ☎ 800-224-3838. The number for Lost and Found is ☎ 407-224-4244.

EARLY ENTRY AND UNIVERSAL EXPRESS

UNIVERSAL NO LONGER OPERATES an early-entry program. The Universal Express program is actually two programs, one for Universal hotel guests and one available to everyone. Concerning the latter, there is a basic program, available to all guests at no additional charge (that operates much like Disney's FASTPASS), and an enhanced program that costs extra.

UNIVERSAL EXPRESS PROGRAMS AVAILABLE TO ALL GUESTS

THE BASIC PROGRAM WORKS LIKE THIS: theme-park guests are issued Universal Express return tickets at kiosks set near the entrances of popular attractions. These return tickets have a one-hour time window printed on them, good for admission during that prescribed time period to the Express queue at a particular attraction. This special queue bypasses much of the main line, and those waiting in it have priority over the proles stuck in the regular queue.

Once you obtain a basic program Express pass, you can't get another until: (1) the time window for you to use your first pass has begun; or (2) two hours after the time you were issued the first pass. The transaction time—the time when you actually obtained the first pass—is printed on the bottom of the pass. So, if your return window is more than two hours away, you can get a second Universal Express pass before you've used the first.

Be advised that the Universal Express machines are somewhat temperamental. Originally, you had to slide your admission pass through a slot to be scanned. When that didn't work very well, Universal disconnected the scanning slot, and placed the scanner lower down on the machine. Currently you place your admission in a glove-compartment-sized opening on the front of the machine. Unfortunately, the opening is large and the scanner requires the admission to be placed in a very specific spot in order to be read. Many guests don't hit the spot and think the machine is on the blink. It's a trial-and-error situation, but you need to move your pass around in the opening until you chance upon the sweet spot. Once the card is read you can obtain your Universal Express pass.

If you're willing to drop a little extra cash, you can upgrade to Universal Express Plus. Universal Express Plus allows you to use the Express entrance one time only at each designated Universal Express attraction. With the Plus feature there are no return windows, so you can visit attractions at your convenience. Universal Express Plus is good only for the date of purchase *at one park,* and can only be used by one person.

unofficial **TIP**
Don't like to wait, and don't mind paying extra not to? Shell out for Universal Express Plus.

Universal Express Plus is available for $15 over and above your admission most of the year, and for $25 during peak seasons. You can purchase Universal Express Plus at the theme-park's ticket windows, just outside the front gates. Once in the Universal Studios theme park, Universal Express Plus is available at the Back to the Future Store, the Cartoon Store, Shaiken's Souvenirs, and Nickstuff. Inside Islands of Adventure you can buy Universal Express Plus at Jurassic Outfitters, Toon Extra, Treasures of Poseidon, the Marvel Alterniverse Store, and at Port Merchants Cart. As of the time of his writing, Universal Express Plus was not available on the Internet.

Universal Express Program Available to Universal Resort Guests

The Universal Express program for Universal resort guests allows guests to bypass the regular line anytime, and as often as desired, by simply showing their room key. This perk far surpasses any perk accorded guests of Disney resorts.

How Universal Express Impacts Crowd Conditions at the Attractions

This system dramatically affects crowd movement (and touring plans) in the Universal parks, since all guests can access the Express line to some degree. A woman from York-town, Virginia, writes:

> People in the [Express] line were let in at a rate of about ten to one over the regular line folks. This created bottle-necks and long waits for people who didn't have the express privilege at the very times when it is supposed to be easier to get around! The fallout from this was that we just kind of poked around until noon, then found basically no wait for ANYTHING (even Spider-Man) in the afternoon.

Unfortunately, especially for attractions that were created before Universal Express was conceived, the Universal Express kiosks are sometimes stuffed in an awkward corner or hidden off to the side. Park guests often crowd around the kiosks, trying to figure out what attraction their pass is for, what time slot to choose, and where the actual express line is. As a woman from Nashua, New Hampshire, complains:

> We had to figure out that we needed to go to the terminals at a location other than the ride itself . . . We were in a "mosh pit" in the heat trying to get to the terminals!

SINGLES LINES

AND THERE'S YET ANOTHER OPTION: the singles line. Several attractions have this special line for guests riding alone. As Universal employees will tell you, this line is often even faster than the Express line. We strongly recommend you use the singles line or the Express line whenever possi-ble, as it will decrease your overall wait and leave more time for repeat rides or just bumming around the parks.

UNIVERSAL, KIDS, AND SCARY STUFF

ALTHOUGH THERE'S PLENTY FOR YOUNGER CHILDREN to enjoy at the Universal parks, the majority of the major attractions have the potential for wigging out kids under 8 years of age. At Universal Studios Florida, forget Revenge of the Mummy, *Twister*, *Earthquake*, Jaws, Men in Black, Back to the Future, and *Terminator 2: 3-D*. The first part of the ride is a little intense for a few preschoolers, but the end is all happi-ness and harmony. Interestingly, very few families report problems with *Beetlejuice's Rock 'n' Roll Graveyard Revue* or *The Universal Horror Make-up Show*. Any-thing not listed is pretty benign.

unofficial **TIP**
If you've got tots ages 7 or younger, consider that many of Universal's attractions can be frightening for little ones.

At Universal's Islands of Adventure, watch out for The Incredible Hulk Coaster, Dr. Doom's Fearfall, The Adventures of Spider-Man, the Jurassic Park River Adventure, Dueling Dragons, and *Poseidon's Fury*. Popeye & Bluto's Bilge-Rat Barges is wet and wild, but most younger children handle it well. Dudley Do-Right's Ripsaw Falls is a toss-up, to be considered only if your kids liked water-flume rides. The *Sinbad* stunt show includes some explosions and startling special effects, but once again, children tolerate it well. Nothing else should pose a problem.

UNIVERSAL STUDIOS FLORIDA

UNIVERSAL CITY STUDIOS INC. has run a studios tour and movie-theme tourist attraction for more than 30 years, predating all Disney parks except Disneyland. In the early 1980s, Universal announced plans to build a new theme-park complex in Florida. But while Universal labored over its new project, Disney jumped into high gear and rushed its own studios/theme park onto the market, beating Universal by about two years.

NOT TO BE MISSED AT UNIVERSAL STUDIOS FLORIDA	
Back to the Future	Terminator 2: 3-D
Earthquake—The Big One	Jaws
Men in Black Alien Attack	Shrek 4-D
Revenge of the Mummy	

Universal Studios Florida opened in June 1990. At that time, it was almost four times the size of Disney-MGM Studios (Disney-MGM has since expanded somewhat), with much more of the facility accessible to visitors. Like its sister facility in Hollywood, Universal Studios Florida is spacious, beautifully landscaped, meticulously clean, and delightfully varied in its entertainment. Rides are exciting and innovative and, as with many Disney rides, focus on familiar and/or beloved movie characters or situations.

On Universal Studios Florida's *E.T.* ride, you escape the authorities on a flying bike and leave Earth to visit *E.T.*'s home planet. In Jaws, the persistent great white shark makes heart-stopping assaults on your small boat, and in *Earthquake—The Big One,* special effects create one of the most realistic earthquake simulation ever produced. Guests also ride in a Delorean-cum-time machine in yet another chase, this one based on the film *Back to the Future,* and fight alien bugs with zapper guns in Men in Black. New attractions based on the *Jimmy Neutron* and *Shrek* movies raised the entertainment stakes even higher. Universal opened in spring 2004 their most ambitious attraction to date: Revenge of the Mummy. Replacing longtime Universal Studios fixture Kong-frontation and based on *The Mummy* film franchise, it's a combination roller coaster/dark ride with maglev coaster tracks, robotics technology adapted from the Mars lander, and a pyrotechnic "ceiling of flame."

While these rides incorporate state-of-the-art technology and live up to their billing in terms of excitement, creativity, uniqueness, and special effects, some lack the capacity to handle the number of guests who frequent major Florida tourist destinations. If a ride has great appeal but can accommodate only a small number of guests per ride or per hour, long lines form. It isn't unusual for the wait to exceed an hour and a quarter for the *E.T.* ride.

unofficial **TIP**
Be forewarned: Universal's rides, while thrilling, can have longer-than-usual waits, and tend to break down—call ahead to see what's open.

Happily, most shows and theater performances at Universal Studios Florida are in theaters that accommodate large numbers of people. Since many shows run continuously, waits usually don't exceed twice the show's performance time (15–30 minutes).

Universal Studios Florida is laid out in an upside-down L configuration. Beyond the main entrance, a wide boulevard stretches past several shows and rides to a New York City backlot set. Branching off this pedestrian thoroughfare to the right are five streets that access other areas of the studios and intersect a promenade circling a large lake.

The park is divided into six sections: Production Central, New York, Hollywood, San Francisco/Amity, Woody Woodpecker's Kid Zone, and World Expo. Where one section begins and another ends is blurry, but no matter. Guests orient themselves by the major rides, sets, and landmarks and refer, for instance, to "New York," "the waterfront," "over by *E.T.,*" or "by Mel's Diner." The area of Universal Studios Florida open to visitors is about the size of Epcot.

The park offers all standard services and amenities, including stroller and wheelchair rental, lockers, diaper-changing and infant-nursing facilities, car assistance, and foreign-language assistance. Most of the park is accessible

Universal Studios

1. *Animal Planet Live!*
2. Back to the Future— The Ride
3. *Beetlejuice's Rock 'n' Roll Graveyard Revue*
4. The Boneyard
5. *A Day in the Park with Barney*
6. Earthquake—The Big One
7. E.T. Adventure
8. Fear Factor Live
9. Fievel's Playland
10. *The Horror Make-Up Show*
11. Jaws
12. Jimmy Neutron's Nicktoon Blast
13. Lucy, A Tribute
14. Men in Black Alien Attack
15. Nickelodeon Studios Walking Tours
16. Revenge of the Mummy
17. *Shrek 4-D*
18. Sound Stage 54
19. *Terminator 2: 3-D*
20. Twister
21. Woody Woodpecker's Kid Zone

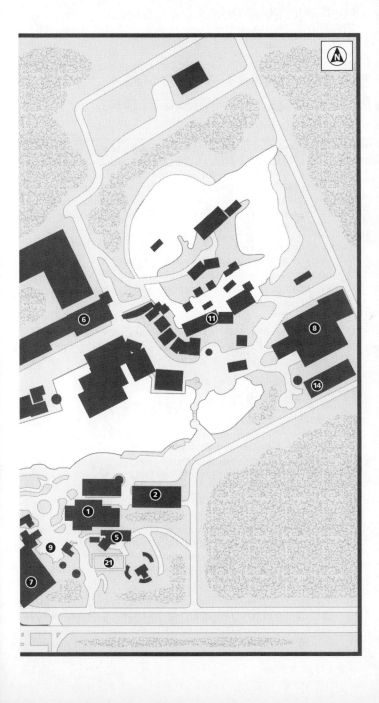

to disabled guests, and TDDs are available for the hearing impaired. Almost all services are in the Front Lot, just inside the main entrance.

UNIVERSAL STUDIOS FLORIDA ATTRACTIONS

Animal Planet Live! (Universal Express)

APPEAL BY AGE	PRESCHOOL ★★★★	GRADE SCHOOL ★★★★	TEENS ★★★
YOUNG ADULTS ★★★		OVER 30 ★★★	SENIORS ★★★½

What it is Animal tricks and comedy show based on the popular cable network's programs. **Scope and scale** Major attraction. **When to go** After you have experienced all rides. **Author's rating** Cute lil' critters; ★★★. **Duration of presentation** 20 minutes. **Probable waiting time** 25 minutes.

DESCRIPTION AND COMMENTS This show aims to build on the popularity of Animal Planet's various TV programs and characters, integrating video segments from the TV shows with live sketches, jokes, and animal tricks performed onstage. The idea is to create eco-friendly family entertainment that mirrors the themes of Animal Planet programming. Several of the animal thespians are veterans of television and movies, and many were rescued from shelters. Audience members can participate as well: where else will you get the chance to hold an eight-foot albino reticulated python in your lap?

TOURING TIPS Check the daily entertainment schedule for show times. You shouldn't have any trouble getting in to this show. Save it for mid or late afternoon.

Back to the Future—The Ride (Universal Express)

APPEAL BY AGE	PRESCHOOL †	GRADE SCHOOL ★★★★	TEENS ★★★★
YOUNG ADULTS ★★★★		OVER 30 ★★★★	SENIORS ★★½

† Sample size too small for an accurate rating.

What it is Flight-simulator thrill ride. **Scope and scale** Headliner. **When to go** First thing in the morning after Mummy and Men in Black. **Special comments** Rough ride; may induce motion sickness. Must be 40 inches tall to ride. **Author's rating** Not to be missed, if you have a strong stomach; ★★★★. **Duration of ride** 4½ minutes. **Loading speed** Moderate.

DESCRIPTION AND COMMENTS Guests in Doc Brown's lab get caught up in a high-speed chase through time that spans a million years. An extremely intense simulator ride, Back to the Future is similar to Star Tours and Body Wars at Walt Disney World but is much rougher and more jerky. Though the story does-n't make much sense, the visual effects are wild and powerful. The vehicles (Delorean time machines) in Back to the Future are much smaller than those of Star Tours and Body Wars, so the ride feels more personal and less like a group experience

TOURING TIPS As soon the park opens, guests stampede to Mummy, Men in Black, and Back to the Future. Our recommendation: be there when the park opens, and join the rush. If you don't ride before 10:20 a.m., your wait may be exceptionally long. *Note:* sitting in the rear seat of the car makes the ride more realistic.

Motion Sickness

WARNING!

Beetlejuice's Rock 'n' Roll Graveyard Revue (Universal Express)

APPEAL BY AGE	PRESCHOOL ★★★★	GRADE SCHOOL ★★★★	TEENS ★★★★
YOUNG ADULTS ★★★½		OVER 30 ★★★½	SENIORS ★★★½

What it is Rock-and-roll stage show. **Scope and scale** Almost major attraction. **When to go** At your convenience. **Author's rating** Outrageous; ★★★½. **Duration of presentation** 18 minutes. **Probable waiting time** None.

DESCRIPTION AND COMMENTS High-powered rock-and-roll stage show stars Beetlejuice, Frankenstein, the Bride of Frankenstein, Wolfman, Dracula, and a pair of fly girls called Hip and Hop. The show features contemporary dance and pop songs rather than classic rock. High-energy, silly, bawdy, and generally funnier than it has any right to be, the long running *Revue* just keeps plugging along.

TOURING TIPS Mercifully, this attraction is under cover.

A Day in the Park with Barney (Universal Express)

APPEAL BY AGE	PRESCHOOL ★★★★½	GRADE SCHOOL ★★★	TEENS ★★
YOUNG ADULTS ★★½		OVER 30 ★★★	SENIORS ★★★

What it is Live character stage show. **Scope and scale** Major children's attraction. **When to go** Anytime. **Author's rating** A great hit with preschoolers; ★★★★. **Duration of presentation** 12 minutes plus character greeting. **Probable waiting time** 15 minutes.

DESCRIPTION AND COMMENTS Barney, the purple dinosaur of Public Television fame, leads a sing-along with the help of the audience and sidekicks Baby Bop and BJ. A short preshow gets the kids lathered up before they enter Barney's Park (the theater).

Interesting theatrical effects include wind, falling leaves, clouds and stars in the simulated sky, and snow. After the show, Barney exits momentarily to allow parents and children to gather along the stage. He then returns and moves from child to child, hugging each and posing for photos.

TOURING TIPS If your child likes Barney, this show is a must. It's happy and upbeat, and the character greeting that follows is the best organized we've seen in any theme park. There's no line and no fighting for Barney's attention. Just relax by the rail and await your hug. There's also a great indoor play area nearby, designed especially for wee tykes.

Earthquake—The Big One (Universal Express)

APPEAL BY AGE	PRESCHOOL ★★★	GRADE SCHOOL ★★★★	TEENS ★★★★
YOUNG ADULTS ★★★★		OVER 30 ★★★★	SENIORS ★★★★

What it is Combination theater presentation and adventure ride. **Scope and scale** Major attraction. **When to go** In the morning or late afternoon. **Special comments** May frighten young children. **Author's rating** Not to be missed; ★★★★. **Duration of presentation** 20 minutes. **Loading speed** Moderate.

DESCRIPTION AND COMMENTS Film shows how miniatures are used to create special effects in earthquake movies, followed by a demonstration of how miniatures, blue screen, and matte painting are integrated with live-action stunt sequences (starring audience volunteers) to create a realistic final product. Afterward, guests board a subway from Oakland to San Francisco and experience an earthquake—the big one. Special effects range from fires and runaway trains to exploding tanker trucks and tidal waves. This is Universal's answer to Disney-MGM's Catastrophe Canyon. The special effects are comparable, but the field of vision is better at Catastrophe Canyon. Nonetheless, *Earthquake* is one of Universal's more compelling efforts.

TOURING TIPS Experience *Earthquake* after tackling the park's other rides.

E. T. Adventure (Universal Express)

APPEAL BY AGE	PRESCHOOL ★★★★	GRADE SCHOOL ★★★★	TEENS ★★★
YOUNG ADULTS ★★★		OVER 30 ★★★½	SENIORS ★★★½

What it is Indoor adventure ride based on the *E.T.* movie. **Scope and scale** Major attraction. **When to go** Before noon; before 10 a.m. if you have small children. **Author's rating** A happy reunion: ★★★½. **Duration of ride** 4½ minutes. **Loading speed** Moderate.

DESCRIPTION AND COMMENTS Guests aboard a bicycle-like conveyance escape with E.T. from earthly law-enforcement officials and then journey to E.T.'s home planet. The attraction is similar to Peter Pan's Flight at the Magic Kingdom but is longer and has more elaborate special effects and a wilder ride.

TOURING TIPS Most preschoolers and grade-school children love E.T. We think it worth a 20- to 30-minute wait, but nothing longer. Lines build quickly after 10 a.m., and waits can be more than two hours on busy days. Ride in the morning or late afternoon. Guests who balk at sitting on the bicycle can ride in a comfortable gondola.

A mother from Columbus, Ohio, writes about horrendous lines at E.T.:

The line for E.T. took two hours! The rest of the family waiting out-side thought that we had gone to E.T.'s planet for real.

A woman from Richmond, Virginia, objects to how Universal represents the waiting time:

We got into E.T. without much wait, but the line is very deceptive. When you see a lot of people waiting outside and the sign says "ten-minute wait from this point," it means ten minutes until you are inside the building. But there's a very long wait inside [before] you get to the moving vehicles.

Fear Factor Live

APPEAL BY AGE	PRESCHOOL ★	GRADE SCHOOL ★★	TEENS ★★★★
YOUNG ADULTS ★★★		OVER 30 ★★★	SENIORS ★½

What it is Live version of the gross-out stunt television show on NBC. **Scope and scale** Headliner. **When to go** 6 to 8 shows daily; crowds are smallest at the first and second-to last shows. **Author's rating** Great fun if you love the TV show; ★★★.

DESCRIPTION AND COMMENTS In each show, park guests compete against each other in several extreme stunts. The stunts—like drinking bug smoothies, scaling tall walls and swimming in a tank full of eels—were developed with help from the brains behind Fear Factor and are no less creepy than the ones you see on TV.

If you don't want to be onstage, you can still play an inter-active role in the audience by controlling cannons that blast contestants with water, air, and other such things (like hard rubber balls . . . ouch!). Prepare to be grossed out—much like the massive coasters here, parts of this show are not for the faint of heart or anyone with a weak stomach; many of the stunts may be too intense for kids younger than six years.

TOURING TIPS Apparently, the odds are more in your favor for get-ting into Harvard than being chosen to appear on the TV ver-sion of Fear Factor, so if you've ever wanted a chance to test your mettle, the live show may be your big chance. Participants for the physical stunts are chosen early in the morning outside the theater, so be sure to head there first thing if you want to be a contestant. The victims—er, contestants—for the ick-factor stunts, like the bug smoothie drinking, are chosen directly from the audience. Sit close to the front and wave your hands like crazy when it comes time for selection.

Fievel's Playland

| APPEAL BY AGE | PRESCHOOL ★★★★ | GRADE SCHOOL ★★★★ | TEENS — |
| YOUNG ADULTS | — | OVER 30 — | SENIORS — |

What it is Children's play area with water slide. **Scope and scale** Minor attraction. **When to go** Anytime. **Author's rating** A much-needed attraction for preschoolers; ★★★★. **Probable waiting time** 20–30 minutes for the water slide; otherwise, no waiting.

DESCRIPTION AND COMMENTS Imaginative playground features ordinary household items reproduced on a giant scale, as a mouse would experience them. Preschoolers and grade-schoolers can climb nets, walk through a huge boot, splash in a sardine-can fountain, seesaw on huge spoons, and climb onto a cow skull. Most of the playground is reserved for preschoolers, but a water slide/raft ride is open to all ages.

TOURING TIPS Walk into Fievel's Playland without waiting, and stay as long as you want. Younger children love the oversized items, and there's enough to keep teens and adults busy while little ones let off steam. The water slide/raft ride is open to everyone but is extremely slow-loading and carries only 300 riders per hour. With an average wait of 20–30 minutes, we don't think the 16-second ride is worth the trouble. Also, you're highly likely to get soaked.

Lack of shade is a major shortcoming of the entire attraction. Don't go during the heat of the day.

Jaws (Universal Express)

| APPEAL BY AGE | PRESCHOOL ★★½ | GRADE SCHOOL ★★★★ | TEENS ★★★★ |
| YOUNG ADULTS ★★★★ | | OVER 30 ★★★★ | SENIORS ★★★★ |

What it is Adventure boat ride. **Scope and scale** Headliner. **When to go** Before 11 a.m. or after 5 p.m. **Special comments** Will frighten young children. **Author's rating** Not to be missed; ★★★★. **Duration of ride** 5 minutes. **Loading speed** Fast. **Probable waiting time** per 100 people ahead of you 3 minutes. **Assumes** All 8 boats are running.

DESCRIPTION AND COMMENTS Jaws delivers five minutes of nonstop action, with the huge shark repeatedly attacking. A West Virginia woman, fresh from the Magic Kingdom, told us the shark is "about as pesky as that witch in Snow White." While the story is entirely predictable, the shark fairly realistic and as big as a boxcar, what makes the ride unique is its sense of journey. Jaws builds an amazing degree of suspense. It isn't just a cruise into the middle of a pond where a rubber fish assaults the boat interminably. Add inventive sets and powerful special effects, and you have a first-rate attraction.

A variable at Jaws is the enthusiasm and acting ability of your boat guide. Throughout the ride, the guide must set the tone, elaborate the plot, drive the boat, and fight the shark. Most guides are quite good. They may overact, but you can't fault them for lack of enthusiasm. Consider also that each guide repeats this wrenching ordeal every eight minutes.

TOURING TIPS Jaws is well designed to handle crowds. People on the boat's left side tend to get splashed more.

A mother of two from Williamsville, New York, who believes our warning about getting wet should be more strongly emphasized, has this to say:

Your warning about the Jaws attraction . . is woefully understated. Please warn your readers—we were seated on the first row of the boat. My nine-year-old sat at the end of the boat (first person on the far left), and I was seated next to him. We were wary of these seats as I had read your warning, but I felt prepared. NOT!!!! At that moment the water came flooding over the left front side of the boat, thoroughly drenching the two of us and filling our sneakers with water. Unfortunately for us, this was only our third attraction of the day (9:30 a.m.) and we still had a long day ahead of us. It was a rather chilly and windy 62-degree day. We went to the restrooms, removed our shorts, and squeezed out as much water as we could, but we were very cold and uncomfortable all day. This will be our most vivid and lasting memory of our day at Universal Studios!!!

A dad from Seattle suggests that getting wet takes a backseat to being terrified:

Our eight-year-old was so frightened by Jaws that we scrapped the rest of the Universal tour and went back to E.T. An employee said she wouldn't recommend it to anyone under ten. Maybe you should change "may frighten small children" to "definitely will scare the pants off most children."

Jimmy Neutron's Nicktoon Blast (Universal Express)

APPEAL BY AGE	PRESCHOOL ★★★	GRADE SCHOOL ★★★★	TEENS ★★★
YOUNG ADULTS ★★★		OVER 30 ★★½	SENIORS ★★

What it is Cartoon science demonstration and simulation ride. **Scope and scale** Major attraction. **When to go** The first hour after park opening or after 5 p.m. **Author's rating** Incomprehensible but fun ★★★.

Duration of ride A little over 4 minutes. **Loading speed** Moderate to slow. **Probable waiting time per 100 people ahead of you** 5 minutes. **Assumes** All 8 simulators in use.

DESCRIPTION AND COMMENTS This ride features motion simulators that move and react in synch with a cartoon projected onto a huge screen. Based on the Nickelodeon movie *Jimmy Neutron: Boy Genius,* this attraction replaced The Funtastic World of Hanna-Barbera. In addition to Jimmy, the attraction features a mob of other characters from Nickelodeon, including Sponge-Bob SquarePants, the Rugrats, the Fairly Odd Parents, and the Wild Thornberrys. The story, inasmuch as Universal explains it, takes place in two parts. First, guests are invited to participate in a demonstration of Jimmy's newest invention, which is stolen before the demonstration can proceed. After that, an alien plot is revealed, and guests are strapped into motion-simulator vehicles in order to help Jimmy rescue his invention and defend the Earth. In practice, the plot is absolutely incomprehensible (at least to an adult). All we can report after riding about a dozen times is that there is a frenetic high-speed chase punctuated by an abundance of screaming (also incomprehensible) in piercing, very high pitched, cartoony voices.

TOURING TIPS This attraction is drawing sizeable crowds primarily because its new, and because its next door to the new *Shrek 4-D* attraction. We think Jimmy Neutron is at best a so-so effort, and not much of an improvement over its predecessor. Except for avid *Jimmy Neutron* cartoon fans, in other words, it's expendable. If you can't live without it, ride during the first hour the park is open, after 5 p.m., or use Universal Express. Be aware that a very small percentage of riders suffer motion sickness. Stationary seating is available and is mandated for persons less than 40 inches tall.

Lucy, a Tribute

APPEAL BY AGE	PRESCHOOL ★	GRADE SCHOOL ★★	TEENS ★★
YOUNG ADULTS ★★★	OVER 30 ★★★		SENIORS ★★★

What it is Walk-through tribute to Lucille Ball. **Scope and scale** Diversion. **When to go** Anytime. **Author's rating** A touching remembrance; ★★★ **Probable waiting time** None.

DESCRIPTION AND COMMENTS The life and career of comedienne Lucille Ball are spotlighted, with emphasis on her role as Lucy Ricardo in the long-running television series *I Love Lucy.* Well designed and informative, the exhibit succeeds admirably in recalling the talent and temperament of the beloved redhead.

TOURING TIPS See Lucy during the hot, crowded midafternoon, or on your way out of the park. Adults could easily stay 15–30 minutes. Children, however, get restless after a couple of minutes.

Men in Black Alien Attack (Universal Express)

APPEAL BY AGE	PRESCHOOL †	GRADE SCHOOL ★★★★½	TEENS ★★★★★
YOUNG ADULTS ★★★★★		OVER 30 ★★★★★	SENIORS ★★★★

† Sample size too small for an accurate rating.

What it is Interactive dark thrill ride. **Scope and scale** Super headliner. **When to go** In the morning after Revenge of the Mummy. **Special comments** May induce motion sickness. Must be 42 inches tall to ride. **Author's rating** Buzz Lightyear on steroids; not to be missed; ★★★★½. **Duration of ride** 2½ minutes. **Loading speed** Moderate to fast.

DESCRIPTION AND COMMENTS Based on the movie of the same name, Men in Black brings together actors Will Smith and Rip Torn (as Agent J and MIB Director Zed) for an interactive sequel to the hit film. The story line has you volunteering as a Men in Black (MIB) trainee. After an introduction warning that aliens "live among us" and articulating MIB's mission to round them up, Zed expands on the finer points of alien spotting and familiarizes you with your training vehicle and your weapon, an alien "zapper." Following this, you load up and are dispatched on an innocuous training mission that immediately deteriorates into a situation where only you are in a position to prevent aliens from taking over the universe. Now, if you saw the movie, you understand that the aliens are mostly giant, exotic bugs and cockroaches and that zapping the aliens involves exploding them into myriad gooey body parts. Thus, the meat of the ride (no pun intended) consists of careening around Manhattan in your MIB vehicle and shooting aliens. The technology at work is similar to that used in the Spider-Man attraction at Universal's Islands of Adventure, which is to say that it's both a wild ride and one where movies, sets, robotics, and your vehicle are all integrated into a fairly seamless package.

Men in Black is interactive in that your marksmanship and ability to blast yourself out of some tricky situations will determine how the story ends. Also, you are awarded a personal score (like Disney's Buzz Lightyear's Space Ranger Spin) and a score for your car. There are about three dozen possible outcomes and literally thousands of different ride experiences determined by your pluck, performance, and in the final challenge your intestinal fortitude.

TOURING TIPS Each of the 120 or so alien figures has sensors that activate special effects and respond to your zapper. Aim for the eyes and keep shooting until the aliens' eyes turn red.

Also, many of the aliens shoot back, causing your vehicle to veer or spin. In the mayhem, you might fail to notice that another vehicle of guests runs along beside you on a dual track. This was included to instill a spirit of competition for anyone who finds blowing up bugs and saving the universe less than stimulating. Note that at a certain point, you can shoot the flashing "vent" on top of this other car and make them spin around. Of course, they can do the same to you . . . .

Although there are many possible endings, the long lines at this headliner attraction will probably dissuade you from experiencing all but one or two. To avoid a long wait, hotfoot it to MIB immediately after riding Mummy the first 30 minutes the park is open.

Nickelodeon Studios–Nick Live!

**APPEAL BY AGE PRESCHOOL ★★½ GRADE SCHOOL ★★★★ TEENS ★★★
YOUNG ADULTS ★★★ OVER 30 ★★★ SENIORS ★★★**

What it is Nickelodeon Studios Tour and show. **Scope and scale** Minor attraction. **When to go** As per the show times in the handout park map. **Author's rating** ★★★. **Duration of tour** 36 minutes. **Probable waiting time** 30–45 minutes.

DESCRIPTION AND COMMENTS The tour examines set construction, soundstages, wardrobe, props, lighting, video production, and special effects. Much of this information is presented more creatively in the *Horror Make-Up Show* production, but the Nickelodeon tour is tailored for kids. They're made to feel supremely important; their opinions are used to shape future Nickelodeon programming.

Nick Live! is a short version of the TV show, where guests play strange games being tested for possible inclusion on Nickelodeon. Adding some much-needed zip, the show ends with a lucky child getting "slimed." If you don't understand, consult your children.

TOURING TIPS While grade-schoolers, especially, enjoy this tour, it's expendable for everyone else. Go on a second day or second visit at Universal.

Revenge of the Mummy (Universal Express)

**APPEAL BY AGE PRESCHOOL ★★ GRADE SCHOOL ★★★★ TEENS ★★★★★
YOUNG ADULTS ★★★★½ OVER 30 ★★★★ SENIORS ★★★½**

What it is Combination dark ride and roller coaster. **Scope and scale** Super headliner. **When to go** The first hour the park is open or after 6 p.m. **Special comments** 48-inch minimum-height requirement. **Author's rating** Killer! ★★★★½. **Duration of ride** 3 minutes. **Probable waiting time per 100 people ahead of you** 7 minutes. **Loading speed** Moderate.

DESCRIPTION AND COMMENTS Revenge of the Mummy replaced Kongfrontation in the New York section of the park in spring 2004. It's kinda hard to wrap your mind around the attraction, but trust us when we say you're in for a very strange experience. Here, quoting Universal, are some of the things you can look forward to:

- Authentic Egyptian catacombs
- High-velocity show immersion system (we think this has something to do with very fast baptism)
- Magnet-propulsion launch wave system
- A "Brain Fire" (!!!!) that hovers [over guests] with temperatures soaring to 2,000 degrees Farenheit
- Canoptic jars containing grisly remains

Reading between the lines, Revenge of the Mummy is an indoor dark ride based on the Mummy flicks, where guests fight off "deadly curses and vengeful creatures" while flying through Egyptian tombs and other spooky places on a high-tech roller coaster. The special effects are cutting edge, integrating the best technology from such attractions as *Terminator 2: 3-D,* Spider-Man (the ride), and Back to the Future, with groundbreaking visuals. It's way cool.

The queuing area serves to establish the story line: You're in a group touring a set from the Mummy films when you enter a tomb where the fantasy world of film gives way to the real thing. Along the way you are warned about a possible curse. The visuals are rich and compelling as the queue makes its way to the loading area where you board a sort of clunky, jeep-looking vehicle. The ride begins as a slow, very elaborate dark ride, passing through various chambers including one where flesh-eating scarab beetles descend on you. Suddenly your vehicle stops, then drops backwards and rotates. Here's where the aforementioned "magnet-propulsion launch wave system" comes in. In more ordinary language, this means you're shot at high speed up the first hill of the roller coaster part of the ride. We don't want to ruin your experience by divulging too much, but the coaster part of the ride offers its own panoply of surprises. We will tell you this, however: there are no barrell rolls or any upside-down stuff. And though it's a wild ride by anyone's definition, the emphasis remains as much on the visuals, robotics, and special effects as on the ride itself.

TOURING TIPS Revenge of the Mummy has a very low riders-per-hour capacity for a super-headliner attraction, and especially for the park's top draw. Waits, even using Universal Express, will run longer than an Academy Awards show. Your only prayer for a tolerable wait is to be on hand when the park opens and sprint immediately to the Mummy. One fallback is to use Universal Express, but even with Univeral Express expect a sizeable wait after 11 a.m. A second option is to use the singles line. This is often more expedient than Universal Express. Concerning motion sickness, if you can ride Space Mountain without ill effect, you should be fine on Revenge of the Mummy.

Shrek 4-D (Universal Express)

APPEAL BY AGE PRESCHOOL ★★★★ GRADE SCHOOL ★★★★½ TEENS ★★★★½
YOUNG ADULTS ★★★★½ OVER 30 ★★★★½ SENIORS ★★★★½

What it is 3-D movie. **Scope and scale** Headliner. **When to go** The first hour the park is open or after 4 p.m. **Author's rating** Warm, fuzzy mayhem; ★★★★½. **Duration of presentation** 20 minutes.

DESCRIPTION AND COMMENTS Based on characters from the hit movie *Shrek*, the preshow presents the villain from the movie, Lord Farquaad, as he appears on various screens to describe his posthumous plan to reclaim his lost bride, Princess Fiona, who married Shrek. The plan is posthumous since Lord Farquaad ostensibly died in the movie, and it's his ghost making the plans, but never mind. Guests then move into the main theater, don their 3-D glasses, and recline in seats equipped with "tactile transducers" and "pneumatic air propulsion and water spray nodules capable of both vertical and horizontal motion." As the 3-D film plays, guests are also subjected to smells relevant to the on-screen action (oh boy).

Technicalities aside, *Shrek* is a real winner. It's irreverent, frantic, laugh-out-loud funny, and iconoclastic. Concerning the latter, the film takes a good poke at Disney with Pinnocchio, the Three Little Pigs, and Tinkerbelle (among others) all sucked into the mayhem. The film quality and 3-D effects are great, and like the feature film, it's sweet without being sappy. Plus, in contrast to Disney's *Honey, I Shrunk the Audience* or *It's Tough to Be a Bug!*, *Shrek 4-D* doesn't generally frighten children under 7 years of age.

TOURING TIPS Universal claims they can move 2,400 guests an hour through *Shrek 4-D*. However, its popularity means that Express passes for the day may be gone as early as 10 a.m., and waits in the regular line may exceed an hour. Bear that in mind when scheduling your day.

Street Scenes

APPEAL BY AGE PRESCHOOL ★★★ GRADE SCHOOL ★★★★½ TEENS ★★★★½
YOUNG ADULTS ★★★★½ OVER 30 ★★★★★ SENIORS ★★★★★

What it is Elaborate outdoor sets for making films. **Scope and scale** Diversion. **When to go** Anytime. **Special comments** You'll see most sets without special effort as you tour the park. **Author's rating** One of the park's great assets; ★★★★★ **Probable waiting time** No waiting.

DESCRIPTION AND COMMENTS Unlike at Disney-MGM Studios, all Universal Studios Florida's backlot sets are accessible for guest inspection. They include New York City streets, San Francisco's waterfront, a New England coastal town, Rodeo Drive, and Hollywood Boulevard.

TOURING TIPS You'll see most as you walk through the park.

Terminator 2: 3-D Battle Across Time

APPEAL BY AGE	PRESCHOOL ★★★	GRADE SCHOOL ★★★★	TEENS ★★★★★
YOUNG ADULTS ★★★★★		OVER 30 ★★★★★	SENIORS ★★★★

What it is 3-D thriller mixed-media presentation. **Scope and scale** Super headliner. **When to go** After 3:30 p.m. **Special comments** The nation's best theme-park theater attraction; very intense for some preschoolers and grade-schoolers. **Author's rating** Furiously paced high-tech experience; not to be missed; ★★★★★. **Duration of presentation** 20 minutes, including an 8-minute preshow. **Probable waiting time** 20–40 minutes.

DESCRIPTION AND COMMENTS The *Terminator* "cop" from *Terminator 2* morphs to life and battles Arnold Schwarzenegger's T-100 cyborg character. If you missed the *Terminator* flicks, here's the plot: A bad robot arrives from the future to kill a nice boy. Another bad robot (who has been reprogrammed to be good) pops up at the same time to save the boy. The bad robot chases the boy and the rehabilitated robot, menacing the audience in the process.

The attraction, like the films, is all action, and you really don't need to understand much. What's interesting is that it uses 3-D film and a theater full of sophisticated technology to integrate the real with the imaginary. Images seem to move in and out of the film, not only in the manner of traditional 3-D, but also in actuality. Remove your 3-D glasses momentarily and you'll see that the guy on the motorcycle is actually onstage.

We've watched this type of presentation evolve, pioneered by Disney's *Captain EO, Honey, I Shrunk the Audience,* and *Muppet-Vision 3-D. Terminator 2: 3-D,* however, goes way beyond lasers, with moving theater seats, blasts of hot air, and spraying mist. It creates a multidimensional space that blurs the boundary between entertainment and reality. Is it seamless? Not quite, but it's close. We rank *Terminator 2: 3-D* as not to be missed and consider it the absolute best theme-park theater attraction in the United States. If *Terminator 2: 3-D* is the only attraction you see at Universal Studios Florida, you'll have received your money's worth.

TOURING TIPS The 700-seat theater changes audiences about every 19 minutes. Even so, because the show is hot, expect to wait about 30–45 minutes. The attraction, on Hollywood Boulevard near the park's entrance, receives huge traffic during morning and early afternoon. By about 3 p.m., however, lines diminish somewhat. Though you'll still wait, we recommend holding off on *Terminator 2: 3-D* until then. If you can't stay until late afternoon, see the show first thing in the morning. Families with young children should know that the violence characteristic of the *Terminator* movies is largely absent from the attraction. There's suspense and action but not much blood and guts.

Twister (Universal Express)

APPEAL BY AGE   PRESCHOOL ★★   GRADE SCHOOL ★★★★   TEENS ★★★★
YOUNG ADULTS ★★★★   OVER 30 ★★★★   SENIORS ★★★★

What it is Theater presentation featuring special effects from the movie *Twister*. **Scope and scale** Major attraction. **When to go** Should be your first show after experiencing all rides. **Special comments** High potential for frightening young children. **Author's rating** Gusty; ★★★½. **Duration of presentation** 15 minutes. **Probable waiting time** 26 minutes.

DESCRIPTION AND COMMENTS *Twister* combines an elaborate set and special effects, climaxing with a five-story-tall simulated tornado created by circulating more than 2 million cubic feet of air per minute.

TOURING TIPS The wind, pounding rain, and freight-train sound of the tornado are deafening, and the entire presentation is exceptionally intense. School children are mightily impressed, while younger children are terrified and overwhelmed. Unless you want the kids hopping in your bed whenever they hear thunder, try this attraction yourself before taking your kids.

Universal Horror Make-Up Show (Universal Express)

APPEAL BY AGE   PRESCHOOL ★★★   GRADE SCHOOL ★★★½   TEENS ★★★½
YOUNG ADULTS ★★★½   OVER 30 ★★★½   SENIORS ★★★½

What it is Theater presentation on the art of make-up. **Scope and scale** Major attraction. **When to go** After you have experienced all rides. **Special comments** May frighten young children. **Author's rating** A gory knee-slapper; ★★★½. **Duration of presentation** 25 minutes. **Probable waiting time** 20 minutes.

DESCRIPTION AND COMMENTS Lively, well-paced look at how make-up artists create film monsters, realistic wounds, severed limbs, and other unmentionables. Funnier and more upbeat than many Universal Studios presentations, the show also presents a wealth of fascinating information. It's excellent and enlightening, if somewhat gory.

TOURING TIPS Exceeding most guests' expectations, the *Horror Make-Up Show* is the sleeper attraction at Universal. Its humor and tongue-in-cheek style transcend the gruesome effects, and most folks (including preschoolers) take the blood and guts in stride. It usually isn't too hard to get into.

Woody Woodpecker's Nuthouse Coaster and Curious George Goes to Town Playground

APPEAL BY AGE	PRESCHOOL ★★★★	GRADE SCHOOL —	TEENS —
YOUNG ADULTS —		OVER 30 —	SENIORS —

What it is Interactive playground and kid's roller coaster. **Scope and scale** Minor attraction. **When to go** Anytime. **Author's rating** A good place to let off steam; ★★★.

DESCRIPTION AND COMMENTS Rounding out the selection of other nearby kid-friendly attractions, this KidZone offering consists of Woody Woodpecker's Nuthouse Coaster and an interactive playground called Curious George Goes to Town. The child-sized roller coaster is small enough for kids to enjoy but sturdy enough for adults, though its moderate speed might unnerve some smaller children (the minimum height to ride is 36 inches). The Curious George playground exemplifies the Universal obsession with wet stuff; in addition to innumerable spigots, pipes, and spray guns, two giant roof-mounted buckets periodically dump a thousand gallons of water on unsuspecting visitors below. Kids who want to stay dry can mess around in the foam-ball playground, also equipped with chutes, tubes, and ball-blasters.

TOURING TIPS After its unveiling, Universal employees dubbed this area "Peckerland." Visit the playground after you've experienced all the major attractions.

UNIVERSAL STUDIOS FLORIDA ONE-DAY TOURING PLAN

THIS PLAN IS FOR ALL VISITORS. If a ride or show is listed that you don't want to experience, skip that step and proceed to the next. Move quickly from attraction to attraction and, if possible, don't stop for lunch until after Step 9. Minor street shows occur at various times and places throughout the day; check the daily schedule for details.

BUYING ADMISSION TO UNIVERSAL STUDIOS FLORIDA

One of our big gripes about Universal Studios is that there are never enough ticket windows open in the morning to accommodate the crowd. You can arrive 45 minutes before official opening time and still be in line to buy your admission when the park opens. Therefore, we strongly recommend you buy your admission in advance. Passes are available by mail from Universal Studios at ☎ 800-224-3838. They are also sold at the concierge desk or attractions box office of many Orlando-area hotels. If your hotel doesn't offer tickets, try Guest Services at the Doubletree Hotel ☎ 407-351-1000, at the intersection of Major Boulevard and Kirkman Avenue.

unofficial **TIP**
Pay before you play: buy your tickets to Univeral Studios before you arrive at the park to avoid long lines at the ticket windows.

Many hotels that sell Universal admissions don't issue actual passes. Instead, the purchaser gets a voucher that can be redeemed for a pass at the theme park. Fortunately, the voucher-redemption window is separate from the park's ticket sales operation. You can quickly exchange your voucher for a pass and be on your way with little or no wait.

TOURING PLAN

1. Call ☎ 407-363-8000 the day before your visit for the official opening time.

2. On the day of your visit, eat breakfast and arrive at Universal Studios Florida 20–25 minutes before opening time with your admission pass or an admission voucher in hand.
   If you have a voucher, exchange it for a pass at the voucher-redemption window. Pick up a map and the daily entertainment schedule.

3. Line up at the turnstile. Ask any attendant whether any rides or shows are closed that day. Adjust the touring plan accordingly.

4. When the park opens, go straight down the Plaza of the Stars. Pass Rodeo Drive on your right. When you reach Nickelodeon Way on your left, you should be standing between Jimmy Neutron's Nicktoon Blast on your left and *Shrek 4-D* on your right. If both are up and running, try to get a Universal Express pass for *Shrek 4-D* usable later in the day (around lunchtime if possible). If you can't get a *Shrek 4-D* pass for that time period, don't sweat it; *Shrek 4-D* has

a large enough capacity to keep lines moving even on crowded days. Plan to return to the altogether-expendable Jimmy Neutron later in the day, using Universal Express.

5. Proceed toward the back of the park (past SoundStage 54) to the New York section and ride Revenge of the Mummy.

6. Now head to Men in Black: Alien Attack. From Revenge of the Mummy, proceed with the lagoon on your right along the Embarcadero, along Amity Avenue, and over the bridge to get there. If you're leaving from Jimmy Neutron's Nictkoon Blast or *Shrek 4-D,* take a left on Rodeo Drive to Hollywood Boulevard, pass Mel's Diner (on your left), and (keeping the lagoon on your left) go directly to Men in Black. Ride.

7. After Men in Black, backtrack to Back to the Future and ride.

8. Exit left and pass the International Food Bazaar. If crowds are heavy, this might be about time for lunch, for your *Shrek 4-D* Universal Express pass, or both. If you want to keep going, continue bearing left past *Animal Planet Live!* and go to the E.T. Adventure Ride.

9. Retrace your steps toward Back to the Future. Keeping the lagoon on your left, cross the bridge to Amity. Ride Jaws.

10. Exit and turn left down The Embarcadero. Ride *Earthquake– The Big One,* which is right next door to Jaws.

11. Work your way back toward the main entrance. Is it time for your Universal Express window for *Shrek 4-D* yet? If so, see *Shrek 4-D.* If not, take a breather and have lunch. Unless your *Shrek 4-D* time window is a long way off, see that show before moving on to Step 12.

12. If you're still intact after various alien assaults, a bike ride to another galaxy, a shark attack, an earthquake, and an encounter with a smelly ogre, take on a tornado. Return to the New York set and see *Twister.* The line will appear long but should move quickly as guests are admitted inside.

13. If you haven't already eaten, do so now. Work in your *Shrek 4-D* visit if that hasn't come along yet.

14. At this point you have four major attractions yet to see:

   Animal Planet Live!
   Beetlejuice's Rock 'n' Roll Graveyard Revue
   Fear Factor Live
   The Gory Gruesome and Grotesque Horror Make-Up Show
   Terminator 2: 3-D

   Animal Planet Live!, the *Beetlejuice* show, *Fear Factor Live,* and the *Horror Make-Up Show* are performed several times daily, as listed in the entertainment schedule. Plan the remainder of your itinerary according to the next listed shows for these presentations. Try to see *Terminator 2: 3-D* after 3:30 p.m., but whatever you do, don't miss it.

15. Our touring plan doesn't include the Nickelodeon Studios Tour–*Nick Live!,* Woody Woodpecker's KidZone, or *A Day in the Park with Barney.* If you have school-age children in your party, consider taking the Nickelodeon tour in late afternoon or on a second day at the park. If you're touring with preschoolers, see *Barney* after you ride E. T., and then head for KidZone.

16. This concludes the touring plan. Spend the remainder of your day revisiting your favorite attractions or inspecting sets and street scenes you may have missed. Also, check your daily entertainment schedule for live performances that interest you.

UNIVERSAL'S ISLANDS *of* ADVENTURE

WHEN UNIVERSAL'S ISLANDS OF ADVENTURE theme park opened in 1999, it provided Universal with enough critical mass to actually compete with Disney. Universal finally has on-site hotels, a shopping and entertainment complex, and two major theme parks. Doubly interesting is that the new Universal park is pretty much just for fun—in other words, a direct competitor to Disney's Magic Kingdom, the most visited theme park in the world. How direct a competitor is it? Check out the box on the facing page for a comparison.

And though it may take central Florida tourists awhile to make the connection, here's what will dawn on them when they finally do: Universal's Islands of Adventure is a state-of-the-art park competing with a Disney park that is more than 25 years old and has not added a new super-headliner attraction for many years.

Of course, that's only how it looks on paper. The reality, as they say, is still blowing in the wind. The Magic Kingdom, after all, is graceful in its maturity and much beloved. And then there was the question on everyone's mind: could Universal really pull it off? Recalling the disastrous first year that the Universal Studios Florida park experienced, we held our breath to see if Islands of Adventure's innovative, high-tech attractions would work. Well, not only did they work, they were up and running almost two months ahead of schedule. Thus, the clash of the titans is once again hot. Universal is coming on strong with the potential of sucking up three days of a tourist's week (more, if you include Universal's strategic relationship with SeaWorld and Busch Gardens). And that's more time than anyone has spent off the Disney campus for a long, long time.

> *unofficial* **TIP**
> Roller coasters at Islands of Adventure are the real deal, and not for the feint of heart, nor for little ones.

Through it all, Disney and Universal spokesmen downplay their fierce competition, pointing out that any new theme park or attraction makes central Florida a more marketable destination. Behind closed doors, however, it's a Pepsi/Coke–type rivalry that will keep both companies working hard to gain a competitive edge. The good news, of course, is that this competition translates into better and better attractions for you to enjoy.

BEWARE OF THE WET AND WILD

ALTHOUGH WE HAVE DESCRIBED UNIVERSAL'S Islands of Adventure as a direct competitor to the Magic Kingdom, there is one major qualification you should be aware of. Whereas most Magic Kingdom attractions are designed to be enjoyed by guests of any age, attractions at Islands of Adventure are largely created for an under-40 population. The roller coasters at Universal are serious with a capital "S," making Space Mountain and Big Thunder Mountain look about as tough as Dumbo. In

> *unofficial* **TIP**
> Several attractions at Islands of Adventure will drench you to the bone, so beware.

fact, seven out of the nine top attractions at Islands are thrill rides, and of these, there are three that not only scare the bejeezus out of you but also drench you with water.

For families, there are three interactive playgrounds as well as six rides that young children will enjoy. Of the thrill rides, only the two in Toon Lagoon (described later) are marginally appropriate for young children, and even on these rides your child needs to be fairly stalwart.

ISLANDS OF ADVENTURE VERSUS THE MAGIC KINGDOM	
ISLANDS OF ADVENTURE	**MAGIC KINGDOM**
Six Islands (includes Port of Entry)	Seven Lands (includes Main Street)
Two adult roller-coaster attractions	Two adult roller-coaster attractions
A Dumbo-type ride	Dumbo
One flume ride	One flume ride
Toon Lagoon character area	Mickey's Toontown character area

Islands of Adventure

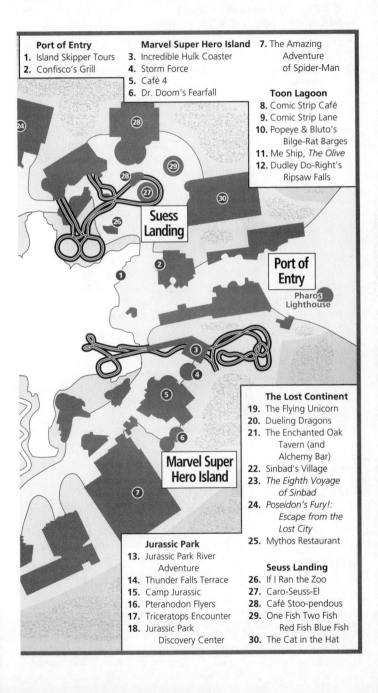

Port of Entry
1. Island Skipper Tours
2. Confisco's Grill

Marvel Super Hero Island
3. Incredible Hulk Coaster
4. Storm Force
5. Café 4
6. Dr. Doom's Fearfall
7. The Amazing Adventure of Spider-Man

Toon Lagoon
8. Comic Strip Café
9. Comic Strip Lane
10. Popeye & Bluto's Bilge-Rat Barges
11. Me Ship, *The Olive*
12. Dudley Do-Right's Ripsaw Falls

Jurassic Park
13. Jurassic Park River Adventure
14. Thunder Falls Terrace
15. Camp Jurassic
16. Pteranodon Flyers
17. Triceratops Encounter
18. Jurassic Park Discovery Center

The Lost Continent
19. The Flying Unicorn
20. Dueling Dragons
21. The Enchanted Oak Tavern (and Alchemy Bar)
22. Sinbad's Village
23. *The Eighth Voyage of Sinbad*
24. *Poseidon's Fury!: Escape from the Lost City*
25. Mythos Restaurant

Seuss Landing
26. If I Ran the Zoo
27. Caro-Seuss-El
28. Café Stoo-pendous
29. One Fish Two Fish Red Fish Blue Fish
30. The Cat in the Hat

GETTING ORIENTED AT
ISLANDS OF ADVENTURE

BOTH UNIVERSAL THEME PARKS are accessed via the Universal CityWalk entertainment complex. Crossing CityWalk from the parking garages, you can bear right to Universal Studios Florida or left to Universal's Islands of Adventure.

Universal's Islands of Adventure is arranged much like the World Showcase section of Epcot, in a large circle surrounding a lake. Unlike Epcot, however, the Islands of Adventure theme areas evidence the sort of thematic continuity pioneered by Disneyland and the Magic Kingdom. Each land, or island in this case, is self-contained and visually consistent in its theme, though you can see parts of the other islands across the lake.

Passing through the turnstiles, you first encounter the Moroccan-style Port of Entry, where you will find Guest Services, lockers, stroller and wheelchair rentals, ATM banking, lost and found, and, of course, shopping. From the Port of Entry, moving clockwise around the lake, you can access Marvel Super Hero Island, Toon Lagoon, Jurassic Park, the Lost Continent, and Seuss Landing. You can crisscross the lake on small boats, but otherwise there is no in-park transportation.

NOT TO BE MISSED AT ISLANDS OF ADVENTURE

The Incredible Hulk Coaster	Dueling Dragons
The Adventures of Spider-Man	Poseidon's Fury!
Jurassic Park River Adventure	

ISLANDS *of* ADVENTURE ATTRACTIONS
MARVEL SUPER HERO ISLAND

THIS ISLAND, WITH ITS FUTURISTIC and retro-future design and comic book signage, offers shopping and attractions based on Marvel Comics characters.

The Amazing Adventures of Spider-Man
(Universal Express)

APPEAL BY AGE PRESCHOOL ★★★ GRADE SCHOOL ★★★★½ TEENS ★★★★★
YOUNG ADULTS ★★★★★ OVER 30 ★★★★★ SENIORS ★★★★

What it is Indoor adventure simulator ride based on Spider-Man. **Scope and scale** Super headliner. **When to go** Before 10 a.m. **Special**

comments Must be 40 inches tall to ride. **Author's rating** Our choice for the best attraction in the park; ★★★★★. **Duration of ride** 4½ minutes. **Loading speed** Fast.

DESCRIPTION AND COMMENTS Covering 1.5 acres and combining moving ride vehicles, 3-D film, and live action, Spider-Man is frenetic, fluid, and astounding. The visuals are rich, and the ride is wild, but not jerky. Although the attractions are not directly comparable, Spider-Man is technologically on a par with Disney-MGM's Tower of Terror, which is to say that it will leave you in awe. As a personal aside, we love both and would be hard pressed to choose one over the other.

The storyline is that you are a reporter for the *Daily Bugle* newspaper (where Peter Parker, aka Spider-Man, works as a mild-mannered photographer), when it's discovered that evil villains have stolen (I promise I'm not making this up) the Statue of Liberty. You are drafted on the spot by your cantankerous editor to go get the story. After speeding around and being thrust into "a battle between good and evil," you experience a 400-foot "sensory drop" from a skyscraper roof all the way to the pavement. Because the ride is so wild and the action so continuous, it's hard to understand the plot, but you're so thoroughly entertained that you don't really care. Plus, you'll want to ride again and again. Eventually, with repetition, the story line will begin to make sense.

TOURING TIPS Ride first thing in the morning after The Incredible Hulk Coaster or in the hour before closing.

Dr. Doom's Fearfall (Universal Express)

APPEAL BY AGE	PRESCHOOL —	GRADE SCHOOL ★★★	TEENS ★★★★
YOUNG ADULTS ★★★½		OVER 30 ★★★	SENIORS —

What it is Lunch liberator. **Scope and scale** Headliner. **When to go** Before 9:15 a.m. **Special comments** Must be 52 inches tall to ride. **Author's rating** More bark than bite; ★★★. **Duration of ride** 40 seconds. **Loading speed** Slow.

DESCRIPTION AND COMMENTS Here you are (again) strapped into a seat with your feet dangling and blasted 200 feet up in the air and then allowed to partially free-fall back down. If you are having trouble forming a mental image of this attraction, picture the midway game where a macho guy swings a sledgehammer, propelling a metal sphere up a vertical shaft. At the top of the shaft is a bell. If the macho man drives the sphere high enough to ring the bell, he wins a prize. Got the idea? OK, on this ride you are the metal sphere.

The good news is this ride looks much worse than it actually is. The scariest part by far is the apprehension that builds as you sit, strapped in, waiting for the thing to launch. The blasting up and free-falling down parts are really very pleasant.

TOURING TIPS We've seen glaciers that move faster than the line to Dr. Doom. If you want to ride without investing half a day, be one of the first in the park to ride. Fortunately, if you're on hand at opening time, being among the first isn't too difficult (mainly because the nearby Hulk and Spider-Man attractions are bigger draws).

The Incredible Hulk Coaster (Universal Express)

APPEAL BY AGE PRESCHOOL ★ GRADE SCHOOL ★★★★★ TEENS ★★★★★
YOUNG ADULTS ★★★★   OVER 30 ★★★★   SENIORS ★★½

What it is Roller coaster. **Scope and scale** Super headliner. **When to go** Before 9:30 a.m. **Special comments** Must be 54 inches tall to ride. **Author's rating** A coaster-lover's coaster; ★★★★½. **Duration of ride** 1½ minutes. **Loading speed** Moderate.

DESCRIPTION AND COMMENTS There is, as always, a story line, but for this attraction it's of no importance whatsoever. What you need to know about this attraction is simple. You will be shot like a cannonball from 0 to 40 miles per hour in two seconds, and then you will be flung upside down 100 feet off the ground, which will, of course, induce weightlessness. From there it's a mere seven rollovers punctuated by two plunges into holes in the ground before you're allowed to get out and throw up.

Seriously, the Hulk is a great roller coaster, perhaps the best in Florida, providing a ride comparable to Montu (Busch Gardens) with the added thrill of an accelerated launch (instead of the more typical uphill crank). Plus, like Montu, the ride is smooth. You won't be jarred and whiplashed on the Incredible Hulk.

TOURING TIPS The Hulk gives Spider-Man a run as the park's most popular attraction. Ride first thing in the morning. Universal provides electronic lockers near the entrance of the Hulk to deposit any items that might depart your person during the Hulk's seven inversions. Program the number of your locker into the terminal and follow the instructions. You'll receive a slip of paper with a code you can enter when you return to retrieve your stuff. The locker is free if you only use it for a short time. If you leave things in the locker for a couple of hours, however, you'll have to pay a modest rental charge. When you reach the boarding area, note that there is a separate line for those who want to ride in the first row.

Storm Force Accelatron (Universal Express)

APPEAL BY AGE PRESCHOOL ★★★½ GRADE SCHOOL ★★★ TEENS ★★★
YOUNG ADULTS ★★★   OVER 30 ★★★   SENIORS ★★★

What it is Indoor spinning ride. **Scope and scale** Minor attraction. **Special comments** May induce motion sickness. **When to go** Before

10:30 a.m. **Author's rating** Teacups in the dark; ★★★. **Duration of ride** 1½ minutes. **Loading speed** Slow.

DESCRIPTION AND COMMENTS Storm Force is a spiffed-up indoor version of Disney's nausea-inducing Mad Tea Party. Here you spin to the accompaniment of a simulated thunderstorm and swirling sound and light. There's a story line that loosely ties this midway-type ride to the Marvel Super Hero theme area, but it's largely irrelevant and offers no advice on keeping your lunch down.

TOURING TIPS Ride early or late to avoid long lines. If you're prone to motion sickness, keep your distance.

TOON LAGOON

TOON LAGOON IS CARTOON ART translated into real buildings and settings. Whimsical and gaily colored, with rounded and exaggerated lines, Toon Lagoon is Universal's answer to Mickey's Toontown Fair in the Magic Kingdom. The main difference between the two toon lands is that (as you will see) you have about a 60 percent chance of drowning at Universal's version.

Comic Strip Lane

What it is Walk-through exhibit and shopping/dining venue. **Scope and scale** Diversion. **When to go** Anytime.

DESCRIPTION AND COMMENTS This is the main street of Toon Lagoon. Here you can visit the domains of Beetle Bailey, Hagar the Horrible, Krazy Kat, the Family Circus, and Blondie and Dagwood, among others. Shops and eateries tie into the cartoon strip theme.

TOURING TIPS This is a great place for photo ops with cartoon characters in their own environment. It's also a great place to drop a few bucks in the diners and shops, but you probably already figured that out.

Dudley Do-Right's Ripsaw Falls
(Universal Express)

APPEAL BY AGE	PRESCHOOL ★★½	GRADE SCHOOL ★★★★	TEENS ★★★½
YOUNG ADULTS ★★★		OVER 30 ★★★½	SENIORS ★★½

What it is Flume ride. **Scope and scale** Major attraction. **When to go** Before 11 a.m. **Special comments** Must be 44 inches tall to ride. **Author's rating** A minimalist Splash Mountain; ★★★½. **Duration of ride** 5 minutes. **Loading speed** Moderate.

DESCRIPTION AND COMMENTS Inspired by the *Rocky and Bullwinkle* cartoon series, this ride features Canadian Mountie Dudley Do-Right as he attempts to save Nell from evil Snidely Whiplash. Story line aside, it's a flume ride, with the inevitable big drop at the end. Universal claims this is the first flume ride to "send riders plummeting 15 feet below the surface of the water." No need to bring diving gear—in reality you're just plummeting into a tunnel.

The only problem with this attraction is that everyone inevitably compares it to Splash Mountain at the Magic Kingdom. The flume is as good as Splash Mountain's, and the final drop is a whopper, but the theming and the visuals aren't even in the same league. The art, sets, audio, and jokes at Dudley Do-Right are minimalist at best; it's Dudley Do-Right's two-dimensional approach versus Splash Mountain's three-dimensional presentation. Taken on its own terms, however, Dudley Do-Right is a darn good flume ride.

TOURING TIPS This ride will get you wet, but on average not as wet as you might expect (it looks worse than it is). If you want to stay dry, however, arrive prepared with a poncho or at least a big garbage bag with holes cut out for your head and arms. After riding, take a moment to gauge the timing of the water cannons that go off along the exit walk. This is where you can really get drenched. While younger children are often intimidated by the big drop, those who ride generally enjoy themselves. Ride first thing in the morning after experiencing the Marvel Super Hero rides.

Me Ship, The Olive

APPEAL BY AGE	PRESCHOOL ★★★★	GRADE SCHOOL ★★★½	TEENS ½
YOUNG ADULTS ½		OVER 30 ½	SENIORS —

What it is Interactive playground. **Scope and scale** Minor attraction. **When to go** Anytime. **Author's rating** Colorful and appealing for kids; ★★★.

DESCRIPTION AND COMMENTS *The Olive* is Popeye's three-story boat come to life as an interactive playground. Younger children can scramble around in Sweet Pea's Playpen, while older sibs shoot water cannons at riders trying to survive the adjacent Bilge-Rat raft ride.

TOURING TIPS If you're into the big rides, save this for later in the day.

Popeye & Bluto's Bilge-Rat Barges (Universal Express)

APPEAL BY AGE	PRESCHOOL ★★★	GRADE SCHOOL ★★★★½	TEENS ★★★
YOUNG ADULTS ★★★★		OVER 30 ★★★½	SENIORS ★★½

What it is Whitewater raft ride. **Scope and scale** Major attraction. **When to go** Before 10:30 a.m. **Special comments** Must be 42 inches tall to ride. **Author's rating** Bring your own soap; ★★★★. **Duration of ride** 4½ minutes. **Loading speed** Moderate.

DESCRIPTION AND COMMENTS This sweetly named attraction is a whitewater raft ride that includes an encounter with an 18-foot-tall octopus. Engineered to ensure that everyone gets drenched, the ride even provides water cannons for highly intelligent nonparticipants ashore to fire at those aboard. The rapids are rougher and more interesting, and the ride longer, than the Animal Kingdom's Kali River Rapids. But nobody surpasses Disney for visuals and theming, though the settings of these two attractions (cartoon set and Asian jungle river, respectively) are hardly comparable.

TOURING TIPS If you didn't drown on Dudley Do-Right, here's a second chance. You'll get a lot wetter from the knees down on this ride, so use your poncho or garbage bag and ride barefoot with your britches rolled up. In terms of beating the crowds, ride the barges in the morning after experiencing the Marvel Super Hero attractions and Dudley Do-Right. If you are lacking foul weather gear or forgot your trash bag, you might want to put off riding until last thing before leaving the park. Most preschoolers enjoy the raft ride. Those who are frightened react more to the way the rapids look as opposed to the roughness of the ride.

JURASSIC PARK

JURASSIC PARK (FOR ANYONE WHO'S BEEN ASLEEP FOR 20 YEARS) is a Steven Spielberg film franchise about a fictitious theme park with real dinosaurs. Jurassic Park at Universal's Islands of Adventure is a real theme park (or at least a section of one) with fictitious dinosaurs.

Camp Jurassic

APPEAL BY AGE	PRESCHOOL ★★★	GRADE SCHOOL ★★★	TEENS —
YOUNG ADULTS —		OVER 30 —	SENIORS —

What it is Interactive play area. **Scope and scale** Minor attraction. **When to go** Anytime. **Author's rating** Creative playground, confusing layout; ★★★.

DESCRIPTION AND COMMENTS Camp Jurassic is a great place for children to cut loose. Sort of a Jurassic version of Tom Sawyer Island, kids can explore lava pits, caves, mines, and a rain forest.

TOURING TIPS Camp Jurassic will fire the imaginations of the under-13 set. If you don't impose a time limit on the exploration, you could be here awhile. The layout of the play area is confusing and intersects the queuing area for the Pteranodon Flyers. If your child accidentally lines up for the Pteranodons, he'll be college age before you see him again.

Discovery Center

APPEAL BY AGE	PRESCHOOL ★★½	GRADE SCHOOL ★★★½	TEENS ★★★
YOUNG ADULTS ★★★		OVER 30 ★★★	SENIORS ★★★

What it is Interactive natural history exhibit. **Scope and scale** Minor attraction. **When to go** Anytime. **Author's rating** ★★★.

DESCRIPTION AND COMMENTS The Discovery Center is an interactive, educational exhibit that mixes fiction from the movie *Jurassic Park,* such as using fossil DNA to bring dinosaurs to life, with various skeletal remains and other paleontological displays. One exhibit allows guests to watch an animatronic raptor being hatched. Another allows you to digitally "fuse" your DNA with a dinosaur to see what the resultant creature would look like. Other exhibits include dinosaur egg scanning and identification and a quiz called "You Bet Jurassic."

TOURING TIPS Cycle back after experiencing all the rides or on a second day. Most folks can digest this exhibit in 10–15 minutes.

Jurassic Park River Adventure (Universal Express)

APPEAL BY AGE	PRESCHOOL ★★★	GRADE SCHOOL ★★★★½	TEENS ★★★★½
YOUNG ADULTS ★★★★		OVER 30 ★★★★	SENIORS ★★★½

What it is Indoor/outdoor adventure ride based on the *Jurassic Park* movies. **Scope and scale** Super headliner. **When to go** Before 11 a.m. **Special comments** Must be 42 inches tall to ride. **Author's rating** Better than its Hollywood cousin; ★★★★. **Duration of ride** 6½ minutes. **Loading speed** Fast.

DESCRIPTION AND COMMENTS Guests board boats for a water tour of Jurassic Park. Everything is tranquil as the tour begins, and the boat floats among large herbivorous dinosaurs such as brontosaurus and stegosaurus. Then, as word is received that some of the carnivores have escaped their enclosure, the tour boat is accidentally diverted into Jurassic Park's maintenance facilities. Here, the boat and its riders are menaced by an assortment of hungry meat eaters led by the ubiquitous T-Rex. At the climactic moment, the boat and its passengers escape by plummeting over an 85-foot drop billed as the "longest, fastest, steepest water descent ever built" (did anyone other than me notice the omission of the word wettest?).

TOURING TIPS Though the boats make a huge splash at the bottom of the 85-foot drop, you don't get all that wet. Unfortunately, before the boat leaves the dock, you must sit in the puddles left by previous riders. Once underway there's a little splashing, but nothing major until the big drop at the end of the ride. When you hit the bottom, however, enough water will cascade into the air to extinguish a three-alarm fire. Fortunately, not all that much lands in the boat.

Young children must endure a double whammy on this ride. First, they are stalked by giant, salivating (sometimes spitting) reptiles, and then they're sent catapulting over the falls. Unless your children are fairly stalwart, wait a year or two before you spring the River Adventure on them.

Pteranodon Flyers

APPEAL BY AGE	PRESCHOOL ★★★	GRADE SCHOOL ★★★	TEENS ★
YOUNG ADULTS ★½		OVER 30 ★★★	SENIORS ★½

What it is Slow as Christmas. **Scope and scale** Minor attraction. **When to go** When there's no line. **Author's rating** All sizzle, no steak; ½. **Duration of ride** 1¼ minutes. **Loading speed** Slower than a hog in quicksand.

DESCRIPTION AND COMMENTS This attraction is Islands of Adventure's biggest blunder. Engineered to accommodate only 170 persons per hour (about half the hourly capacity of Dumbo!), the ride swings you along a track that passes over a small part of Jurassic Park. We recommend that you skip this one. Why? Because the Jurassic period will probably end before you reach the front of the line! And your reward for all that waiting? A one minute and fifteen second ride. Plus, the attraction has a name that nobody over 12 years old can pronounce.

TOURING TIPS Photograph the pteranodon as it flies overhead. You're probably looking at something that will someday be extinct.

THE LOST CONTINENT

THIS AREA IS AN EXOTIC MIX of Silk Road bazaar and ancient ruins, with Greco-Moroccan accents. And you thought your decorator was nuts. Anyway, this is the land of mythical gods, fabled beasts, and expensive souvenirs.

Dueling Dragons (Universal Express)

APPEAL BY AGE	PRESCHOOL —	GRADE SCHOOL ★★★★	TEENS ★★★★
YOUNG ADULTS ★★★★		OVER 30 ★★★★	SENIORS ★★

What it is Roller coaster. **Scope and scale** Headliner. **When to go** Before 10:30 a.m. **Special comments** Must be 54 inches tall to ride. **Author's rating** Almost as good as the Hulk coaster; ★★★★. **Duration of ride** 1¾ minutes. **Loading speed** Moderate.

DESCRIPTION AND COMMENTS This high-tech coaster launches two trains (Fire and Ice) at the same time on tracks that are closely intertwined. Each track is differently configured so that you get a different experience on each. Several times, a collision with the other train seems imminent, a catastrophe that seems all the more real because the coasters are inverted (i.e., suspended from above so that you sit with your feet dangling). At times, the two trains and their passengers are separated by a mere 12 inches.

Because this is an inverted coaster, your view of the action is limited unless you are sitting in the front row. This means that most passengers miss seeing all these near collisions. But don't worry; regardless of where you sit, there's plenty to keep you busy. Dueling Dragons is the highest coaster in the park and also claims the longest drop at 115 feet, not to mention five inversions. And like the Hulk, it's a nice smooth ride all the way.

Coaster cadets argue about which seat on which train provides the wildest ride. We prefer the front row on either train, but coaster loonies hype the front row of Fire and the last row of Ice.

TOURING TIPS The good news about this ride is that you won't get wet unless you wet yourself. The bad news is that wetting yourself comes pretty naturally. The other bad news is that the queuing area for Dueling Dragons is the longest, most convoluted affair we've ever seen, winding endlessly through a maze of subterranean passages. After what feels like a comprehensive tour of Mammoth Cave, you finally emerge at the loading area where you must choose between riding Fire or Ice. Of course, at this critical juncture, you're as blind as a mole rat from being in the dark for so long. Our advice is to follow the person in front of you until your eyes adjust to the light. Try to ride during the first 90 minutes the park is open. Warn anyone waiting for you that you might be a while. Even if there is no line to speak of, it takes 10–12 minutes just to navigate the caverns and not much less time to exit the attraction after riding. However, if lines are low, park employees will open special doors marked "Re-entry to Fire" or "Re-entry to Ice" (depending on what coaster you just rode) that allow you to get right back to the head of the queue and ride again. Finally, if you don't have time to ride both Fire and Ice, be advised that the *Unofficial* crew unanimously prefers Fire to Ice.

The Eighth Voyage of Sinbad (Universal Express)

APPEAL BY AGE	PRESCHOOL ★★★	GRADE SCHOOL ★★★½	TEENS ★★½
YOUNG ADULTS ★★★		OVER 30 ★★★	SENIORS ★★½

What it is Theater stunt show. **Scope and scale** Major attraction. **When to go** Anytime as per the daily entertainment schedule. **Author's rating** Not inspiring; ★★. **Duration of presentation** 17 minutes. **Probable waiting time** 15 minutes.

DESCRIPTION AND COMMENTS A story about Sinbad the Sailor is the glue that (loosely) binds this stunt show featuring water explosions, ten-foot-tall circles of flame, and various other daunting eruptions and perturbations. The show reminds us of those action movies that substitute a mind-numbing succession of explosions, crashes, and special effects for plot and character development. Concerning *Sinbad,* even if you bear in mind that it's billed as a stunt show, the production is so vacuous and redundant that it's hard to get into the action. Fans of the *Hercules and Xena* TV shows might appreciate the humor more than the average showgoer.

TOURING TIPS See *Sinbad* after you've experienced the rides and the better-rated shows. The theater seats 1,700; performance times are listed in the daily entertainment schedule.

The Flying Unicorn (Universal Express)

APPEAL BY AGE	PRESCHOOL ★★★★½	GRADE SCHOOL ★★★½	TEENS ★★
YOUNG ADULTS ★★		OVER 30 ★	SENIORS ★

What it is Children's roller coaster. **Scope and scale** Minor attraction. **When to go** Before 11 a.m. **Author's rating** A good beginner's coaster; ★★★. **Duration of ride** 1 minute. **Loading speed** Slow.

DESCRIPTION AND COMMENTS A child-sized roller coaster through a forest setting, the Unicorn provides a nonthreatening way to introduce young children to the genre.

TOURING TIPS This one loads very slowly. Ride before 11 a.m.

Poseidon's Fury! Escape from the Lost City (Universal Express)

APPEAL BY AGE	PRESCHOOL ★★	GRADE SCHOOL ★★★★	TEENS ★★★★
YOUNG ADULTS ★★★★		OVER 30 ★★★★	SENIORS ★★★★

What it is High-tech theater attraction. **Scope and scale** Headliner. **When to go** After experiencing all the rides. **Special comments** Audience stands throughout. **Author's rating** Much improved; ★★★★. **Duration of presentation** 17 minutes including preshow. **Probable waiting time** 25 minutes.

DESCRIPTION AND COMMENTS In the first incarnation of this story, the Greek gods Poseidon and Zeus duked it out, with Poseidon as the heavy. Poseidon fought with water, and Zeus fought with fire, though both sometimes resorted to laser beams and smoke machines. In the new version, the rehabilitated Poseidon now tussles with an evil wizardish guy, and everybody uses fire, water, lasers, smoke machines, and angry lemurs (*Note:* lemurs are not actually used—just seeing if you're paying attention.) As you might have inferred, the new story is somewhat incoherent, but the special effects are still amazing, and the theming of the preshow areas is quite imposing. The plot unravels in installments as you pass through a couple of these areas and finally into the main theater. Though the production is a little slow and plodding at first, it wraps up with quite an impressive flourish. There's some great technology at work here. *Poseidon* is by far and away the best of the Islands of Adventure theater attractions.

TOURING TIPS If you are still wet from Dudley Do-Right, the Bilge-Rat Barges, and the Jurassic Park River Adventure, you might be tempted to cheer the evil wizard's flame jets in hopes of finally drying out. Our money, however, is on Poseidon. It's legal in Florida for theme parks to get you wet, but setting you on fire is frowned upon.

Frequent explosions and noise may frighten younger children, so exercise caution with preschoolers. Shows run continuously if the technology isn't on the blink. We recommend catching *Poseidon* after experiencing your fill of the rides.

SEUSS LANDING

A TEN-ACRE THEME AREA based on Dr. Seuss's famous children's books. Like at Mickey's Toontown in the Magic Kingdom, all of the buildings and attractions replicate a whimsical, brightly colored cartoon style with exaggerated features and rounded lines. There are three rides at Seuss Landing (described below) and an interactive play area, If I Ran the Zoo, populated by Seuss creatures.

Caro-Seuss-El (Universal Express)

APPEAL BY AGE	PRESCHOOL ★★★★	GRADE SCHOOL ★★★★	TEENS —
YOUNG ADULTS —	OVER 30 —		SENIORS —

What it is Merry-go-round. **Scope and scale** Minor attraction. **When to go** Before 10:30 a.m. **Author's rating** Wonderfully unique; ★★★½. **Duration of ride** 2 minutes. **Loading speed** Slow.

DESCRIPTION AND COMMENTS Totally outrageous, the Caro-Seuss-El is a full-scale, 56-mount merry-go-round made up exclusively of Dr. Seuss characters.

TOURING TIPS Even if you are too old or don't want to ride, this attraction is worth an inspection. Whatever your age, chances are good you'll see some old friends. If you are touring with young children, try to get them on early in the morning.

The Cat in the Hat (Universal Express)

APPEAL BY AGE	PRESCHOOL ★★★★	GRADE SCHOOL ★★★★	TEENS ★★★
YOUNG ADULTS ★★★½		OVER 30 ★★★½	SENIORS ★★★½

What it is Indoor adventure ride. **Scope and scale** Major attraction.
When to go Before 11:30 a.m. **Author's rating** Seuss would be proud;
★★★½. **Duration of ride** 3½ minutes. **Loading speed** Moderate.

DESCRIPTION AND COMMENTS Guests ride on "couches" through 18
   different sets inhabited by animatronic Seuss characters, including The Cat in the Hat, Thing 1,Thing 2, and the beleaguered
   goldfish who tries to maintain order in the midst of bedlam. Well
   done overall, with nothing that should frighten younger children.
TOURING TIPS This is fun for all ages. Try to ride early.

One Fish, Two Fish, Red Fish, Blue Fish (Universal Express)

APPEAL BY AGE	PRESCHOOL ★★★★	GRADE SCHOOL ★★★★	TEENS ★★★
YOUNG ADULTS ★★★		OVER 30 ★★★	SENIORS ★★★

What it is Wet version of Dumbo the Flying Elephant. **Scope and scale**
Minor attraction. **When to go** Before 10 a.m. **Author's rating** Who
says you can't teach an old ride new tricks?; ★★★½. **Duration of ride**
2 minutes. **Loading speed** Slow.

DESCRIPTION AND COMMENTS Imagine Dumbo with Seuss-style fish
   instead of elephants and you've got half the story. The other
   half of the story involves yet another opportunity to drown.
   Guests steer their fish up or down 15 feet in the air while traveling in circles. At the same time, they try to avoid streams of
   water projected from "squirt posts." A catchy song provides
   clues for avoiding the squirting.
      Though ostensibly a children's ride, the song and the chal-
   lenge of steering your fish away from the water jets make this
   attraction fun for all ages.
TOURING TIPS We don't know what it is about this theme park and
   water, but you'll get wetter than at a full-immersion baptism.

ISLANDS *of* ADVENTURE ONE-DAY TOURING PLAN

BE AWARE THAT IN THIS PARK there are an inordinate
number of attractions that will get you wet. If you want to
experience them, come armed with ponchos, large plastic
garbage bags, or some other protective covering. Failure to
follow this prescription will make for a squishy, sodden day.

This plan is for groups of all sizes and ages and includes thrill rides that may induce motion sickness or get you wet. If the plan calls for you to experience an attraction that does not interest you, simply skip that attraction and proceed to the next step. Be aware that the plan calls for some back-tracking. If you have young children in your party, customize the plan to fit their needs.

1. Call ☎ 407-363-8000, the main information number, the day before your visit for the official opening time. Try to purchase your admission sometime prior to the day you intend to tour.

2. On the day of your visit, eat breakfast and arrive at the Islands of Adventure turnstiles 20–30 minutes before opening time. Park, buy your admission (if you did not purchase it in advance), and wait at the turnstiles to be admitted.

3. While at the turnstile, ask an attendant whether any rides or shows are closed that day. Adjust the touring plan accordingly.

4. When the park opens, go straight through the Port of Entry and take a left, crossing the bridge into Marvel Super Hero Island. At Super Hero Island, bear left to The Incredible Hulk Coaster.

5. Ride Incredible Hulk.

6. Exiting Hulk, hustle immediately to The Adventures of Spider-Man, also in Marvel Super Hero Island.

7. Dr. Doom's Fearfall, to the left of Spider-Man, is sort of a poor man's Tower of Terror. What's more, it loads about as fast as molasses on a shingle. We suggest you skip it. However, if you're bound and determined to ride, now's the time. *Note:* Steps 8–10 involve attractions where you will get wet. If you're not up for a soaking this early in the morning, skip ahead to Step 11, but be advised that you may have a bit of a wait at the Toon Lagoon attractions later in the day.

8. Continuing clockwise around the lake, depart Super Hero Island and cross into Toon Lagoon.

9. In Toon Lagoon, ride Dudley Do-Right's Ripsaw Falls.

10. Also in Toon Lagoon, subject yourself to Popeye & Bluto's Bilge-Rat Barges.

11. After the barge ride, continue your clockwise circuit around the lake, passing through Jurassic Park without stopping. Continue to the Lost Continent.

12. At the Lost Continent, ride both tracks of Dueling Dragons.

13. While at the Lost Continent, experience *Poseidon's Fury! Escape from the Lost City.*

14. Depart the Lost Continent, moving counterclockwise around the lake, and enter Jurassic Park.

15. In Jurassic Park, try the Jurassic Park River Adventure.
16. Also in Jurassic Park, check out Triceratops Encounter.
17. Return to the Lost Continent. Check the daily entertainment schedule for the next performance of *The Eighth Voyage of Sinbad* stunt show. If a show is scheduled to begin within 30 minutes or so, go ahead and check it out. Otherwise, skip ahead to Step 18 and work *Sinbad* in later.
18. From the Lost Continent, move clockwise around the lake to Seuss Landing. Ride The Cat in the Hat.
19. At this point, you will have done all the big stuff. Spend the rest of your day experiencing attractions you bypassed earlier or re-peating ones you especially enjoyed.

DINING *at* UNIVERSAL ORLANDO

ONE OF OUR CONSTANT GRIPES about theme parks is the food. To many guests hustling through the parks, dining is a low priority—they don't mind the typically substandard fare and high prices because their first objective is to see the sights and ride the rides. This is certainly understandable, but the *Unofficial Guide* team is made up of big fans of big eating. It's our opinion that there's no reason not to expect quality food and service when theme parks invest so much elsewhere in design, production, and development.

> **unofficial TIP**
> You may be pleas-antly surprised by the quality of the food at Universal Studios Orlando.

The good news is that food in Universal is almost always a cut above and a step ahead of what you can find at Walt Disney World and other parks. More variety, bet-ter preparations, and more current trends are generally the rule at Universal. Counter-service and fast-food offerings are comparable to Disney. To help you make choices for sit-down meals at breakfast, lunch, or dinner, we've provided profiles of Universal's full-service places, most of which are located in the CityWalk complex. For information about CityWalk's night-club scene, see the Universal Orlando CityWalk section in Part Ten, After Dark.

In addition to these restaurants, the three Loews hotels on Universal's property offer various full-service dining opportunities. At the Portofino Bay resort, you'll find Mama Della's, with Italian comfort food served in a casual dining space where Mama is in charge. Trattoria del Porto offers many of the same type of dishes but without Mama's interference. For more upscale dining, there's Delfino Riviera, serving Ligurian (from the northwestern region of Italy on the Ligurian Sea) specialties in a romantic atmosphere that includes a strolling guitarist. Across the way is the Hard Rock Hotel's The Palm, a link in the chain of steakhouses based on the original in New York and its characteristic wall caricatures. The Hard Rock also hosts Sunset Grill, a casual and vaguely Californian eatery that has had difficulty finding its niche.

The Royal Pacific brings the second Orlando restaurant from Emeril Lagasse, this one called Emeril's Tchoup Chop. The name is pronounced "chop chop" ("Tchoup" is short for Tchoupitoulas, the street that Lagasse's main New Orleans restaurant is on), and the cuisine is a stylized version of Hawaiian dishes. The food gets mixed reviews, but most people love the decor. Royal Pacific also has good light bites at Jake's American Bar, as well as Islands Dining Room, the hotel's version of a coffee shop.

Counter-service fast food is available throughout Universal Studios Orlando. The food compares in quality to McDonald's, Arby's, or Taco Bell, but is more expensive, though often served in larger portions.

THE COST OF COUNTER-SERVICE FOOD

To help you develop your dining budget, here are prices of common counter-service items. Sales tax isn't included.

FOOD	PRICE
Barbecue platter	$7.49–$11.99
Brownie (with nuts)	$2.49
Cereal	$2.50
Cheeseburger platter	$5.99
Chicken finger platter	$7.49
Chips	$2.49
Cookie	$2.12
Deli sandwich	$6.49–$6.99
Entree salad	$5.99–$7.99
Grilled chicken sandwich platter	$6.99
Ice cream	$4.49
Individual pizza	$6.49–$6.79
Kid's meal	$5.99–$6.99
Burger or chicken	$6.49–$6.99
Muffin	$2.29

THE COST OF COUNTER-SERVICE FOOD (CONTINUED)

FOOD	PRICE
Plate of fruit	$7.24
Popcorn	$2.29
Souvenir bucket	$4.49
Refill	$1.99
Pretzel	$2.19
Side of fries	$2.79
Slice of pie	$3.49
Slice of pizza	$3.49–$3.99
Soup of the day	$2.98
Veggie burger platter	$5.89
DRINKS	
Cappuccino	$2.29
Cocoa	$1.49
Coffee	$1.89
Hot tea	$1.59
Souvenir mug	$4.99
Large beer	$4.99
Souvenir beer cup	$7.49
Orange juice	$1.89
Milk	$2.02

UNIVERSAL ORLANDO RESTAURANTS

NAME	CUISINE	OVERALL RATING	COST	QUALITY RATING	VALUE RATING
CITYWALK					
Emeril's Orlando	American	★★★★½	Exp	★★★★★	★★★
Pastamore	Italian	★★★	Inexp/ Mod	★★★★	★★★★
NBA City	American	★★★	Mod	★★★★	★★★
Hard Rock Café	American	★★★	Mod	★★★½	★★★★
Jimmy Buffet's Margaritaville	Caribbean/ American	★★½	Mod	★★★½	★★★
Pat O'Brien's	Cajun	★★	Inexp	★★★½	★★★★
Bob Marley	Jamaican/ Caribbean	★★	Inexp	★★★½	★★★
NASCAR Café	American	★★	Mod	★★★	★★
PORTOFINO BAY					
Bice	Italian	★★★★½	Exp	★★★½	★★★★½

UNIVERSAL ORLANDO RESTAURANTS (CONTINUED)

NAME	CUISINE	OVERALL RATING	COST	QUALITY RATING	VALUE RATING
PORTOFINO BAY (CONTINUED)					
Delfino Riviera	Italian	★★★½	Exp	★★★★★	★★★
Trattoria del Porto	Italian	★★½	Mod	★★★½	★★★
ROYAL PACIFIC					
Jake's American Bar	American	★★★	Mod	★★★★	★★★★
Emeril's Tchoup Chop	Pacific Rim	★★★	Mod	★★★½	★★★
ISLANDS					
Mythos	Steak/ Seafood	★★★	Mod/ Exp	★★★★	★★★
Confisco Grille	American	★★½	Exp	★★★½	★★★
HARD ROCK					
The Palm	Steak	★★★	Exp	★★★½	★★★
The Kitchen	American	★★	Mod	★★★½	★★
STUDIOS					
Lombard's Landing	Seafood	★★½	Mod	★★★½	★★★
Finnegan's	Irish	★★	Mod	★★★	★★

UNIVERSAL ORLANDO RESTAURANT PROFILES

BELOW ARE PROFILES for full-service restaurants found in Universal Studios Florida, Islands of Adventure, and the CityWalk complex.

Bice ★★★★½

| ITALIAN | EXPENSIVE | QUALITY ★★★★ | VALUE ★★★★ |

Royal Pacific Hotel; ☎ 407-503-DINE

Customers Locals and tourists. **Reservations** Recommended. **When to go** Dinner. **Entree range** $17–$42. **Payment** AE, D, DC, MC, V. **Service rating** ★★★★★. **Friendliness rating** ★★★★. **Parking** Valet or self-parking; $5 charge for valet. **Bar** Full service. **Wine selection** Very good. **Dress** Resort dressy. **Disabled access** Good. **Hours** Sunday–Thursday, 5:30–10:30 p.m., Friday and Saturday, 5:30–11:30 p.m.

SETTING AND ATMOSPHERE Wood and marble floors, crisp white linens, opulent flower arrangements and waiters in black suits give Bice ("beach-ay") the feeling of a formal restaurant, but there is nothing stiff or fussy about the space or the staff. It is immaculately clean, beautifully lit, and relatively quiet even when it's crowded.

HOUSE SPECIALTIES Menu changes seasonally; selections may include prosciutto with fresh melon and baby greens; homemade braised beef sparerib ravioli with spinach in mushroom-marsala sauce; veal Milanese with cherry tomatoes and arugula; pistachio semifreddo.

ENTERTAINMENT AND AMENITIES Piano in bar.

SUMMARY AND COMMENTS This is part of a chain of very upscale and quite impressive restaurants found in New York, Tokyo, and Las Vegas and other international locales. The food is incredibly fresh, well prepared, and elegant, and the service is top notch. But be prepared: even a modest meal will put a dent in your wallet, and even though the food and service are definitely worth it, it may be too expensive for many vacationers. If you want to try a variety of things on the menu, split a salad, appetizer, or pasta dish (traditionally eaten before the entree) between two people for a starter; portions are large enough for sharing and the staff is more than happy to accommodate.

Bob Marley—A Tribute to Freedom ★★½

JAMAICAN/CARIBBEAN   INEXPENSIVE   QUALITY ★★★½   VALUE ★★★

CityWalk; ☎ 407-224-2262

Customers Locals and tourists. **Reservations** Not accepted. **When to go** Early evening. **Entree range** $7–$8. **Payment** AE, D, MC, V. **Service rating** ★★. **Friendliness rating** ★★★. **Parking** Universal Orlando garage. **Bar** Full service. **Wine selection** Poor. **Dress** Casual; dreadlocks if you have them. **Disabled access** Good. **Hours** Monday–Friday, 4 p.m.–2 a.m.; Saturday and Sunday, 2 p.m.–2 a.m.

SETTING AND ATMOSPHERE The space, said to be fashioned after Bob Marley's island home, gives one the feeling of sitting on a porch or verandah and watching entertainment on a backyard stage. Most of the area is open to the elements, although there are shelters from the occasional rainstorm.

HOUSE SPECIALTIES Jerk-marinated chicken breast; smoky white-cheddar cheese fondue; Jamaican vegetable patties; beef patties.

ENTERTAINMENT AND AMENITIES Live reggae; cover charge after 8 p.m.

SUMMARY AND COMMENTS There is much more emphasis put on the music than the food here, although you can manage a palatable bite to eat while listening to some good tunes. Sure, you're allowed to get up and dance.

Confisco Grille ★★½

AMERICAN	EXPENSIVE	QUALITY ★★★½	VALUE ★★★

Islands of Adventure/Port of Entry; ☎ 407-363-8000

Customers Park guests. **Reservations** Accepted. **When to go** Anytime. **Entree range** $11–$18. **Payment** AE, D, DC, MC, V. **Service rating** ★★. **Friendliness rating** ★★. **Parking** Universal Orlando garage. **Bar** Full service. **Wine selection** Moderate. **Dress** Casual. **Disabled access** Good. **Hours** 11:30 a.m. until park closing; also features a character breakfast featuring Spider-Man several mornings throughout the year. Call for details.

SETTING AND ATMOSPHERE A way station on the road to Morocco, perhaps? Actually, it's meant to look like a customs house.

HOUSE SPECIALTIES Pad thai; selection of salads; beef and chicken fajitas, grilled sandwiches.

SUMMARY AND COMMENTS It's clear that the Universal food gurus put all their efforts into the counter-service eateries located throughout the park. Confisco Grille and Mythos are the only full-service restaurants in the park, and each offers a modest dining experience. They're fine for those times when you just can't stand in another line, even if it is just to get food.

Emeril's Orlando ★★★½

AMERICAN	EXPENSIVE	QUALITY ★★★	VALUE ★★★

CityWalk; ☎ 407-224-2424

Customers Locals and park guests. **Reservations** Required. **When to go** Early or late evening. **Entree range** $18–$32. **Payment** AE, D, DC, MC, V. **Service rating** ★★★★. **Friendliness rating** ★★★★. **Parking** Universal Orlando garage; valet parking available, check with restaurant about validation. **Bar** Full service. **Wine selection** Very good. **Dress** Casual to dressy. **Disabled access** Good. **Hours** Sunday–Thursday, 11:30 a.m.–2:30 p.m. and 5:30–10 p.m.; Friday and Saturday, 11:30 a.m.–2:30 p.m. and 5:30–11 p.m.

SETTING AND ATMOSPHERE The main dining room is two stories high and features hardwood floors, wooden beams, and stone walls, all of which act as sounding boards for the noisy dining room. Sliding glass doors lead to the kitchen, where Emeril may or may not be cooking (probably not). Part of the kitchen is open, and there are eight seats at a food bar. These are some of the best seats in the house and shouldn't be turned down if offered.

HOUSE SPECIALTIES The menu changes frequently. Signature items that might be available include oyster stew; farm-raised quail; "a study of duck;" and lobster cheesecake.

SUMMARY AND COMMENTS Owner Emeril Lagasse gained popularity from his show on Food Network, and his restaurants were instant hits. But the food proves he's more than a flash in the proverbial pan. Lagasse also has restaurants in New Orleans and Las Vegas, so it's unlikely he will be on the premises, though he does visit sometimes. *Note:* Reservations can be hard to come by unless booked weeks in advance. To get a table on the same day as your visit, call the restaurant at 3:15 p.m. Reservations that have not been confirmed by that time are canceled and made available to callers.

Emeril's Tchoup Chop ★★★★

AMERICAN	EXPENSIVE	QUALITY ★★★★	VALUE ★★★

Royal Pacific; ☎ 407-503-CHOP

Customers Locals and park guests. **Reservations** Recommended. **When to go** Dinner. **Entree range** $23–$34. **Payment** AE, D, DC, MC, V. **Service rating** ★★★. **Friendliness rating** ★★★★. **Parking** Valet or self-parking; $5 charge. **Bar** Full service. **Wine selection** Good. **Dress** Resort dressy. **Disabled access** Good. **Hours** Lunch: Monday–Sunday, 11:30 a.m.–2 p.m.; dinner: Sunday–Thursday, 5:30–10 p.m.; Friday and Saturday. 5:30–11 p.m.

SETTING AND ATMOSPHERE It's a cool, attractive, Polynesian-themed room reminiscent of a giant tiki bar, complete with bamboo, waterfalls, sculpted gardens, and giant woks in full view.

HOUSE SPECIALTIES Wok-seared orange sake glazed duck; Thai-style Caesar salad; braised Kobe beef short ribs; banana-cream pie; banana cheesecake.

SUMMARY AND COMMENTS This beautiful room serves up Far-East specialties with some flair, although service can sometimes be a bit slow. The food is tasty, but again, quite pricey. To stick to a tighter budget, go at lunchtime and try the lighter options like the entree-sized soups and salads, and skip dessert.

Finnegan's ★★

IRISH	MODERATE	QUALITY ★★★	VALUE ★★

Universal Studios/New York; ☎ 407-363-8000

Customers Park guests. **Reservations** Priority seating. **When to go** Anytime. **Entree range** $10–$16. **Payment** AE, D, DC, MC, V. **Service rating** ★★. **Friendliness rating** ★★. **Parking** Universal Orlando garage. **Bar** Full service. **Wine selection** Ireland is not really known for its wines; good beer selection, though. **Dress** Casual. **Disabled access** Good. **Hours** Daily, 11 a.m. until park closing.

SETTING AND ATMOSPHERE Fashioned after an Irish pub, albeit one built as a movie set. Along with the requisite pub-like accoutrements—tin ceiling, belt-driven paddle fans—are movie lights and half walls that suggest the back of scenery flats.

HOUSE SPECIALTIES Shepherd's pie; fish and chips; Irish stew; bangers and mash; shrimp Scargo; Irish coffee.

ENTERTAINMENT AND AMENITIES Singer.

SUMMARY AND COMMENTS The fare is modest, but the entertainment is fun and the beer is cold. Add to that the fact that this is only one of two spots in Universal Studios park where you can get a waiter to bring food to you, and the pub fare starts to look a bit more attractive.

Hard Rock Café ★★★

AMERICAN	MODERATE	QUALITY ★★★½	VALUE ★★★★

CityWalk; ☎ 407-351-7625

Customers Locals and tourists. **Reservations** Not accepted. **When to go** Afternoon or evening. **Entree range** $8–$18. **Payment** AE, D, DC, MC, V. **Service rating** ★★★. **Friendliness rating** ★★. **Parking** Universal Orlando garage. **Bar** Full service. **Wine selection** Moderate. **Dress** Casual. **Disabled access** Good. **Hours** Daily, 11 a.m.–2 a.m.

SETTING AND ATMOSPHERE This is the biggest HRC in the world (or in the Universe, as they like to say in this part of town). Shaped like the Coliseum, the two-story dining room is a massive museum of rock art memorabilia. The circular center bar features a full-size Cadillac spinning overhead. If you need to be told this is a noisy restaurant, you've never been to a Hard Rock Café before. Everyone, however, should visit a Hard Rock at least once.

HOUSE SPECIALTIES Pig sandwich; charbroiled burgers; barbecued ribs; rock and roll pot roast; grilled fajitas; T-bone steak.

OTHER RECOMMENDATIONS Hot fudge brownie; chocolate-chip cookie pie.

ENTERTAINMENT AND AMENITIES Rock 'n' roll records and memorabilia.

SUMMARY AND COMMENTS Most people complain about a burger that costs $7.59. But this is a good burger—half a pound—and it comes with fries. And all the rest of the food is equally as good, which is why Hard Rock Café remains the theme restaurant that everyone else wants to imitate.

Jake's American Bar ★★

ASIAN, AMERICAN	MODERATE	QUALITY ★★	VALUE ★★

Royal Pacific Hotel; ☎ 407-503-DINE

Customers Hotel guests. **Reservations** Not accepted. **When to go** Early evening. **Entree range** $9.50–$20. **Payment** AE, D, DC, MC, V. **Service rating** ★★. **Friendliness rating** ★★★. **Parking** Valet or self-park; $5 charge for valet. **Bar** Full service. **Wine selection** Average. **Dress** resort casual. **Disabled access** Good. **Hours** Daily, 2–11 p.m.; bar, 2 p.m.–2 a.m.

SETTING AND ATMOSPHERE Run-of-the-mill hotel bar and restaurant.

HOUSE SPECIALTIES Pu Pu platter; Brandi's BBQ baby back ribs; steak sandwich; Fly Away Roaster.

ENTERTAINMENT AND AMENITIES Thursday and Sunday, karaoke from 8:30 p.m.–12:30 a.m.; Friday and Saturday, solo guitarist from 8:30–11:30 p.m.

SUMMARY AND COMMENTS This is a viable option if you're staying in the hotel, but as far as special meals go, this place doesn't deliver—and really isn't meant to. For a quick meal, this spot is convenient but doesn't merit a visit if you're not already in the area.

Jimmy Buffett's Magaritaville   ★★★

CARIBBEAN/AMERICAN	MODERATE	QUALITY ★★★½	VALUE ★★★

CityWalk; ☎ 407-224-2155

Customers Local and tourist parrotheads. **Reservations** Not accepted. **When to go** Early evening. **Entree range** $8–$17. **Payment** AE, D, DC, MC, V. **Service rating** ★★★. **Friendliness rating** ★★★. **Parking** Universal Orlando garage. **Bar** Full service. **Wine selection** Minimal. **Dress** Flowered shirts, flip-flops. **Disabled access** Good. **Hours** Daily, 11 a.m.–2 a.m.

SETTING AND ATMOSPHERE Two-story dining space with many large-screen TVs playing Jimmy Buffett music videos and scenes from his live performances. A volcano above one of the bars occasionally erupts to spew margaritas down the slope into a giant blender.

HOUSE SPECIALTIES Cheeseburgers, of course; conch fritters; Yucatán quesadillas with whole-wheat tortillas; New Orleans nachos; key-lime pie.

ENTERTAINMENT AND AMENITIES Live music on the porch early; band on inside stage late evening.

SUMMARY AND COMMENTS This is a relaxing, festive place but it's not always worth the wait (especially if it's two hours, which it has been known to be). The atmosphere, though, is like a taste of the beach without having to travel to the coast. If the line for a table is outrageous, see if you can sidle up to the bar for a margarita and appetizers, which is just as much if not more fun than actually having a full meal. This place is wildly popular with Jimmy Buffet fans standing in line just to get a beeper so they can stand in line some more and wait for a table.

The Kitchen ★★★★

| AMERICAN | EXPENSIVE | QUALITY ★★★ | VALUE ★★★ |

Hard Rock Hotel; ☎ **407-503-**DINE

Customers Tourists. **Reservations** Recommended. **When to go** Dinner. **Entree range** $15–$25. **Payment** AE, D, DC, MC, V. **Service rating** ★★½. **Friendliness rating** ★★★★. **Parking** Valet or self-parking; $5 charge. **Bar** Full service. **Wine selection** Good. **Dress** Casual. **Disabled access** Good. **Hours** Daily, 7 a.m.–11 p.m.

SETTING AND ATMOSPHERE Taking on the appearance of the spacious kitchen in a rock megastar's mansion, The Kitchen's walls are adorned with culinary-themed memorabilia from the Hard Rock Hotel's many celebrity guests.

HOUSE SPECIALTIES Seared ahi tuna; chicken chorizo quesadillas; Kobe beef burger; maple-glazed cedar-plank salmon; meatloaf; key lime tart

ENTERTAINMENT AND AMENITIES Rock stars occasionally visit to cook their specialties; signed aprons and rock memorabilia on the walls.

SUMMARY AND COMMENTS Though we must admit our expectations weren't too high for this Hard Rock venture, we were pleasantly surprised with the food and service here. Though expensive, the food is actually quite good and the setting is pretty fun. The Kobe beef burger will set you back about $17 but the regular version is just as tasty and much less expensive. Visiting rock stars often perform cooking demonstrations of their favorite dishes at the Chef's Table, so call ahead to see if any rock stars will be in the kitchen—you may find yourself having dinner with Joan Jett or Bob Seger. If dinner is a little out of your price range but you still want the experience, go for the $13.95 brunch buffet, which includes a host of fresh, yummy selections and an omelet station.

Islands Dining Room ★★★

| CARIBBEAN | MODERATE | QUALITY ★★★ | VALUE ★★★ |

Royal Pacific Hotel; ☎ **407-503-**DINE

Customers Hotel guests. **Reservations** Suggested for character dining and during holiday weekends. **When to go** Breakfast, character dinners. **Entree range** breakfast, $8.50–$19.50; lunch, $12–$21; dinner, $12–$30. **Payment** AE, D, DC, MC, V. **Service rating** ★★★. **Friendliness rating** ★★★. **Parking** Valet or self-park; $5 charge for valet. **Bar** Full service. **Wine selection** Average. **Dress** Casual. **Disabled access** Good. **Hours** Daily, 6 a.m.–10 p.m.

SETTING AND ATMOSPHERE Pretty standard hotel dining room; big and open, and always spotless.

HOUSE SPECIALTIES Guava-barbecue shredded pork on goat-cheese grits; roasted almond and mixed-berry pancakes; Tahitian French toast à l'orange; herb-crusted ahi tuna; panko-crusted chicken breast; islands sushi sampler for two.

ENTERTAINMENT AND AMENITIES Character dining available on select evenings; call ahead to confirm.

SUMMARY AND COMMENTS Breakfast here is a treat—the specialties are all tasty and (surprisingly) moderately priced. Lunch and dinner are good, too, but with all the other restaurants around, especially if you're spending the day in the parks, we suggest having a hearty breakfast here and a lighter lunch elsewhere.

Lombard's Seafood Grille ★★½

SEAFOOD	MODERATE	QUALITY ★★★½	VALUE ★★★

Universal Studios/San Francisco; ☎ 407-363-8000

Customers Park guests. **Reservations** Accepted. **When to go** Anytime. **Entree range** $10–$20. **Payment** AE, D, DC, MC, V. **Service rating** ★★★. **Friendliness rating** ★★. **Parking** Universal Orlando garage. **Bar** Full service. **Wine selection** Good. **Dress** Casual. **Disabled access** Good. **Hours** Daily, 11:30 a.m. until 2 hours before park closes or until park closing, depending on park attendance. Call to verify hours, as there is no set schedule.

SETTING AND ATMOSPHERE Situated on the park's main lagoon, Lombard's looks like a converted wharf-side warehouse. The centerpiece of the brick-walled room is a huge aquarium with bubble-glass windows. A fish-sculpture fountain greets guests.

HOUSE SPECIALTIES Shrimp cioppino ratatouille; ravioli with five cheeses; fried shrimp; fresh fish selections.

SUMMARY AND COMMENTS Lombard's Landing is now more casually focused. Unfortunately, so is the kitchen. There are arguably better food options in the park, but as one of only two full-service restaurants in Universal Studios park, the place can be crowded.

Mama Della's ★★★

ITALIAN	EXPENSIVE	QUALITY ★★★	VALUE ★★★

Portofino Bay Hotel; ☎ 407-503-DINE

Customers Hotel guests. **Reservations** Suggested during high season. **When to go** Dinner. **Entree range** $19–$32. **Payment** AE, D, DC, MC, V. **Service rating** ★★★. **Friendliness rating** ★★★★. **Parking** Valet or self-park; $5 charge for valet. **Bar** Full service. **Wine selection** Good. **Dress** Nice casual. **Disabled access** Good. **Hours** Daily, 5:30–10 p.m.

SETTING AND ATMOSPHERE Just like being in the dining room of a home in Tuscany, with hardwood floors, provincial printed wallpaper, and wooden furniture.

HOUSE SPECIALTIES Baked clams with garlic and oregano; gnochetti with Bolognese sauce; grilled shrimp, scallops, and grouper on cappellini; seared ribeye steak; chocolate praline crunch cake; lemon cheesecake and panna cotta.

ENTERTAINMENT AND AMENITIES Strolling musicians on select nights.

SUMMARY AND COMMENTS This falls on the fancy scale somewhere in between Bice and Trattoria del Porto. Traditional Italian food is served in a comfortable atmosphere conducive of a special meal, but not quite as extravagant as its lavish neighbor, Bice. If you want food (almost) as tasty but for (a bit) less dough, Mama Della's is a great choice.

Mythos ★★★

STEAK/SEAFOOD	MOD/EXP	QUALITY ★★★★	VALUE ★★★

Islands of Adventure/The Lost Continent; ☎ 407-224-4533

Customers Park guests. **Reservations** Accepted. **When to go** Early evening. **Entree range** $10–$18.50. **Payment** AE, D, DC, MC, V. **Service rating** HH. **Friendliness rating** ★★★. **Parking** Universal Orlando garage. **Bar** Full service. **Wine selection** Good. **Dress** Casual. **Disabled access** Good. **Hours** Daily, 11:30 a.m.–3 p.m. or until park closing; call ahead for closing time.

SETTING AND ATMOSPHERE A grotto-like atmosphere to suggest you're eating in a cave. Large picture windows look out over the central lagoon to the Incredible Hulk roller coaster. You can time your meal by coaster launchings.

HOUSE SPECIALTIES Tempura shrimp sushi; coq au vin; cedar-plank salmon; beef filet; risotto of the day.

SUMMARY AND COMMENTS This was originally the park's one stab at fine dining, but few guests seem to be looking for this sort of dining experience, especially after getting soaked on one of the water-based rides. Things are now more casual, but there is still an emphasis on quality. The food is above-average theme-park eats, and the setting provides a pleasant retreat. Make your reservation early if you want to dine here.

NASCAR Café ★★

AMERICAN	MODERATE	QUALITY ★★★	VALUE ★★

CityWalk; ☎ 407-224-7223

Customers Racing fans. **Reservations** Not accepted. **When to go** Anytime. **Entree range** $10–$19. **Payment** AE, D, DC, MC, V. **Service rating** ★★. **Friendliness rating** ★★. **Parking** Universal Orlando garage. **Bar** Full service. **Wine selection** Modest. **Dress** Casual; grease-stained jumpsuits okay. **Disabled access** Good. **Hours** Daily, 10 a.m.–11 p.m.

SETTING AND ATMOSPHERE The dining area is on the second level of this two-story building. As you might expect, the room is decorated with a myriad of memorabilia from the world of NASCAR. A full-sized replica of a race car hangs overhead and occasionally revs up, its wheels spinning, and speakers roar with realistic trackside noise.

HOUSE SPECIALTIES Bill France pork chop; DW Dude filet; Rockingham rib eye; Smoky Mountain barbecue ribs.

SUMMARY AND COMMENTS This is strictly for serious NASCAR fans who can't get enough of it. And the food? With all those signs for motor oil hanging all over the place, do you have to ask?

NBA City ★★★

AMERICAN	MODERATE	QUALITY ★★★	VALUE ★★★

CityWalk; ☎ 407-363-5919

Customers Basketball fans. **Reservations** Not accepted. **When to go** Anytime. **Entree range** $12–$20. **Payment** AE, D, DC, MC, V. **Service rating** ★★★. **Friendliness rating** ★★★. **Parking** Universal Orlando garage. **Bar** Full service. **Wine selection** Modest. **Dress** Casual. **Disabled access** Good. **Hours** Daily, 11 a.m.–11 p.m.

SETTING AND ATMOSPHERE A giant statue of Logoman, the official NBA figure, guards the entrance to the restaurant. The building is designed to resemble an older arena, complete with an overhead track that circles the main dining floor. Booths line the walls, and each has a TV that plays scenes from great basketball games.

HOUSE SPECIALTIES Grilled salmon; double-thick pork chops; chicken stuffed with mozzarella and spinach; New York strip steak.

SUMMARY AND COMMENTS This was originally another concept from the next-door neighbor, Hard Rock Café, but the two entities split soon after this prototype opened. But some of HRC's theme-restaurant quality rubbed off. As themes go, this one is done well. Basketball fans will enjoy the videos and the arcade games in the outer lobby.

Pastamore ★★★½

| ITALIAN | INEXPENSIVE/MODERATE | QUALITY ★★★★ | VALUE ★★★★ |

CityWalk; ☎ 407-224-2244

Customers Park guests. **Reservations** Priority seating. **When to go** Anytime. **Entree range** $10–$20. **Payment** AE, D, MC, V. **Service rating** ★★. **Friendliness rating** ★★★. **Parking** Universal Orlando garage. **Bar** Full service. **Wine selection** Good Italian wines. **Dress** Casual. **Disabled access** Good. **Hours** Daily, 5 p.m.–midnight.

SETTING AND ATMOSPHERE A very hip sort of neoclassic design with high walls of green, purple, and yellow. The ceiling is tiered and features angles and curves that flow through the large space. Romanesque statues and artistic depictions of Italian landscapes dot the room. An open kitchen is at the rear of the restaurant. Outdoor seating is available.

HOUSE SPECIALTIES Veal parmigiana; chicken piccata; veal Marsala; fettuccine Alfredo; mussels marinara; calamari.

SUMMARY AND COMMENTS The kitchen puts forth a decent effort, even though the food is not quite authentic Italian. Family-style dinners, including antipasti, soup, salad, two entrees, and dessert, are available for $19.95 per person. Not a bad deal if you're really hungry. For an even better deal, book the chef's table, which is actually a counter overlooking the open kitchen. For a relatively modest fee, you'll have your own personal chef who will create a special menu.

Pat O'Brien's ★★★

| CAJUN | INEXPENSIVE | QUALITY ★★★½ | VALUE ★★★★ |

CityWalk; ☎ 407-224-2106

Customers Tourists. **Reservations** Not accepted. **When to go** Anytime. **Entree range** $5–$10. **Payment** AE, D, DC, MC, V. **Service rating** ★★. **Friendliness rating** ★★★. **Parking** Universal Orlando garage. **Bar** Full service. **Wine selection** Modest. **Dress** Casual. **Disabled access** Good. **Hours** Daily, 4 p.m.–1 a.m.

SETTING AND ATMOSPHERE A fairly faithful rendition of the original Pat O'Brien's in New Orleans, right down to the fire-and-water fountain in the courtyard. The outdoor dining area is the most pleasant place to eat; inside areas feature a noisy bar and another room with dueling pianos.

HOUSE SPECIALTIES Shrimp gumbo; jambalaya; muffuletta; red beans and rice.

SUMMARY AND COMMENTS The food is surprisingly good, and surprisingly affordable. Be careful about ordering a Hurricane, the restaurant's signature drink. You are automatically charged for the souvenir glass, and if you don't want it, you must turn it in at the bar for a refund.

Trattoria del Porto ★★★

ITALIAN   MODERATE   QUALITY ★★★   VALUE ★★

Portofino Bay Hotel; ☎ 407-503-DINE

Customers Hotel guests. **Reservations** Suggested for dinner. **When to go** Lunch. **Entree range** Lunch, $9–$13.50; dinner, $14–$27. **Payment** AE, D, DC, MC, V. **Service rating ★★★**. **Friendliness rating ★★★**. **Parking** Valet or self-park; $5 charge for valet. **Bar** Full service. **Wine selection** Average. **Dress** Resort casual. **Disabled access** Good. **Hours** 7 a.m.–11 p.m.

SETTING AND ATMOSPHERE Like a boisterous down-home Italian kitchen.

HOUSE SPECIALTIES gnocchi verdi; grouper Milanese; filet mignon; open-faced ravioli with gulf shrimp; pizza Bianca; meatball sandwich.

ENTERTAINMENT AND AMENITIES Character dining available on select evenings; call ahead to confirm.

SUMMARY AND COMMENTS Where Mama Della's succeeds in not feeling like a hotel restaurant, Trattoria del Porto does not. The food is perfectly fine and moderately priced (relatively speaking) but lunch is your best option here. Omelettes at breakfast can set you back more than $10, and dinner options are limited. If the poolside snack bar isn't your thing, or if you must try a meal here, lunch is your best bet.

Wantilan Luau ★★★★

HAWAIIAN   MODERATE   QUALITY ★★★   VALUE ★★★

Royal Pacific Hotel; ☎ 407-503-DINE

Customers Tourists. **Reservations** Accepted. **When to go** Dinner only. **Entree range** $49.50 adults; $29 children ages 3–11. (Prices include tax, gratuity for everyone, and mai tais, wine, and beer for guests ages 21 and older.) **Payment** AE, D, DC, MC, V. **Service rating ★★★**. **Friendliness rating ★★★**.. **Parking** Valet or self-park; $5 charge for valet. **Bar** Mai tais, wine and beer available **Dress** Flowered shirts, beachy casual. **Disabled access** Average. **Hours** Every Saturday night year-round; an additional Friday night show runs from May through early September.

SETTING AND ATMOSPHERE A typical luau setting with tiki torches and wooden tables.

HOUSE SPECIALTIES Buffet includes pit-roasted suckling pig with spiced rum-soaked pineapple purée; guava barbequed short ribs; whole roasted South Pacific wahoo; lomi lomi chicken with Maui onions; tropical fruits.

ENTERTAINMENT AND AMENITIES Polynesian dancing, storytelling, hula dancers, live music.

SUMMARY AND COMMENTS This is a fun diversion and a change of scenery from the other restaurants offered on Universal property. Though dinner is a bit expensive, the entertainment is worth it. A separate children's buffet keeps kids happy with offerings like chicken fingers, macaroni, and pizza.

WET 'N' WILD *and* WATER MANIA *versus* DISNEY WATER PARKS

DISNEY'S WATER PARKS ARE DISTINGUISHED more by their genius for creating an integrated adventure environment than by their slides and individual attractions. At the Disney water parks, both eye and body are deluged with the strange, exotic, humorous, and beautiful. Both Disney water parks are stunningly landscaped. Parking lots, street traffic, and so on are far removed from and out of sight of the swimming areas. Also, each park has its own story to tell, a theme that forms the background for your swimming experience. Once you've passed through the turnstile, you're totally enveloped in a fantasy setting that excludes the outside world.

For many, however, the novelty of the theme is quickly forgotten once they hit the water, and the appreciation of being in an exotic setting gives way to enjoying specific attractions and activities. In other words, your focus narrows from the general atmosphere of the park to the next slide you want to ride. Once this occurs, the most important consideration becomes the quality and number of attractions and activities available and their accessibility relative to crowd conditions. Viewed from this perspective, the non-Disney water parks, especially Wet 'n' Wild, give Disney more than a run for the money.

unofficial **TIP**
Water parks are one area where the heightened thrills of the non-Disney rides may outweigh the decor of the Disney water parks.

GETTING THERE

WET 'N' WILD Wet 'n' Wild is at 6200 International Drive in Orlando, about two miles from Universal Studios Florida and SeaWorld on International Drive at Universal Boulevard. From Interstate 4, take Exit 30A and follow the signs to the park.

WATER MANIA Water Mania is at 6073 West Irlo Bronson Memorial Highway (US 192), a few miles east of the Disney complex in Kissimmee. From the Disney area, take I-4 to Exit 75A and head east for a half mile. The park is across from Celebration (Disney's residential area), near visitor guide marker No. 8. Parking costs $6, although there's no charge for bus parking.

ADMISSION PRICES

DURING WET 'N' WILD'S SUMMER NIGHTS sessions (after 5 p.m. late June–early August) hours are extended until 11 p.m., and a single general admission is $10 off. Summer Nights season passes are $35. You may, of course, stay through Summer Nights' special hours with a general admission pass.

WET 'N' WILD GENERAL ADMISSION

Adults ages 10+ $33.95 + tax
Children ages 3–9 $27.95 + tax
Children under age 3 Free
Seniors $16.98 + tax
Annual Pass $89.95 + tax

WATER MANIA GENERAL ADMISSION

Adults ages 10+ $29.95 + tax
Children ages 3–9 $26.95 + tax
Children under age 3 Free
Annual Pass $49.95 + tax (add $20 for parking pass)

Orlando FlexTicket

This pass is good for up to 14 consecutive days at five parks: Busch Gardens, Universal Studios Florida, Universal Islands of Adventure, CityWalk venues, SeaWorld, and Wet 'n' Wild. Note that Water Mania is not among them. There's also a version that excludes Busch Gardens, so be sure to get the one you want.

FLEXTICKET	
Adults $224.95 + tax	
Children ages 3–9 and seniors ages 50+ $189.95 + tax	
FLEXTICKET WITHOUT BUSCH GARDENS	
Adults $184.95 + tax	
Children ages 3–9 and seniors ages 50+ $150.95 + tax	

ARRIVING

WET 'N' WILD Wet 'n' Wild is open year-round, with seasonal hours.

In the winter, the park is open from 10 a.m.–5 p.m.; spring, from 10 a.m–6 p.m. or 9 a.m.–7 p.m.; summer, from 9 a.m.–9 p.m. (except during Summer Nights, when the park is open until 11 p.m.); and fall, from 10 a.m.–6 p.m. Pools are heated if the park is open at less-than-warm times.

> *un*official **TIP**
> Call ahead if you plan to visit during the colder months because the park may close if it's very cold.

Tubes, towels, and lockers are available for rent for $4, $2, and $5, respectively (with a $2 deposit for each). You can get all three for $9 ($4 deposit). Life vests are free. You can bring your own flotation devices, but you can only use them if they've passed park standards. In addition, there is a little gift shop on the premises where you can stock up on sunscreen, film, and other supplies you might have left behind or run out of. Picnics are allowed, but no glass containers or alcohol are permitted on park grounds.

WATER MANIA Water Mania is open daily from mid-March to late September, with hours typically running 10 a.m.– 5 p.m.

As with all the water parks, you can expect a lot of families with young children, so the prime spots for settling in around the park go quickly. Arrive early, and you'll miss the long entrance lines and find room to stake your claim. Life vests are included with admission but require a small deposit. You may bring your own flotation devices, but be aware that with the exception of the children's areas, they must meet Coast Guard standards for you to use them.

> *un*official **TIP**
> Tubes are provided at each ride that requires one, but you can save time waiting in line for the freebies by renting your own for a small fee.

As a nice touch, you can bring your own picnic lunch to eat under one of the covered pavilions in the wooded (read: shady) picnic area. No glass or alcohol is allowed. You can also rent a shaded cabana with four chairs, four towels, a locker, and two tubes for around $55. Kokomos, the Water Mania gift shop, stocks sunscreen and clothing.

CONTACTING THE WATER PARKS

WET 'N' WILD Wet 'n' Wild has a 24-hour information line, ☎ 800-992-WILD, or visit its Web site at **www.wetnwild.com**.

WATER MANIA For more information on Water Mania, call ☎ 800-527-3092 or visit **www.watermania-florida.com**.

A FLUME-*to*-FLUME COMPARISON

THE FOLLOWING CHART PROVIDES a sense of what each water park offers, inside and outside Walt Disney World. In standard theme-park jargon, the water parks refer to their various features, including slides, as "attractions." Some individual attractions consist of several slides. If each slide at a specific attraction is different, we count them separately. Runoff Rapids at Blizzard Beach, for example, offers three corkscrew slides, each somewhat different. Because most guests want to experience all three, we count each individually. At the Toboggan Racers attraction (also at Blizzard Beach), there are eight identical slides, side by side. There's no reason to ride all eight, so we count the whole attraction as one slide.

FLUMES	BLIZZARD BEACH	TYPHOON LAGOON	WET 'N' WILD	WATER MANIA
Vertical Speed Body Slide	1	1	2	1
Vertical Speed Tube Slide	1	–	–	1
Twisting Body Slide	–	–	1	–
Camel Hump Body Slide	1	–	1	–
Camel Hump Mat Slide	1	–	–	–
Camel Hump Tube Slide	–	–	1	2
Corkscrew Mat Slide	–	–	1	1
Corkscrew Body Slide	–	3	1	–
Open Corkscrew Tube Slide	3	4	2	1
Dark Corkscrew Tube Slide	1	–	2	2

FLUMES	BLIZZARD BEACH	TYPHOON LAGOON	WET 'N' WILD	WATER MANIA
1–3 Person Raft Flume	3	2	3	2
4–5 Person Raft Flume	1	1	3	1
TOTAL SLIDES	12	11	17	11
OTHER ATTRACTIONS				
Interactive Water Ride	1	1	1	1
Wave Pool	1	1	1	1
Surf Pool	–	1	1	1
Snorkeling Pool	–	1	–	
Lazy River	1	1	1	1
Isolated Children's Area	2	2	2	4
OTHER ATTRACTIONS TOTAL	5	7	6	8
TOTAL SLIDES AND ATTRACTIONS	17	18	23	19

Do the numbers tell the story? In the case of Wet 'n' Wild, they certainly do. If you can live without the Disney theme setting and story line, Wet 'n' Wild offers more attractions and more variety than any of the other parks. Plus, throughout the summer, Wet 'n' Wild is open until 11 p.m., offering live bands and dancing nightly. Even if you don't care about the bands or dancing, summer nights are more comfortable, lines for the slides are shorter, and you don't have to worry about sunburn.

Did we mention the giant toilet bowl? Wet 'n' Wild has an attraction, dubbed The Storm. The ride actually looks like a lot of fun, but in all honesty it strongly resembles a huge commode. Riders wash down a chute to gain speed, then circle around a huge bowl before dropping into a pool below. This must be how that goldfish you flushed in third grade felt.

unofficial **TIP**
Wet 'n' Wild's later summer hours may mean shorter lines for the slides in the evenings.

Generally speaking, during the day, you'll find Water Mania the least crowded of the parks, followed by Wet 'n' Wild. The Disney parks quite often sell out by about 11 a.m. This is followed by long waits for all of the slides.

Although not approaching Disney's standard for aesthetic appeal and landscaping, both Wet 'n' Wild and Water Mania are clean and attractive. In the surf and wave pool department, Disney's Typhoon Lagoon wins hand down.

Whereas its surf lagoon produces six-foot waves that you can actually body surf, the wave pools at the other parks offer only "bobbing" action. All of the parks have outstanding water-activity areas for younger children, and each park features at least one unique attraction: Wet 'n' Wild has an interactive ride where you control your speed and movements with water blasts; Blizzard Beach has a 1,200-foot water bobsled; Water Mania has a surfing wave; and at Typhoon Lagoon you can snorkel among live fish.

Prices for one-day admission are about the same at Blizzard Beach, Typhoon Lagoon, and Wet 'n' Wild, and slightly less at Water Mania. Discount coupons are often available in free local visitor magazines for Wet 'n' Wild and Water Mania.

PART TEN

AFTER DARK

DINNER THEATERS

CENTRAL FLORIDA PROBABLY HAS MORE dinner attractions than anywhere else on Earth. The name "dinner attraction" is something of a misnomer, because dinner is rarely the attraction. These are audience-participation shows or events with food served along the way. They range from extravagant productions where guests sit in arenas at long tables to intimate settings at individual tables. Don't expect terrific food, but if you're looking for something entertaining outside of Walt Disney World, consider one of these.

If you decide to try a non-Disney dinner show, scavenge local tourist magazines from brochure racks and hotel desks outside the World. These free publications usually have discount coupons for area shows.

THE SHOWS

Arabian Nights
6225 West Irlo Bronson Highway, Kissimmee (US 192 just east of I-4); ☎ 407-239-9223

Show times Sunday–Tuesday, 7:30 p.m.; Wednesday–Saturday, 8:30 p.m.; only 1 show nightly. **Reservations** Can usually be made through the day of the show. **Cost** $39.59; $20.33 ages 3–11. **Discounts** Discount coupons in local magazines, AAA, seniors. **Type of seating** Long rows of benches at tables flanking either side of a large riding arena. All seats face the action. **Menu** Salad, prime rib or chicken breast, mixed vegetables, garlic mashed potatoes, and sheet cake. Children's alternative is chicken fingers with mashed potatoes. **Vegetarian alternative** Lasagna. **Beverages** Unlimited beer, wine, tea, coffee, and soft drinks.

DESCRIPTION AND COMMENTS Horses and riders present equestrian skills and trick riding with costumes, music, and theatrical lighting. The loose story line involves a princess who spots a handsome prince, who then disappears. A genie appears to grant her three wishes, which, of course, she uses to try to find the stud on the steed. For some reason, she doesn't just tell the genie to produce the guy front and center. They travel the world over—and back in time—to look for him. The search takes them anywhere they might find horses: the circus, the Wild West, the set of *Ben Hur.* In all, horses perform to musical accompaniment.

If you are an unbridled horse fan, you're going to think you've died and gone to heaven. Fifty horses, including Lipizzans, palominos, quarter horses, and Arabians, perform 22 acts. The stunts are impressive, and a great deal of skill and timing is employed to pull them off. But after a while the tricks start to look the same, and only the costumes and the music are different. The ending, however, has been changed from a pandering patriotic ploy to a beautiful snowy scene where the horses gambol freely about the arena. It's truly a lovely sight.

The prime rib is edible, and the lasagna alternative is fine. The salad is unappealing, as is the dessert.

Capone's Dinner & Show
4740 West US 192, Kissimmee; ☎ 407-397-2378

Show times 8 p.m. nightly; changes seasonally. **Reservations** Need to make reservations several days in advance. **Cost** $40; $24 ages 4–12 (does not include tax or tip). **Discounts** Florida residents, AAA, seniors, military, hospitality workers. **Type of seating** Long tables with large groupings facing an elevated stage; some smaller tables for parties of two to six. **Menu** Buffet with lasagna, baked ziti, spaghetti, baked chicken, baked ham, boiled potatoes, tossed salad, and brownies. **Vegetarian alternative** Spaghetti, ziti, pasta salad. **Beverages** Unlimited beer, wine, soft drinks, coffee, and tea.

DESCRIPTION AND COMMENTS The audience, attending a celebration for mobster Al Capone at a 1930s speakeasy in Chicago, enters through a secret door using a password. The show is a musical of sorts, with most songs from other sources sung by cast members to recorded accompaniment. The story revolves around Miss Jewel—the speakeasy's hostess, who loves Detective Marvel, the only cop in Chicago that Capone can't buy—and one of the show's floozies and her gambling boyfriend. (Can you say *Guys and Dolls?*)

The audience parades through the buffet line before the show; seconds are invited. The food, which had been passable in the past, should now just be passed up. During a recent visit the plastic flowers above the buffet were in dire need of dusting.

For a musical, this show employs a lot of nonsingers. Even the dancing is second-rate. The waiters—who speak with tough-guy accents and kid around with guests—did more to entertain the children than at any other show. Still, the theme is a bit too adult for families.

Dolly Parton's Dixie Stampede
8251 Vineland Avenue, Orlando; ☎ 866-443-4943

Show times 6:30 Sunday–Thursday, 6:30 and 8:30 Saturdays. **Reservations** Can generally be made up to the day of the show. **Cost** $46.99; $19.99 ages 4–11. **Discounts** Discounts seasonally. **Type of seating** Long rows of chairs at tables surrounding a large riding arena. All seats face the show. **Menu** Rotisserie chicken, pork loin, creamy vegetable soup, corn on the cob, half a baked potato, biscuit, and apple-filled pastry. **Vegetarian alternative** Lasagna, fruit bowl (the soup is not vegetarian). **Beverages** Unlimited soft drinks, two alcoholic beverages per guest (beer or wine).

DESCRIPTION AND COMMENTS Pass the cheese, please. This somewhat hokey show isn't exactly Broadway quality, but it is fun to see. Fifty minutes before the show begins, there's an opening act that changes nightly. Possible acts include a husband-and-wife juggling team, a kooky cowboy, and beautiful horses. The preshow, however, is painfully corny; if you do arrive early, stroll through the outdoor stables to see the horses before the show.

The story, set in the Civil War–era Deep South, is contrived, but the real treat is the impressive stunts performed on horseback. The animals are striking and the handlers are quite entertaining. The music and acting are both average and the set, though cute, is not remarkable.

The food is very ordinary, though the portions are generous and nothing is bad; the specialty fruit drink is exceedingly sweet, and we do not recommend it. However, the boot-shaped novelty glasses are a kitschy and fun souvenir.

Makahiki Luau
SeaWorld, 7007 SeaWorld Drive, Orlando; ☎ 800-327-2420

Show times 6:30 p.m. nightly. **Reservations** Need to make reservations at least 3 days in advance; reservations can be made online; payment is due at time of booking. **Cost** $42.95; $27.95 ages 3–9;

under age 3 free with a reservation. **Discounts** Discounts seasonally. **Type of seating** Long tables; no separation from other parties. **Menu** Fruit "pu pu" platter, salad, mahi mahi in piña colada sauce, Hawaiian chicken, sweet-and-sour pork, fried rice, vegetables, and a seasonal dessert. **Vegetarian alternative** Mixed vegetables, sticky rice. **Beverages** One complimentary mai tai; full cash bar. This is the only show to offer just one cocktail, an odd thing, considering the park is owned by Anheuser-Busch, which makes practically all the beer in the world.

DESCRIPTION AND COMMENTS The Makahiki Luau has the appearance of a touring lounge act that might play the Ramada Inn circuit in the Midwest. Even the venue, a large, dark room with a very low ceiling, looks like a motel lounge. In this musical revue featuring singers, dancers, and fire twirlers, a Don Ho–esque singer is given way too much time. The dancers perform well, and the fire twirler who ends the show is impressive, but there is otherwise little excitement.

The food is more varied than at many shows. The mahi mahi is good, but the fruit platter is fairly uninteresting. The food is served family-style, and you may share a platter with another family.

The service is not very attentive. Audience participation is minimal, and children probably will be bored.

kids Medieval Times Dinner and Tournament

4510 East US 192, Kissimmee; ☎ 800-229-8300

Show times Vary according to season and nights. **Reservations** Best to make reservations a week ahead. **Cost** $48.95; $32.95 ages 3–11 (does not include tax or tip). **Discounts** Seniors, military, AAA, hotel employees, travel agents. You get free admission on your birthday; valid ID required for proof. **Type of seating** Arena-style, in rows that face the riding floor. **Menu** Garlic bread, vegetable soup, whole roasted chicken, spare ribs, herb-basted potatoes, and strudel. Everything is eaten by hand. **Vegetarian alternative** Lasagna, or raw veggies with dip plate. **Beverages** Two rounds of beer, sangria, or soft drinks; cash bar available.

DESCRIPTION AND COMMENTS A tournament set 900 years in the past pits six knights against each other. Audience members are seated in areas corresponding to the color of the knights' pennants and are encouraged to cheer for their knight and boo his opponents. Part of the tournament is actual competition. The knights perform stunts, including hitting a target with a lance or collecting rings on a lance while riding horseback. After each event, successful knights receive carnations from the queen to toss to young ladies in their sections.

After a while, the tournament takes on a choreographed feel—and with good reason. It comes down to a fight to the finish until only one knight is left standing. There are cheating knights who pull others off their horses and hand-to-hand combat with maces, battle-axes, and swords. The winning knight selects a fair maiden from the audience to be his princess.

The food is remarkable only in that you eat it with your hands, including a whole chicken you must pull apart. The chicken is good, the ribs a little tough.

The show is good, and the knights give 100 percent (the bruises they must get!). The sword fights are so realistic that sparks fly off the metal blades. Audience participation reaches a fevered pitch, with each section cheering for its knight and calling for the death of the dastardly opponents. It's amazing how bloodthirsty people can be after they've ripped a chicken apart with their bare hands.

With all the horses, jousting, and fighting, children shouldn't be bored, though parents of very young children might be concerned about the violence.

Pirates Dinner Adventure
6400 Carrier Drive, Orlando; ☎ 407-248-0590

Show times 7:45 p.m. nightly. **Reservations** Can be made up to the day of the show. **Cost** $44.95; $27.50 ages 3–11 (does not include tax or tip). **Discounts** Florida residents, AAA, AARP, military. **Type of seating** Arena-style. **Menu** Salad, beef and roasted chicken, fresh vegetables, ice cream and apple cobbler; children's alternative is chicken fingers. **Vegetarian alternative** Lasagna. **Beverages** Unlimited beer, wine, and soft drinks.

DESCRIPTION AND COMMENTS Audience members are told to arrive long before the doors are open to the auditorium. In the meantime, guests mill about and look over maritime memorabilia and nosh on assorted appetizers. As show time approaches, a "host pirate" leads the audience members in song and dance, and a man demonstrates his fire-eating skills. Later, audience members will recall that this man had the best meal of the evening. The dining area features a life-size pirate ship surrounded by water.

The set is impressive, and during the evening pirates swoop from overhead, race around the ship in boats powered by electric motors, toss balls into a net with the help of audience volunteers, and bounce on a trampoline that's part of the ship. What's mystifying is that there doesn't seem to be a reason for any of this. The sound system is poor, and it was difficult to tell what was going on and why. Audience members sit in color-coded sections and are encouraged to cheer for pirates wearing their colors as they compete against each other. There's plenty to interest kids. Adults might be interested, too, if the story were easier to follow.

Sleuths Mystery Show

**Republic Square, 7508 Republic Drive, Orlando;
☎ 407-363-1985**

Show times Vary nightly; 6 p.m., 7:30 p.m., or 9 p.m. **Reservations** Can be made up to the day of the show. **Cost** $46.95; $23.95 ages 3–11 (does not include tax or tip). **Discounts** Florida residents, AAA, seniors, students, Disney employees, travel agents, military, hospitality employees, full-blooded Chippewa Native Americans. **Type of seating** Large round tables that seat 8–10; some smaller tables. **Menu** Cheese spread and crackers; assorted hot and cold hors d'oeuvres, tossed salad; choice of Cornish hen, prime rib (at an extra $3 charge), or lasagna; veggies and a baked potato; mystery dessert. **Vegetarian alternative** Cheese lasagna. **Beverages** Unlimited beer, wine, or soft drinks.

DESCRIPTION AND COMMENTS Sleuths perform a repertory of murder mysteries the audience must solve. Audience participation is key to the enjoyment. Guests are part of the show from the moment they enter the theater. Actors in character direct seating and try to drop clues as to who and what their parts are in the play. Although they work from a script, much of the show is ad-libbed. Unfortunately, the cast tends to be of limited talent and incapable of ad-libbing well. Each table must choose a spokesman and prepare a question for the actors as they try to solve the murder. Unless you come with a large group, you probably will find yourself interacting with strangers.

The cheese spread and crackers—one crock and one basket for the entire table—is about as cheesy an appetizer as you'll find. The salad is a bigger joke than any of the actors produce. The prime rib was tough during our visit, and the Cornish hen had little meat.

You'll probably have more fun if you go with a large group and occupy your own table. Older children might find the show interesting, but younger ones will probably be bored.

UNIVERSAL ORLANDO CITYWALK

CITYWALK IS A SHOPPING, DINING, AND ENTERTAIN-MENT venue that doubles as the entrance plaza for the Universal Studios and Islands of Adventure theme parks. Situated between the parking complex and the theme parks, CityWalk is heavily trafficked all day but truly comes alive at night.

In the evening, CityWalk is Universal's answer to Walt Disney World's Pleasure Island. Like its rival, CityWalk offers a number of nightclubs to sample, but where Disney and Church Street tend to create their own clubs, many of CityWalk's entertainment and restaurant venues depend on well-known brand names. At CityWalk you'll find a Hard Rock Cafe and concert hall; Jimmy Buffet's Margaritaville; a Motown Cafe; NBA City, a sports bar; a NASCAR Café; a branch of New Orleans' famous Pat O'Brien's club; and a reggae club that celebrates the life and music of Bob Marley. The Groove, a high-tech disco, City Jazz, a jazz club that turns into Bonkerz Comedy Club Thursday through Saturday nights, and the Latin Quarter, a space dedicated to the food, music, and culture of all 21 Latin nations, operate without big-name tie-ins.

Another CityWalk distinction is that most of the clubs are also restaurants, or alternatively, most of the restaurants are also clubs. Although there's a lot of culinary variety, restaurants and nightclubs are different animals. Sight lines, room configuration, acoustics, intimacy, and atmosphere—important considerations in a nightclub—are not at all the same in a venue designed to serve meals. Although it's nice to have all that good food available, the club experience is somewhat dulled. Working through the lineup, Pat O'Brien's, The Groove, and City Jazz/Bonkerz Comedy Club are more nightclub than restaurant, whereas Margaritaville is more restaurant than club. Bob Marley's and the Latin Quarter are about half and half. The Hard Rock Live, NASCAR Café, NBA City, Emeril's, and Pastamore are restaurants.

GETTING THERE

THE UNIVERSAL FLORIDA COMPLEX can be accessed via Kirkman Road from I-4, Exit 75B. Driving from the Walt Disney World area, take I-4 Exit 74A onto Sand Lake Road heading north (away from International Drive) and turn right onto Turkey Lake Road. Follow the signs to the Turkey Lake Road entrance.

Universal Orlando—CityWalk

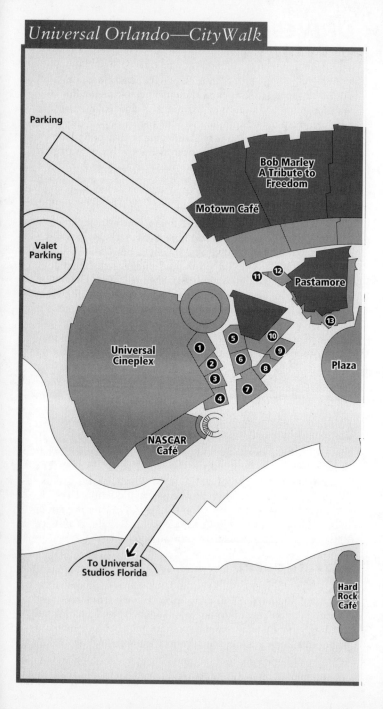

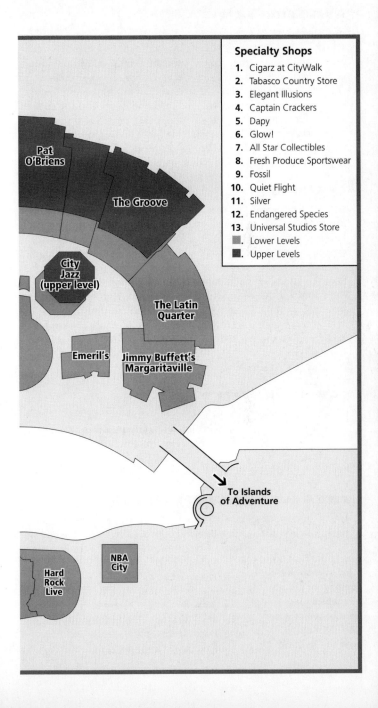

Specialty Shops

1. Cigarz at CityWalk
2. Tabasco Country Store
3. Elegant Illusions
4. Captain Crackers
5. Dapy
6. Glow!
7. All Star Collectibles
8. Fresh Produce Sportswear
9. Fossil
10. Quiet Flight
11. Silver
12. Endangered Species
13. Universal Studios Store
- Lower Levels
- Upper Levels

ADMISSION PRICES

CITYWALK'S PARTY PASS ALL-CLUB ACCESS is $9.95, which gets you into all the clubs (you can also pay $13 and add a movie). Otherwise, you can pay individual cover charges at each club; these tend to run $3–$6 apiece. Given this price range, getting the all-access pass makes the most sense unless you intend to visit just one club. The Orlando FlexTicket allows free entry to all of the venues. Not into the club scene? The Meal and Movie Deal is $19.95 and includes—what else?—dinner at one of the CityWalk restaurants (you choose from a special menu) and a movie.

ARRIVING

ONCE WITHIN THE UNIVERSAL COMPLEX, you'll be directed to park in one of two multitiered parking garages. Parking runs about $8 for cars and $10 for RVs. Be sure to write down the location of your car before heading out of the garages—the evening will end on a considerably brighter note if you avoid wandering about the garages searching for the rental car. An alternative, if you're out for a special occasion or just want to have everything taken care of, Universal also offers valet parking (2 hours) for $7; $14 for over 2 hours. After 6 p.m. parking is free, with the exception of valet services. From the garages, moving sidewalks transport you directly to CityWalk.

CONTACTING CITYWALK

CONTACT CITYWALK GUEST SERVICES at ☎ 407-224-2691, or visit their Web site at **www.citywalk.com.** Keep in mind, though, that CityWalk personnel may not be up on individual club doings, so your best bet may be to contact specific clubs directly when you reach the Orlando area.

CITYWALK VERSUS PLEASURE ISLAND

JUST AS UNIVERSAL'S ISLANDS OF ADVENTURE theme park allows for more direct competition with Disney's Magic Kingdom, CityWalk squares off with Pleasure Island in the field of nightlife entertainment.

unofficial **TIP**
If you're into club-hopping, or just not sure which place you want to spend your wild night out at, head to CityWalk.

As the underdog, CityWalk tries to catch the wave of the hottest fads in nightclubs and dining. Pleasure Island tends more toward themes and trends with long-established general appeal. Because Pleasure Island has the vast pool of Disney World guests to draw from, CityWalk aggressively tries to attract locals in addition to tourists. Overall, Pleasure Island caters to guests who might like to indulge in a little clubbing on their vacation but normally don't make a habit of pub-crawling. CityWalk presents a flashy buffet of premiere nightclubs and restaurants that you might normally find scattered around a large metropolis.

HOW CITYWALK AND PLEASURE ISLAND COMPARE	
CITYWALK	PLEASURE ISLAND
Next to Universal's theme parks. Parking decks free after 6 p.m.	Next to Downtown Disney. Parking is hectic
About $10 (all clubs included)	About $21
Half local/half tourist; mostly ages 20–30	Mostly older teens or curious older adults
Nine restaurants	Four restaurants
Three dance clubs	Seven dance clubs
Five live music venues	Three live music venues
Upscale mall fare shopping	Disney memorabilia; hipster clothing

One key difference is that the larger CityWalk is not as physically enclosed as Pleasure Island because it serves as an open portal to the Universal parks. In addition, the CityWalk clubs don't have cover charges until about 9 p.m. So, if you're not interested in jumping around, arrive early, pick the club you like best, and settle in for the rest of the night. More than at Pleasure Island, several CityWalk establishments are both restaurants and clubs, allowing you to have dinner and dance the night away under the same roof. Both complexes have outdoor areas featuring frequent live music, festivals, and other events; both also have large multiscreen move theaters.

All that said, which entertainment complex you might prefer depends on individual tastes. Hence we provide a chart comparing the high points of each.

In addition to the clubs and restaurants, there are (of course) shops and a Universal Cineplex multiscreen movie theater. In regard to the clubs, you can pay a cover in each one you visit or opt for a more expensive passport to all the clubs. Because the all-access pass is only $10—less than half the admission to Disney's Pleasure Island—we recommend going with that option rather than fooling with individual cover charges. Mini-profiles on each of the nightclubs begin on page 210.

METROPOLIS AND MATRIX

THOUGH NOT A REAL THREAT to either Pleasure Island or CityWalk, and certainly not on the scale of the departed Church Street Station, this new pair of conjoined nightclubs does offer an upscale double venue that's convenient to shopping and lodging and yet has no affiliation with the theme parks. The clubs are located on an upper level of the Pointe Orlando shopping complex at 9101 International Drive; parking is available in the adjacent deck. A single cover charge (usually about $10) gets you admission to both clubs, and you can walk back and forth freely. Metropolis is the more chic of the two, with fancy pool tables and several conversation pits bulging with overstuffed sofas and chairs. A small dance floor borders the expansive bar for those who wish to bust a move. Patrons are a little more laid-back than those at the neighboring club. Across the way, Matrix is a straight-ahead dance factory, with a much larger floor, fewer seats, and a generally flashier vibe (not to mention a high-tech lighting rig and pounding sound). Locals, club kids, and other nightlife denizens gravitate here first, then wander over to Metropolis to chill out and relax for a bit.

unofficial TIP
If you're looking for non-Disneyesque nightlife, head to Metropolis and/or Matrix.

Both clubs host rotating theme nights, with college night and Latin night being especially popular. Hours are typically 9 p.m.–2 a.m., Wednesday–Sunday (Matrix) and 9 p.m.–2 a.m., Thursday–Sunday (Metropolis), with occasional extra open nights seasonally. Call ☎ 407-370-3700 for more details, or check out **www.metropolismatrix.com.**

CITYWALK CLUBS

Bob Marley—A Tribute to Freedom
What it is Reggae restaurant and club. **Hours** 4 p.m.–2 a.m. Monday through Friday 2 p.m.–2 a.m. Saturday and Sunday. **Cuisine** Jamaican-influenced appetizers and main courses. **Entertainment** Reggae bands in the outdoor gazebo after 8 p.m. **Cover** $5 after 7 p.m. nightly (more for special acts)

COMMENTS This club is a re-creation of Marley's home in Kingston, Jamaica, and contains a lot of interesting Marley memorabilia. The courtyard is the center of action. Must be age 21 or over after 10 p.m.

City Jazz
What it is Jazz club and themed restaurant/comedy club. **Hours** 8 p.m.–1 a.m. Sunday through Thursday; 7 p.m.–2 a.m. Friday and Saturday. **Cuisine** No food. **Entertainment** Live jazz. National stand-up comics appear onstage Thursday–Sunday nights. **Cover** $5; some ticketed events higher.

COMMENTS Jazz club that's also home to *Down Beat* magazine's Jazz Hall of Fame museum (open 3–6 p.m.).

The Groove
What it is High-tech disco. **Hours** 9 p.m.–2 a.m. **Cuisine** No food. **Entertainment** DJ plays dance tunes. Sometimes there are live bands. **Cover** $5.

COMMENTS Guests must be age 21 or older to enter this très chic club designed to look like an old theater in the midst of restoration. There are seven bars and several themed cubbyholes for getting away from the thundering sound system. Dancers are barraged with strobes, lasers, and heaven knows what else.

Hard Rock Live
What it is Live music concert hall and club. **Hours** 7 p.m. until closing. **Cuisine** Limited menu. **Entertainment** House band performs weekdays with big-name groups taking over on weekends. **Cover** $10 for house band. Cover varies for name acts.

COMMENTS Great acoustics, comfortable seating, and good sight lines make this the best concert venue in town. House band is excellent. By the by, the Hard Rock Live concert hall and the Hard Rock Café restaurant are separate facilities.

Jimmy Buffett's Margaritaville
What it is Key West–themed restaurant and club. **Hours** Daily, 11 a.m.–2 a.m. **Cuisine** Caribbean, Florida fusion, and American. **Entertainment** Live rock and island-style music after 10 p.m. **Cover** $5 after 10 p.m.

COMMENTS Jimmy's is a big place with three bars that turns into a nightclub after 10 p.m. If you eat dinner here, you'll probably want to find another vantage point when the band cranks up.

Latin Quarter
What it is Latin salsa-themed restaurant and live music hall. **Hours** 11:30 a.m.–10 p.m. Monday through Friday; noon–2 a.m. Saturday and Sunday. **Cuisine** Latin American. **Entertainment** Live salsa band nightly. **Cover** $5 after 10 p.m.

COMMENTS Primarily a restaurant with entertainment on the side. Live salsa music (and often dancing) are performed in sets throughout the night.

Pat O'Brien's Orlando

What it is Dueling pianos sing-along club and restaurant. **Hours** 4 pm.–2 a.m. **Cuisine** Cajun. **Entertainment** Dueling pianos and sing-alongs. **Cover** $5 after 6 p.m. for piano bar only.

COMMENTS A clone of the famous New Orleans club of the same name. You can dine in the courtyard or on the terrace without paying a cover. You must be age 21 or over to hang out here.

ACCOMMODATION INDEX

RESTAURANT INDEX

SUBJECT INDEX